The Official

EB5 ,

The Official EB-5 Guidebook, Fifth Edition

Copyright © 2019 by EB5 Affiliate Network, LLC

151 Calle San Francisco, San Juan, Puerto Rico 00901

www.EB5AffiliateNetwork.com

1-800-288-9138

About EB5 Affiliate Network

EB5 Affiliate Network (EB5AN) is the preferred vendor for new EB-5 regional center setup and for access to approved EB-5 regional centers. EB-5 project financing is a quickly growing industry that is highly fragmented. There is substantial room for creative solutions in terms of overall EB-5 project strategy, investment design, and structure.

Our team has extensive experience in business strategy, investment evaluation, securities, tax, and immigration law. Our team has advised Fortune 500 companies on growth and investment strategies and has worked on some of the largest IPOs, securities offerings, and private equity buyouts in recent memory. We have helped provide the opportunity for thousands of foreign nationals to successfully immigrate to the United States and transition to the American lifestyle while creating thousands of jobs for Americans.

Our goal is to work together with committed partners in the EB-5 space who are interested in creating economically feasible, financially sound, and marketable EB-5 projects that can be successfully funded by accredited overseas investors.

Quick Statistics on Our Team

Global Presence: The EB5AN team consists of multi-lingual and cross-cultural industry professionals from around the world, including India, Brazil, and China, key markets for EB-5 investor financing. Our team is on the ground, literally, which gives our team prescient, up-to-date information on the EB-5 investor and related financial markets, allowing us to provide strategic and informed advice to our clients on what is required to successfully fund a project in any climate.

Business strategy: Our team has advised Fortune 500 companies in the hospitality, real estate, finance, media, manufacturing, transportation, and travel industries on strategic business initiatives ranging from supply chain sensitivities, portfolio review, greenfield market manufacturing strategy, vertical integration, and consumer pricing strategy. We understand how businesses work and how to frame a compelling and realistic investment story.

Economic analysis: Our team includes economists by training. We utilize the most up-to-date economic analysis software and statistical methods available that have been recognized and approved by USCIS. In addition, we provide free industry-recognized tools, including our national TEA map and RIMS II job calculator, in an effort to increase transparency in the industry.

Private equity investment: Our team has been involved in screening, diligence, and making primary investments in more than $3 billion of private equity transactions.

USCIS approvals: Our company has more than six years of real world experience working with USCIS to gain approvals for regional center designations. The results speak for themselves: We own and operate 15 approved regional centers with coverage of 27 states and Washington, D.C. We have completed more than 200 EB-5 transactions, and we have more than 1,000 investors from more than 40 countries under our regional center network.

Samuel B. Silverman

Sam has extensive real estate development, management, financing, and brokerage experience in Florida, Pennsylvania, California, Georgia, and internationally in the People's Republic of China. Prior to EB5AN, Sam served as the Director of Corporate Strategy and Expansion for Professional Golfer Jack Nicklaus in the People's Republic of China, living full time in Beijing. Sam was also previously employed by the Boston Consulting Group, one of the top management consulting and business strategy firms in the world, where he worked directly with Fortune 500 companies in the food service, media, manufacturing, hospitality, and real estate spaces in the United States, Europe, and Middle East. Sam was honored by *Entrepreneur360 Magazine* and was recognized by *Forbes Magazine* as a National Winner for the Forbes 30 Under 30 List of Social Entrepreneurs. Sam holds a B.A. in economics with a concentration in Mandarin Chinese from Yale University, a certificate in financial accounting from the London School of Economics and Political Science, and an M.B.A. from the Stanford Graduate School of Business.

Michael Schoenfeld

Mike has extensive private equity investment, business diligence, management consulting, and entrepreneurship experience. Prior to EB5AN, Mike worked for AEA Investors, a leading middle-market private equity firm with $10B under management, focused on making control-oriented investments in consumer goods, industrial goods, and business services companies. He invested out of their previous $2.5B middle market private equity fund. His completed transactions include the $2B LBO of 24 Hour Fitness, the leading fitness club operator with over 400 clubs nationwide, and the minority investment in Brand Networks, a leading social media marketing solutions provider. Mike was previously employed by the Boston Consulting Group, one of the top management consulting and business strategy firms in the world, where he worked directly with Fortune 500 companies in the transportation, financial services, industrial goods, information technology, and real estate spaces. Mike was also recognized by

Entrepreneur360 Magazine and named a National Winner on *Forbes Magazine*'s 30 Under 30 List of Social Entrepreneurs. Mike holds a B.A. in economics and a B.S. in business administration from the University of North Carolina at Chapel Hill.

Timothy Y. Shih, Esq.

Tim has extensive legal experience in corporate transactional matters, including complex public and private securities offerings, public and private M&A transactions, banking, and corporate restructuring. Prior to EB5AN, Timothy was an attorney at the law firm of Cravath, Swaine & Moore LLP, one of the top law firms in the world, where he worked with Fortune 500 companies in the hospitality, media, manufacturing, financial, banking, private equity, and real estate spaces. Tim also has extensive experience in the film, media and entertainment industry, having worked as general counsel for an entertainment company in the People's Republic of China. Tim holds a B.S. in computer science from Yale University and a J.D. from the Duke University School of Law.

Table of Contents

Topics for Project Developers

EB-5 Basics

The History of the EB-5 Program

Congress created the opportunity for foreign entrepreneurs to invest in new commercial enterprises in the United States with the passing of the Immigration Act of 1990 (the "Immigration Act"). As part of comprehensive legislative reform with respect to immigration policy, several new categories of immigration visas were enacted with the "EB" preface, indicating the visa category is "employment-based". EB-5 stands for "Employment-Based – Fifth Preference", a very unique and specialized visa category that qualifies certain foreign investors in U.S. commercial enterprises to qualify for a U.S. green card, providing such investor and his or her immediate family the right to live and work in the United States permanently and, if so desire, ultimately attain American citizenship. The intention of the EB-5 Program was to stimulate the U.S. economy through the creation of jobs and, as a result, a minimum requirement of any qualifying investment is that it create at least 10 U.S. jobs per EB-5 investor. In 1992, Congress introduced the Immigrant Investor Pilot Program, also known as the Regional Center Program, which applies specifically to the EB-5 category of visas. This provided guidelines for USCIS to approve EB-5 regional centers to oversee EB-5 investments and monitor job creation with respect to EB-5 projects.

USCIS Overhauls EB-5 Visa Program during the 1990s

In the early stages of the EB-5 Program, many questions were raised and potential issues discovered. Investment projects by nature require a level of trust between the investor and those seeking investment, as well as proper disclosure and good faith between the parties. In addition, the investors themselves are by definition foreign citizens, who themselves may require additional scrutiny purely by nature of their distance from U.S. purview. Ultimately, some bad actors were discovered, as indicated by the discovery of fraud in EB-5 investments in the U.S. District Court case *U.S. v. O'Connor.* Partially as a result of the changing nature of the program and shifting dynamics between the parties involved, the Administrative Appeals Office (AAO) of USCIS was spurred to incorporate additional changes to the program in 1998. Such changes included the requirement that investors prove their investments in the program come from lawful sources. Investors must also demonstrate they are actively involved in their EB-5 projects. Additionally, no guarantee can be offered of the return of capital or any other returns with respect to any EB-5 investments.

Additionally, during the 1990s, four important precedent decisions were handed down in response to attempts by the AAO to regulate new EB-5 applications, which provided further clarity into the judicial standards at play: *Matter of Soffici, Matter of Izummi, Matter of Hsiung,* and *Matter of Ho.* These decisions clarified the types of commercial businesses that may qualify for EB-5 investment, established procedures for administering the investment, and required affirmation that the funding came from legal sources.

Additional Reforms in the 2000s

In an attempt to revitalize the EB-5 Program, the Basic Pilot Program Extension and Expansion Act of 2003 was passed by Congress. An investigation of the EB-5 Program by the Government Accounting Office (GAO) showed that few of the 10,000 visas allocated to the program each year were being granted. The Investor and Regional Center Unit (IRCU) was created in 2005 to oversee the EB-5 Program. IRCU's role included policy creation, case auditing, form design, and the development of regulations, and it has implemented better coordination and reliability within the program.

Additional Changes Summarized

1. In 2009, USCIS established the EB-5 processing center at the California Service Center (CSC), eliminating the previous two centers in California and Texas.
2. In 2009, the Immigrant Investor Pilot Program was extended by President Obama through September 30, 2012.
3. On September 28, 2012, the program was once again extended by President Obama until 2015.
4. From September 2015 through today, the program has received numerous short-term extensions as part of a larger Continuing Resolution. The most recent extension took place on February 15, 2019, extending the program through September 30, 2019.

How EB-5 Capital Works

Since its creation in 1990, the EB-5 visa program has seen tens of thousands of foreign nationals apply for U.S. permanent resident status and billions of dollars of capital deployed into job creating enterprises. However, raising investment capital through the EB-5 visa program is a complicated, multi-year process that requires early, thoughtful planning and professional execution.

The successful structuring and subsequent funding of an investment project with EB-5 capital depends on careful preparation of all required documentation as well as the marketing strategy of the project sponsor. Developing comprehensive and compliant economic, business, and legal documentation is a critical step that is often underestimated by EB-5 applicants and project sponsors. This guidebook is a collection of various resources, feedback, information and relevant material collected or produced by our company over the course of the last four years and represents one of the most comprehensive repositories of information related to the EB-5 industry to date.

Main Parties Involved in the EB-5 Capital Process

The Regional Center: The Regional Center involved in any EB-5 transaction is a USCIS-approved entity usually responsible for, among other things, raising EB-5 capital and counting direct, indirect, and induced job creation that occurs as a result of EB-5 projects. The vast majority of EB-5 projects currently utilize USCIS-designated Regional Centers, instead of the alternative (also known as "direct" EB-5 investments, a topic we will not cover in detail in this book) because the indirect and induced job calculation methodology is an effective and proven way to demonstrate job creation to USCIS that reduces uncertainty, increases transparency, and is more scalable. It should be noted that the main difference between EB-5 Projects utilizing an EB-5 Regional Center versus those using the "direct" model is that Regional Center investments may use an economic model to calculate job creation. "Direct" investments, by contrast, may not, and instead have an evidentiary burden to prove to USCIS that the requisite jobs were created. This information in this book, unless specifically indicated otherwise, assumes Regional Center involvement in the EB-5 transaction.

The New Commercial Enterprise (NCE): The NCE is a term of art defined by USCIS as the entity in which the EB-5 investor will make his or her capital investment for purposes of the EB-5 Program. Typically, this is structured as a newly formed business entity with each investor subscribing as a limited partner or member and the project sponsor acting the general partner or manager of the NCE.

The Job Creating Enterprise (JCE): The JCE is also a term of art defined by USCIS as the entity, typically the EB-5 project entity, that will actually be creating the jobs necessary for the investor to qualify under the EB-5 program.

The EB-5 Investor: The EB-5 Investor is the ultimate end user of the EB-5 program. He or she is the person ultimately desiring to qualify as an immigrant investor under the EB-5 Program by deploying anywhere from $500,000 to $1,000,000 (or such future amounts as determined by USCIS) in investment capital, typically over a 5-year or longer time horizon, into a qualified EB-5 project in the United States. To qualify as an EB-5 project, the investment must create at least 10 jobs that last a minimum of two years.

Required Paperwork for the New Commercial Enterprise and Job Creating Enterprise

Once the NCE is formed, it will typically oversee a securities offering qualifying under certain private placement exemptions and similar exemptions from registration under federal and state securities laws. As many EB-5 securities offerings are private, non-registered offerings, the main disclosure document related to the deal is typically a confidential offering memorandum or private placement memorandum (PPM) that details the material terms of the EB-5 investment. EB-5 investors will then subscribe to the offering by executing a subscription agreement. Once funded with EB-5 investor capital, the NCE will then make an investment in debt or equity, depending on the project structure, into the JCE through which the required 10 jobs per investor will be created.

The NCE and JCE are each required to submit several documents to the USCIS as part of an EB-5 investor's application.

Among other things, the NCE is typically required to submit the following documents:

- USCIS letter of regional center approval designation
- A detailed *Matter of Ho*-compliant business plan
- A targeted employment area (TEA) letter (if the investment is intended to be $500,000 and not $1,000,000, as discussed in detail later in this book)
- An economic report including job creation analysis showing how the required jobs will be created
- Legal offering documents including any PPM or Confidential Offering Memorandum
- Formation documents related to the NCE
- Organizational documents related to the NCE
- Subscription agreement and ancillary documents
- Escrow agreement with capital release terms (if applicable)
- Investment/loan agreement(s) between the NCE and JCE (if applicable)
- Collateral document(s) for the investment/loan
- Additional supporting documentation

The JCE may be required to submit the following:

- Title deed (if the investment is a real estate transaction)

- Credible and recent market analysis or feasibility study
- Bank loan commitment (if applicable)
- Third-party appraisal (if applicable)
- Proof of the project sponsor's capital commitment to the project (if applicable)
- Proof of any other capital or lending instruments to be used in the transaction
- Information on the project sponsor's track record
- Exit strategy for the investment (loan repayment, refinancing, sale, etc.)

Please bear in mind that the lists above are not comprehensive and that each EB-5 investment project is unique and requires a custom set of documents for the project sponsor to accomplish its goals and for each investor to successfully receive USCIS approval of his or her I-526 immigration petition.

Step-by-Step Process for Documenting an EB-5 Project

As noted above, each EB-5 project is different, and no universal solution fits all projects. However, the procedure for assembling a comprehensive and USCIS-compliant set of documents for any EB-5 project is essentially the same.

Step 1: Determine TEA qualification

Since the primary motivation of most EB-5 investors is to receive U.S. permanent residency and not necessarily to achieve a high return on their investment, the overwhelming majority of investors prefer to invest the minimum amount of $500,000 in an EB-5 investment project as opposed to $1,000,000 for projects not located in a targeted employment area (TEA). Therefore, selecting a project located within a TEA is critical in the marketplace today. TEAs are designated areas either located in (i) high unemployment areas with at least 150% of the national average unemployment rate or (ii) rural areas.

Step 2: Determine job creation

Since the primary aim of the EB-5 investor visa program is to provide economic growth in the form of new job creation, the first step in the process is to determine the potential job creation from an investment project. Under the regional center investment model, direct, indirect, and induced jobs will count toward the 10 required jobs per EB-5 investor. This means that job creation will be derived from cost expenditures, project revenues, and the direct employment of workers (W-2 jobs).

For real estate projects, the real estate developer will provide the EB-5 project sponsor with a detailed cost and revenue pro-forma for the development of the project. The EB-5 economist will then determine the number of jobs that the USCIS will attribute to the development of the project.

As pointed out above, for each EB-5 investor that the EB-5 project accepts, at least 10 jobs must be created that last a minimum of two years.

Step 3: Determine target EB-5 capital raise

Once the total number of potential jobs has been determined, that number can be divided by 10 and then multiplied by $500,000 (for EB-5 projects located in TEAs) or $1,000,000 (for EB-5 projects not located in TEAs). For example, if a project is located in a TEA and creates 320 jobs, the project can support a maximum of 32 investors (who each invest $500,000) or a total of $16,000,000 in EB-5 capital investment. The math is relatively simple: 320 jobs created ÷ 10 jobs required per investor = 32 investors × $500,000 per investor = $16,000,000 in total EB-5 capital investment. In this example, the target project can support a total of 32 investors who will all initially receive temporary and eventually permanent green cards, assuming that the project actually does create the required 320 jobs.

Since many investment projects do not ultimately cost exactly the amount initially budgeted or generate exactly the amount of anticipated revenue, building a "job cushion" into the EB-5 project job calculations is important. By creating such a cushion, in the event a project's projected cost estimates and revenue differ from reality, the EB-5 investors may still receive their permanent green cards. If the project ultimately did create less than the required number of jobs per investor, as determined by USCIS, some of the investors (particularly those who filed later) would be at risk of not having their green cards become permanent at the I-829 stage of the EB-5 visa process.

So what does all this mean for determining the EB-5 capital raise for a project today? EB-5 investors are very sensitive to receiving their permanent green cards and successfully demonstrating the required job creation. Therefore, in today's market, it is recommended that EB-5 projects have a job cushion of at least 20%. It is important to note that there is no restriction on the maximum amount of job cushion a project can have. A large project with a small percentage of EB-5 capital could have a job cushion in excess of 300%, which significantly reduces the immigration risk for any EB-5 investors since the project would have to go terribly wrong for the required number of jobs not to be reached.

Step 4: Finalize project documentation and open project escrow account

Once the EB-5 project is fully documented, the project sponsor is responsible for reviewing and approving the final set of investment documents that will be filed by EB-5 investors. After the documentation has been finalized, the project sponsor will work with a major U.S. bank to setup an EB-5 project escrow account for the NCE, to which EB-5 investors will wire their investment funds as they subscribe to the investment offering. While an escrow account is not required by USCIS, it is highly recommended as a measure to ensure investor's funds are properly deployed into the project.

Step 5: Marketing the EB-5 project to investors

Once the escrow account has been opened and the legal documents related to the securities offering have been finalized, the NCE can begin to subscribe investors to the EB-5 project offering. At this point, the project sponsor has several potential options for marketing the project to EB-5 investors: (i) direct marketing by the sponsor to investors overseas, (ii) hiring a registered U.S. broker dealer to manage the EB-5 capital raise, or (iii) partnering with foreign immigration firms overseas that specialize in placing investors in EB-5 projects. The marketing process and decisions related to it involve complex securities law issues, and it is incredibly important to ensure that any decisions related to such marketing are compliant with relevant securities laws in both the United States and the countries in which the investments are marketed. Many EB-5 projects may use an informational seminar format to provide information on the projects, and so it is important to develop a set of marketing materials and have them translated into the local language. Typically, a representative of the NCE will attend these seminars to present the EB-5 project, speak with investors, and answer questions.

Step 6: Subscribing EB-5 investors

Once a new investor decides to invest in a specific EB-5 project, he/she will typically sign a subscription agreement and wire a predetermined amount to the NCE's escrow account. Once investor suitability has been determined according to the procedures set in place by the NCE, the EB-5 investor will work closely with an immigration attorney to prepare his or her I-526 investment petition, which includes as a primary component the documentation tracing the source of the required EB-5 investment funds and indicating that such funds were lawfully obtained.

Step 7: Release of EB-5 capital from project escrow account

Each EB-5 project will decide on its own escrow release structure, which determines when the investors' EB-5 capital will be available or deployed to the NCE to invest in the job creating enterprise. Some EB-5 project sponsors choose to have investor capital released from escrow and available for investment upon submission of the investors' I-526 immigration petitions to USCIS. Other EB-5 project sponsors may choose to have capital released from escrow upon the approval of each individual EB-5 investor. Still others may utilize a hybrid approach where a portion is released on filing, and another portion is released on approval. Determining the correct escrow structure balances several factors including, the desired timing for receipt and subsequent deployment of the capital, an understanding of USCIS processing times, expectations of EB-5 investors, and the overall strategy investment and marketing strategy with respect to the EB-5 project.

Common Mistakes to Avoid

Over the course of the EB-5 program, we have encountered almost every permutation of project structure and we have seen how developers, regional centers, project sponsors, EB-5 investors and all related parties in-between approach a potential EB-5 investment. Below is a nonexclusive list of some of the most frequent mistakes that we encountered.

Inconsistencies across documents within the EB-5 project documentation package

One common mistake is that job creation numbers, projected revenues, and development cost numbers do not match across the business plan, private placement memorandum, and other supporting documentation. This is a critical mistake because USCIS will not approve a set of EB-5 project documents that is not completely consistent across all elements of an investor's I-526 application. These types of errors are common when several different vendors (attorneys, economists, business plan writers, etc.) are involved in assembling the package of EB-5 documentation. Lack of communication between the parties and the failure to oversee integration of disparate components makes this a more common problem than you'd realize. A potential solution to minimize the risk is to engage a single, experienced company to oversee and complete the EB-5 project documentation package in order to minimize these types of critical errors.

Failure to consider the marketability of the EB-5 project given current market conditions

EB-5 projects must be designed and constructed from the beginning with the EB-5 investor marketplace in mind. Since there are more projects desiring EB-5 capital on the market than there are available investors, designing a project with a structure that will be attractive to investors today is vital. In a rapidly changing and evolving marketing environment, having a current knowledge of attractive project structures, capital security, loan terms, escrow release terms, and investment returns is invaluable in presenting an attractive project to potential investors.

Attempts to cut costs by engaging unqualified EB-5 vendors

Yes, many vendors and attorneys will claim to be able to provide the required documentation for an EB-5 project. Be sure to do your due diligence and speak with multiple vendors in the space to determine which EB-5 team will be the most effective at structuring your project and bringing it to market under an approved USCIS regional center. Ask about refund guarantees and check to see what types and how many EB-5 projects the team has been involved with.

Conclusion and Important Takeaways

Deciding to seek EB-5 capital is a significant business decision that should be carefully evaluated according to the size of the project, potential job creation, and EB-5 capital needed. Such a decision should also consider the amount of effort, cost, and planning required on behalf of the project sponsor to put together a successful EB-5 project. Project sponsors must be patient, but the rewards for long-term thinking can be significant. A successful EB-5 project will provide the project developer with valuable, below-market-rate investment capital and will also result in new job creation that stimulates the project's local economy.

Working with or Establishing a Regional Center

Prior to implementation of the Regional Center Program, investors had to directly invest in EB-5 projects and were individually responsible for meeting the job requirements of USCIS. In order to obtain U.S. permanent resident status, which is the primary reason foreign nationals pursue EB-5 investments, an EB-5 investor must, by his or her investment, produce at least 10 jobs that last for no less than two years.

However, within the framework established under the Regional Center Program, EB-5 regional centers make it easier for investors to meet the job creation requirements set forth by USCIS by allowing EB-5 projects to include direct, indirect, and induced jobs when calculating job creation figures. In other words, investing in a project through an EB-5 regional center provides investors with a more favourable and transparent job creation calculation, which allows EB-5 investors to undertake larger projects with greater job cushion than would be feasible in a direct investment.

Additionally, the evidentiary burden for proving jobs differs. Under the regional center model, since jobs are calculated using an econometric model with respect to the expenditures related to the EB-5 project, proving job creation is simply a matter of proving those expenditures actually occurred. Currently there is no requirement under the regional center model to provide additional information regarding actual employees hired, such as W-2 forms, employee verification or other methods. By contrast, a direct EB-5 investment must prove each job was created through W-2 forms and employee verification and must also demonstrate that each job was retained for at least two years.

Furthermore, direct EB-5 investments can include only direct job creation when determining the number of jobs a project creates. Therefore, when indirect or induced jobs need to be included in the job creation calculation, investors must work through a USCIS-approved EB-5 regional center. EB-5 regional center sponsorship can be obtained in two ways: the project developer can seek to establish its own regional center or the developer can work with an existing regional center.

Working with an Existing EB-5 Regional Center

When seeking a USCIS-approved EB-5 regional center to work with, developers must consider the type and location of their project since every EB-5 regional center is limited to a certain geographic region and specific industry sector. These limitations will, in large part, determine which regional centers a developer will be able to work with on a given project.

EB-5 regional center geographic considerations
Over time, the geographic regions approved by USCIS have become smaller, and so newer EB-5 regional centers are likely to have smaller geographic scopes than older regional centers. For instance, some of the older EB-5 regional centers have geographic scopes that span entire states, and in

some cases, multiple states. Newer regional centers, on the other hand, tend to have geographic scopes spanning 10 to fifteen counties, and sometimes even less. Although this is the trend, there are exceptions to this trend.

An EB-5 project seeking sponsorship by a regional center must, therefore, find a regional center whose geographic scope includes the location of the project. If a project's location is outside the approved geographic region of a regional center, that regional center cannot automatically sponsor the project. However, if the geographic boundary is close enough that a compelling argument can be made to USCIS, there is precedent for the expansion of a regional center's geographic scope as part of an individual EB-5 investor's I-526 application.

EB-5 regional center industry (NAICS Code) considerations

In addition to a specific geographic scope, each EB-5 regional center has at least one defined industry sector it is pre-approved to operate in. In the 1990s, these industry designations were defined more loosely, but over time, the classification of industry scope has narrowed. USCIS has adopted the North American Industry Classification System (NAICS), which is used by other federal agencies to classify businesses.

Today, the industry scope of EB-5 regional centers is now more clearly defined by NAICS codes. These NAICS codes are also a critical component of an EB-5 compatible business plan and economic impact report as job creation is typically determined at the NAICS code level. For example, if a hotel project creates ongoing revenues from hotel room rentals, then that revenue would fall under the Accommodation NAICS code which has a specific job multiplier associated with it. This job multiplier would then be multiplied by the projected hotel revenue to determine how many jobs the hotel development could create for EB-5 job calculation purposes.

Prior to the USCIS Policy Memorandum on May 30, 2013, the NAICS industry classification of an EB-5 project had to fall within the approved industry scope of the EB-5 regional center. However, under additional guidance provided pursuant to the 2013 USCIS Policy Memorandum, EB-5 regional centers no longer need to be concerned about which NAICS codes they are pre-approved for as there is no longer a requirement for pre-approved NAICS codes.

To summarize, this means that today an approved regional center can sponsor any type of project involving any NAICS code(s) as long as the project falls within the approved geographic scope of the EB-5 regional center.

EB-5 regional center diligence

The first step in the diligence process for a project developer is to determine which USCIS approved EB-5 regional center(s) have the required geographic coverage to sponsor the EB-5 project. The second step is to interview/diligence the potential EB-5 regional centers that meet the geographic requirements and determine which regional center operator is the best fit for the project. This vetting process should take into consideration the regional center's fees, available services, history, reputation, and track record in the EB-5 space. This process is critical as there are over 750 approved EB-5 regional centers today, but there are no guarantees with respect to how professionally run and operated they are. Additionally, as USCIS requirements have become more stringent over time, there is a risk that many no longer maintain sufficient infrastructure to successfully sponsor EB-5 projects and meet USCIS compliance standards. USCIS has since become active in terminating regional centers that no longer meet their evolving requirements, and it is therefore important to determine the likelihood of a regional center being subject to USCIS action.

The following are key questions to ask when evaluating an EB-5 regional center:

- What is the geographic coverage of your EB-5 regional center(s)?
- When was your EB-5 regional center(s) approved by USCIS? (Approvals after 2014 indicate they were approved after USCIS tightened its requirements)
- How many EB-5 regional centers does your company own/operate?
- Has your EB-5 regional center ever received a Notice of Intent to Deny from USCIS?
- Have any of the EB-5 investors under your EB-5 regional center(s) been denied on an I-526 filing?
- Have any of the EB-5 investors under your EB-5 regional center(s) been denied on an I-829 filing?
- How many EB-5 projects have your regional center/company worked on?
- What services can you provide other than basic EB-5 regional center sponsorship?
- What exactly is included in regional center sponsorship?
- What is the professional background of the principals/owners of the regional center team?
- Do any of the principals/owners of the regional center team have a criminal background or pending legislation against them?
- What are the fees (annual or one-time) for your EB-5 regional center to sponsor my EB-5 project?
- What project documents do you need for diligence purposes and what requirements are needed to determine whether my project can affiliate or join your EB-5 regional center?
- How does your regional center maintain compliance under USCIS and relevant laws?
- What happens to me and my project if the EB-5 regional center is no longer in compliance with USCIS requirements and is issued a Notice of Intent to Terminate?

Applying to Create a Regional Center

All EB-5 regional centers are designated and approved by USCIS. Regional centers are approved by USCIS to make EB-5 investments within a specific geographic area, and each designation is assigned to the specific business entity that owns and operates the regional center. A new EB-5 regional center can be created under the USCIS Immigrant Investor Pilot program by filing an I-924 regional center designation application.

USCIS does not restrict the type of business entity that can file an application for a new regional center, and so an EB-5 regional center application can be filed by any commercial business entity such as a partnership, limited liability company, or corporation. Likewise, USCIS does not restrict the types of projects that an approved regional center can invest in within its approved geographic area. The freedom to make EB-5 investments across the entire spectrum of investment opportunities and the ability to pool direct, indirect, and induced job creation are among the two primary reasons most EB-5 investors prefer investments sponsored by EB-5 regional centers.

Below is a detailed, step-by-step guide for how to successfully apply for and become a new, USCIS-approved EB-5 regional center.

Step 1: Define the scope of the regional center

As owner and operator, you must determine the geographic scope of your regional center and what types of projects your regional center will invest in. Key details that must be included in any regional center application include the following: the location of the future EB-5 investment project, the proposed business model related to the project, estimated required investment amounts, and the amount of total capital needed for the project (both EB-5 capital and other sources of investment capital). A regional center application may include proposals for multiple projects.

It is important to note that you must clearly define the scope of the activities of the regional center and assemble a clear and compliant regional center operational plan. The purpose of this plan is to demonstrate that if approved, you will be able to successfully operate an EB-5 regional center within USCIS guidelines.

Step 2: Hire the right EB-5 regional center application team

Once you have decided to move forward with the preparation of an EB-5 regional center application, the next step is to select an EB-5 team of professionals to work with. This team will assemble all of the required components of the EB-5 regional center application, therefore choosing the right team is incredibly important. There are many vendors, consultants, and attorneys to choose from in the EB-5 space, but you should carefully consider who is the best fit for your specific needs.

Usually, regional center applicants take one of two different approaches when choosing a team of EB-5 professionals: (i) hiring multiple, separate companies and/or attorneys to independently complete each of the major required components and then assembling the final EB-5 application themselves, hoping that all of the numbers match and that the various legal documents and business plans tie together correctly; or (ii) working with a single EB-5 consulting firm that handles the entire process from beginning to end (such as our company, EB5 Affiliate Network).

Working with the best team of EB-5 professionals will help tailor your EB-5 regional center application to your needs as a project sponsor and will likely result in your new EB-5 regional center being approved in the shortest timeframe possible.

Below is a list of most of the key components required as part of a new EB-5 regional center designation application.

- Immigration documents: These documents include a cover letter to USCIS requesting designation as a new EB-5 regional center under the Immigrant Investor Pilot Program and a completed I-924 designation petition—the USCIS form required to setup a new EB-5 regional center.
- Targeted employment area designation: Since most EB-5 investments take place in TEAs, it is important to investigate which areas within your regional center's target geography will qualify as TEAs. Once you've identified your region's TEAs, you will want to state that your regional center will focus its investment activities in those TEAs. A TEA is defined as a rural area or an area with an unemployment rate that is at least 150% of the national average. The benefit of investing in projects within TEAs is that the minimum investment amount is lower per investor (as of the date of this book, $500,000 instead of $1,000,000), which will make the investment more marketable. TEA designation letters are issued on an annual basis and must be obtained from the appropriate state agency.
- Securities documents: An EB-5 regional center application should include a set of securities offering documents that disclose to potential investors the material terms of the EB-5 investment and material information regarding the EB-5 project(s) to be sponsored under the EB-5 regional center.
- Business plan: A key part of the EB-5 regional center application is a business plan that is "Matter of Ho" compliant with USCIS standards, as required by law. This business plan will need to include projected costs, revenues, the exit strategy, market research, competitor analysis information, and other material information with respect to the proposed business investment.
- Job creation report: An EB-5 compliant job report demonstrates how the business described in the EB-5 business plan will create jobs within the regional center's target geographic area. This job report should include specific job calculations for how many jobs the EB-5 project will create if successful, and over what period of time. The report should include all direct, indirect, and induced jobs

15

created as a result of the successful development of the EB-5 project.

Step 3: Complete and file Form I-924 and supporting application documents to set up a new EB-5 regional center

The entire process of assembling your EB-5 regional center application can take anywhere from three weeks to several months depending on the team of EB-5 professionals you choose to engage and your ability to properly compile the information necessary with respect to the application.

At a minimum, an EB-5 regional center application must have an EB-5 compliant business plan, a comprehensive job creation report that meets USCIS requirements, a completed I-924 form, and the appropriate supporting legal documentation. These legal documents include a regional center operating plan and evidence of sufficient capital to operate the regional center in compliance with USCIS requirements.

Once the application is completed, you must sign a set of hard copy application binders with original ink signatures. Then, the completed set of application binders, including the signed I-924 form and a check in the amount of the filing fee made out to "U.S. Department of Homeland Security," will be mailed to the USCIS EB-5 processing unit for new I-924 applications. The appropriate USCIS mailing address and current filing fees for new I-924 applications is available via the USCIS website.

Once the new EB-5 regional center application is approved, your regional center may begin to receive EB-5 capital for projects located within the approved geographic area. Current USCIS processing times are generally available via the USCIS website, but as a general matter, you should expect a new regional center designation to take around 12 months. That being said, our regional centers have historically been approved on average in approximately seven months, so your mileage may vary.

The I-924 application package includes many supporting documents, which vary depending on each applicant's individual circumstances. At a minimum, an I-924 application package should include the following four components:

Component #1: Proof that the regional center will create 10 full-time jobs that will last a minimum of two years for each EB-5 investor who invests in the proposed business. Select forms of evidence may include the following:

- A detailed, *Matter of Ho* compliant business plan
- An economic job report showing how many jobs will be created and over what period of time the job creation will occur
- Offering documents, including the subscription agreement, private placement memorandum (PPM), investor due diligence questionnaire(s), accredited investor questionnaire(s), and IRS tax forms.
- Loan or investment documents reflecting the relationship between the new commercial enterprise (NCE) and the job creating enterprise (JCE)

16

- Limited partnership, limited liability company, or corporate formation and organizational documents for the NCE entity and the entity that will own and operate the new EB-5 regional center
- Detailed and credible financial pro-formas, including projected project costs and revenues demonstrating how the funds will be invested and returned to investors.

Component #2: Supporting evidence that the regional center will be able to meet the ongoing operational requirements of the EB-5 program. Select forms of evidence may include the following:

- Articles of incorporation
- FEIN letter from the IRS
- Escrow agreement
- Drafts of all related contracts
- Bank statements showing sufficient operational capital

Component #3: A detailed plan of all proposed EB-5 project promotional activities of the regional center. Select forms of evidence may include the following:

- Evidence of funds planned for marketing and promotion
- Detailed, line-by-line budget and timeline
- Evidence demonstrating the lawful sources of the regional center's operational and investment capital
- A complete and detailed plan for all marketing operations of the regional center

Component #4: A county map and list of all counties showing the exact geographic coverage of the proposed regional center designation

Be aware of a USCIS request for evidence (RFE)

Since USCIS has the right to ask for additional information from any new EB-5 regional center applicant, it is very important to have a high-quality application that addresses all potential questions a USCIS adjudicator may have about the proposed new regional center. Responding to a USCIS RFE can take several weeks, and the processing time from USCIS for each RFE can be several months, so it is best to try to minimize the odds of receiving an RFE by assembling a high-quality application from the very beginning. Additionally, you are less likely to receive an RFE if you submit business plans and a job creation methodology that has been previously reviewed and approved by USCIS.

Hypothetical, Actual, and Exemplar Project Proposals for Regional Center Applications

Under the EB-5 Program, regional centers are established based on their projected ability to raise capital from foreign investors to develop projects and create jobs in the United States, thereby generating economic growth. Form I-924, which a prospective regional center must submit when seeking formal designation from USCIS, must be accompanied by a project proposal to allow adjudicators to determine whether the center is capable of meeting these goals. A project proposal must additionally accompany any I-526 petitions submitted by the regional center or its associated investors.

Regional centers are required to submit documentation to USCIS regarding three types of projects depending on the stage of planning for the project in question. These three types are hypothetical projects, actual projects, and exemplar projects, which are outlined and discussed in detail below.

Hypothetical Projects versus Actual Projects

A hypothetical project is a project outlined in an I-924 submission but not accompanied by a comprehensive business plan compliant with the guidelines from the *Matter of Ho* decision, which is required for an actual project proposal. Hypothetical projects may include those that have already sought necessary licenses and engaged in other forms of concrete planning as well as truly hypothetical projects, as the distinction from USCIS rests not on the actual status of the project but on whether the submitted documents contain an appropriate business plan.

A hypothetical project proposal outlines the potential impact of a project, including how it will promote economic growth and job creation in the targeted region, and generally how it will accomplish the goals of the EB-5 Program. However, it might not contain the level of detail necessary in an actual project proposal, which includes verifiable evidence of the granting of any necessary licenses and permits and the commitment of funds toward the project, as well as other information to illustrate that a specific project is ready to be implemented.

If a regional center submits what it believes to be an actual project proposal but USCIS finds that the proposal lacks evidence or is otherwise too deficient to be considered actual, the regional center might still be approved based on the hypothetical potential of the project. While actual project approvals are included with the designation letter for a regional center and receive deference in future adjudications, hypothetical projects are simply useful for initial designation decisions. While I-924 submissions can contain a mix of actual and hypothetical projects, the majority of regional center designations in recent years have in fact been based on hypothetical projects.

Hypothetical and actual project proposals are both meant to illustrate how a regional center will raise capital and create jobs. Although these proposals differ in their level of detail and in their significance for later adjudication decisions, both demonstrate to USCIS that the regional center is capable of fulfilling its roles under the EB-5 Program. Both should contain sufficient information in the form of economic projections, market data, and financial analyses to show that the project in question will create the requisite number of jobs. In an actual project proposal, this information would be present through a business plan compliant with *Matter of Ho* guidelines.

Investors should keep in mind that this distinction between hypothetical and actual projects applies only to regional center I-924 proposals. A successful I-526 petition must be supported by a comprehensive business plan detailing an actual project. Regional center representatives should likewise remember that a regional center must submit not only a hypothetical or actual project proposal but also a detailed operational plan for the regional center itself when filing the I-924. A business plan for the regional center is a necessary element of the application for designation.

Exemplar Projects

An exemplar project is an actual project for which the regional center files a sample I-526 petition along with its I-924. For this reason, regional centers with actual projects often file a sample I-526 in an effort to ensure future petitions will receive deference as a result of the approval of the exemplar project. Deference can be crucial in protecting investors if policy changes affect EB-5 Program requirements, for example, and can also cut down on wait times for petition adjudication, as USCIS has no need to review an unchanged business plan in subsequent I-526 petitions after having approved an exemplar. As such, an exemplar project can be a powerful tool in attracting investors.

The exemplar project proposal must include a business plan that comprehensively outlines all elements of the business. It must describe the business and its structure, analyze the target market and competition and show how the business is financially capable of succeeding in that market, accurately calculate the number of indirect and induced jobs the business will create using verifiable economic models, and show that the business has been approved under any relevant federal or state licensing programs. USCIS will review all the organizational documents provided with the sample petition to ensure the project is in compliance with program requirements and able to facilitate the immigration of foreign investors under those guidelines.

Submitting an exemplar project proposal is therefore a logical option for regional centers with an actual project in development at the time the I-924 is filed.

Conclusion

While hypothetical, actual, and exemplar project proposals play different roles in facilitating regional center designation and project approval, regional centers must include with each proposal as much relevant information about a project as possible to encourage a successful adjudication. The decision in *Matter of Ho* provides regional centers and investors with a useful checklist of what USCIS looks for in a successful business plan, but the possibility of changes within the regional center program and the EB-5 Program itself means practitioners should strive to remain aware of evolving plan requirements.

The Basics of Form I-924

Businesses that want to obtain EB-5 regional center status must file Form I-924 with USCIS. Form I-924, Application for Regional Center under the Immigrant Investor Pilot Program, must be approved by USCIS in order for a business entity to be designated as a regional center, enabling them to start receiving capital from foreign nationals for EB-5 projects.

In addition to serving as an application for a business to become designated as an EB-5 regional center, Form I-924 can be used to amend a regional center's designation, which may involve changes to the regional center's organizational structure, geographic scope, or industry scope (NAICS codes). An I-924 can also be filed to obtain approval for an exemplar project.

Accompanying Documentation for Form I-924

Several documents must accompany an I-924 application to provide the necessary evidence to USCIS that the business meets all the criteria for an EB-5 regional center and/or exemplar project. The exact documentation required will depend on the specifics of the application, but some general requirements are listed below.

Regional centers must specify the geographic scope of their activities, and so an I-924 application must demonstrate through a detailed map the proposed area in which the regional center will operate.

The application for regional center designation must also be accompanied by a project (whether hypothetical, actual, or exemplar), and this project's documentation will be used to demonstrate whether the regional center complies with the EB-5 Program's requirements for investments and employment creation. Accompanying documents may include a business plan, financial projections or pro-formas, an economic report, securities documents, due diligence questionnaires, accredited investor questionnaires, subscription agreements, and documents pertaining to the structure of the new commercial enterprise.

Form I-924 must also be accompanied by a description of the anticipated promotional activities of the regional center. Specifically, this might include the marketing plan for attracting EB-5 investors, a proposed budget for marketing, evidence that funds have been allocated for promotion of the regional center, and any descriptions of past, present, or future promotional activities.

Because EB-5 capital must be lawfully obtained, Form I-924 must be accompanied by evidence for how the regional center applicant will ensure investors' funds originate from lawful sources.

The I-924 application must be accompanied by any other documents necessary to prove that the regional center applicant will comply with all EB-5 regulations. Such documentation might include articles of incorporation for the regional center and affiliated new commercial enterprise, contracts or agreements made with other entities expected to engage in activities on the regional center's behalf, and drafts of investment and escrow agreements.

Filing Form I-924

Typically, the Form I-924 is filed by the regional center applicant or an attorney acting on the applicant's behalf, but many other professionals including economists, accountants, and business plan writers are involved in the process. The appropriate USCIS mailing address and current filing fees for new I-924 applications is available via the USCIS website. Processing times vary and are released by USCIS from time to time but as of the date of this book, you should generally expect approximately 12 months for USCIS to process your Form I-924, and after the form is processed, USCIS may request additional information.

Once a business gains USCIS designation as a regional center, it must file Form I-924A each year to maintain this status.

Project Structure

How to Structure an EB-5 Project

A common question received by our team of EB-5 professionals is "What is the typical structure of an EB-5 project?" The answer can be complicated, so we want to share our collective experience resulting from our work across various EB-5 project structures. In addition, we have provided an adjustable mezzanine debt template to serve as a simplified starting point for EB-5 project developers; this can be modified for the specific capital structure of your project. It is worth noting that preferred equity deals are becoming a popular alternative to mezzanine financing and should be considered as well.

Key Parties Involved in an EB-5 Project

The first step in any project structuring discussion is to understand the parties involved in the transaction and to determine which role(s) each party will play. Participants may have several roles in a transaction so it is critical to think through the impact of certain parties fulfilling certain roles.

As a general summary the key participants in an EB-5 deal involve the following:

- Project sponsor (a real estate developer or, for an operating business, the project owner)
- Equity sponsor (often the same as the project sponsor)
- Regional center sponsor
- EB-5 fund manager
  - The EB-5 fund is typically structured as a limited partnership or LLC with investors serving as limited partners or members and the EB-5 fund manager serving as general partner or managing member of the EB-5 fund.
- Project advisors
- Immigration attorney
- Securities attorney
- Business plan writer
- Economist
- Bank/escrow service advisors

Figure 1, which illustrates the different parties involved in an EB-5 deal, the roles they play, their relationship to the project and the project sponsor, and the timing of their involvement in the process, lays the groundwork for an effective business and legal structural approach for a potential project.

Real Estate Development Project				
Typical Project (with or without EB-5)		EB-5 Specific		
Developer	Project Sponsor	RC Sponsor	General Partner	Project Advisors
Role Description & Responsibility				
Group responsible for quarterbacking development deal or operational business, also typically an equity stakeholder in the project	An equity investor, often the key person coordinating the funding of both traditional and EB-5 capital. Sometimes but not always involved in development	Regional Center can act as either the administrative arm or take on a more comprehensive role, including fundraising and serving as GP	The manager of the EB-5 Fund, typically a limited partnership or LLC (New Commercial Enterprise). Responsible for loan administration	Team responsible for ensuring a compliant, complete, and marketable EB-5 offering
Party Who Serves This Function				
Developer or sponsor	Equity investor or manager	USCIS approved Regional Center – either purely as a Regional Center Sponsor or as a more comprehensive partner	Can be the Regional Center, Developer, Migration Agent, or some other third party	Immigration attorney Securities Attorney BP writer Economist Bank / Escrow
Independent from developer?				
No	No	Sometimes – can be independent or related entity	Independence is a benefit here, although may be a related party to developer	Either hired by independent group or developer
Timing of Involvement				
From inception of project	Typically early in project	EB-5 comes in after project has been established and structured. Part of capital stack discussion	During time of EB-5 offering structuring	At the start of EB-5 offering structuring

Figure 1. Roles and responsibilities of parties in an EB-5 project.

EB-5 Project Structuring: Key Decisions

The next key question is "How will EB-5 fit into the capital stack and will the investment function as a loan or an equity investment?" EB-5 investors will always be "equity" investors in some capacity, whether they directly own equity interests in the project or equity interests in the EB-5 fund (often called the "new commercial enterprise" or "NCE"). The NCE can either make a loan to the development company (the "job creating entity" or "JCE") or the NCE can make an equity investment directly into the project. The more common structure is a debt investment because it offers more standardization and protection to investors with a clear path to exit.

If structured as debt, the loan from the NCE into the JCE can take the form of any debt instrument imaginable, with the differing priorities, covenants, and obligations that come with each such type, such as a senior loan, second position loan, or a mezzanine loan. Equity can also be structured in a variety of ways. Capital structuring decisions are deal-specific and must be tailored to the needs of the project, the target investors, and the EB-5 capital's position in the overall capital stack. Some of the key differences between equity versus debt are highlighted below.

Equity

- Investors play a more active role.

- The structure is traditionally used in smaller deals where EB-5 owners are directly involved in management and/or want meaningful returns.
- Equity investments are always subordinated to debt, which increases the risk profile for this type of investment.
- As a general matter, EB-5 investors prefer capital preservation over equity style returns. However, certain investors may be more receptive to traditional equity structures.
- Older deals may have been completed using the equity model before the loan model became more common.

Debt

- Investors play a more passive role.
- This structure is preferred by investors due to the perceived security of debt over equity as a form of investment. The typical EB-5 investor's top priorities are to secure a green card and ensure capital preservation.
- Debt instruments are often secured by collateral and have priority over any equity in the project.
- There is a clear path to exit since debt instruments have a maturity date.
- The loan structure allows for more standard terms, covenants and obligations.
- The NCE typically has various rights with respect to the development of projects.

EB-5 Project Structuring: Key Roles and Responsibilities

After the structure of the deal is determined, the team can begin to decide roles and responsibilities of the involved parties.

Figure 2 serves as a starting point when considering the structure of a project. For illustrative purposes, we're using a mezzanine debt deal framework for a real estate development project, but this can be tailored to meet any project's individual needs.

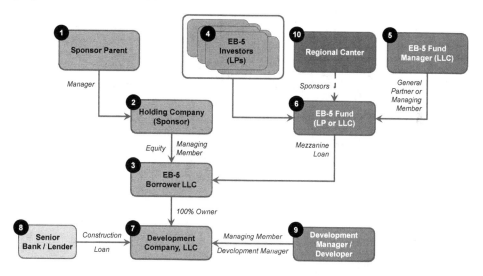

Figure 2. EB-5 project structure.

The key roles of each entity are defined below:

1. Sponsor parent: For a larger real estate developer, this would be the company's recognizable name. This entity may or may not be the owner of the project's (2) holding company. Typically, the (1) sponsor parent will be the manager of the (2) holding company, which is the actual owner of the project. These entities are typically kept separate in order to limit the liability of the (1) sponsor parent across multiple projects. For example, if a (2) holding company were to become insolvent, if structured correctly, the (1) sponsor parent would have protection from liability. If the (1) sponsor parent and the (2) holding company were the same entity, insolvency could jeopardize all projects for the (1) sponsor parent. Having separate entities adds protection for projects and investors and allows for a more organized approach across, in some cases, many projects for a single (1) sponsor parent.

2. Holding company: This company is also referred to as the project sponsor. This is the owner of the development/project. This is the company that owns the (3) EB-5 borrower. Typically, developer equity would be contributed to the project through this company.

3. EB-5 borrower: In a mezzanine debt structure this is the "mezz-co", "mid-co" or "upstream borrower". This entity is specifically formed for the project and its purpose is to borrow the EB-5 funds from the (6) EB-5 fund. This makes the mezzanine loan structurally subordinated to any senior debt. A new (3) EB-5 borrower will typically be formed for each new project and will be specific to that deal.

4. EB-5 investors: The individual (4) EB-5 investors invest into the (6) EB-5 fund by purchasing equity interests in the fund. The combined interests of these investors is pooled to form the (6) EB-5 fund.

5. EB-5 fund manager: This is the manager of the (6) EB-5 fund and is responsible for financial administration of the fund. If the (6) EB-5 fund is a limited partnership, the EB-5 fund manager would serve as the (5) general partner of the EB-5 fund. Similarly, if the (6) EB-5 fund is a limited liability company, the EB-5 fund manager would serve as the managing member or manager of the LLC. The EB-5 fund manager may or may not be affiliated with the (10) regional center or the (7) development company or may be completely independent. The EB-5 fund manager typically has a fiduciary duty to the investors in the (6) EB-5 fund, so if it is affiliated with the (7) development company, such affiliation would need to be disclosed and any conflicts of interest would typically need to be waived by such (4) EB-5 investors.

6. EB-5 fund: (4) EB-5 investors' contributions are pooled together in this (6) EB-5 fund, which is then invested into the project's (7) development company. If the (6) EB-5 fund is a limited partnership, each (4) EB-5 investor purchases partnership interests to become a limited partner in the (6) EB-5 fund. If the (6) EB-5 fund is an LLC, each (4) EB-5 investor purchases equity interests to become a member of the LLC. The rights and roles of limited partners can range from minimal involvement to active voting rights. The (6) EB-5 fund makes either a loan or equity contribution to the (3) EB-5 borrower.

7. Development company: This is the company that directly owns the project assets (land, building, etc.) and is typically the borrower of the senior construction loan, if any. Should there be a mortgage or a secured loan, the (7) development company typically secures the loan because it is the entity that owns the assets of the project.

8. Senior bank/lender: Mezzanine debt deals always involve a (8) senior bank/lender. This lender will have first priority on the (7) development company (assets of the project) and will often record a mortgage on the property. The (8) senior bank/lender and the (6) EB-5 fund should always have an intercreditor agreement which outlines the respective rights of each creditor with respect to the project.

9. Development manager/developer: This entity is responsible for managing the project development. Typically this is the manager of the (7) development company and will oversee tasks including construction, landscaping, etc.

10. Regional center: The (10) regional center typically operates in an administrative capacity with respect to the (6) EB-5 fund. The regional center may be affiliated with the (5) EB-5 fund manager but does not have to be. The

relationship to the (6) EB-5 fund is not an ownership relationship but a service relationship. In some instances, the (10) regional center may be owned by the (7) development company, in such instances, proper disclosures should be given to investors along with any potential conflicts of interest.

Optimizing the structure of an EB-5 project (from an immigration and financial risk perspective) is a complex endeavor and requires the input of a team of knowledgeable advisors with current market data. This illustrative example is meant to serve as a starting point for understanding the key players and structuring decisions involved in the EB-5 process.

Targeted Employment Area (TEA) Designation

In today's EB-5 market, getting an EB-5 project location designated as a TEA is important for successfully attracting EB-5 investors. If an EB-5 project is located in a TEA, the required EB-5 investment amount is only $500,000 dollars as opposed to $1,000,000 for a project not located in a TEA as of the date of this writing. Since the vast majority of EB-5 investors are primarily motivated to invest in an EB-5 project to acquire a green card, they typically have no compelling reason to risk twice as much capital in an EB-5 investment project.

In order to be officially designated as a TEA, an EB-5 project must be located in either (i) a rural area or (ii) a location experiencing a high unemployment rate at least 50% above the national average). When an EB-5 investor submits an I-526 immigration petition, the official TEA letter is included as an exhibit in the petition to demonstrate that the EB-5 project and the investor qualify at the lower TEA investment level. For EB-5 investors who choose to invest in a USCIS-approved regional center, the available projects will most likely be located in a TEA.

Figure 3 illustrates TEA determination for EB-5 projects.

TEA Determination Tree

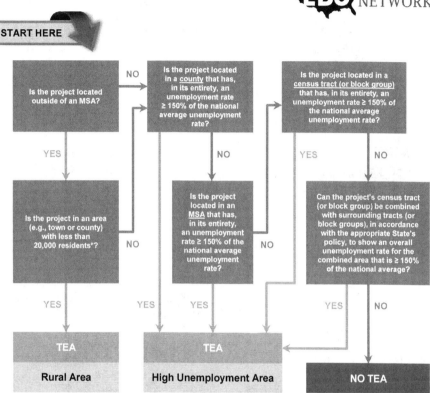

* According to most recent (2010) Census data

Figure 3. TEA determination for EB-5 projects.

1. High Unemployment TEA Designations

To be designated as a high unemployment TEA, an EB-5 project must be located in an area with an unemployment rate of at least 150% of the U.S. national average. For example, since the U.S. national average unemployment rate for 2014 was approximately 6.2%, the required unemployment rate threshold for a high unemployment TEA would be 9.1% (150% of the 6.2% unemployment rate). Additionally, for an EB-5 project to qualify as a high unemployment TEA, it must be in a county or MSA that has a population of 20,000 or more residents.

If an EB-5 project is located in an area that meets the average unemployment requirement listed above and is not within a county or MSA that

31

has a population of 20,000 or more residents, then it can be designated as a high unemployment TEA by the appropriate EB-5 state agency.

USCIS has authorized individual U.S. state agencies (specific departments within each state government) to approve EB-5 project requests for high unemployment TEA designations. EB-5 projects must submit a request to the appropriate EB-5 state agency with supporting data and documentation that the EB-5 project location in question does qualify as a high unemployment TEA under the rules set forth by USCIS as administered and interpreted by the state agency in question. Since USCIS will rely on a properly derived high unemployment TEA designation from the appropriate, authorized EB-5 state agency, this method of high unemployment TEA approval is usually the easiest route for most EB-5 projects.

If an EB-5 project location qualifies as a high unemployment TEA at the time of the EB-5 investor's I-526 submission to USCIS (as recognized by a valid TEA letter from an authorized EB-5 state agency), then it will be recognized by USCIS as an official TEA, and the EB-5 investor will be approved for the reduced TEA investment level.

2. TEA Qualification in Rural Areas

EB-5 project locations must meet a specific set of requirements to qualify as a rural TEA. The EB-5 project in question must not be located within a metropolitan statistical area (MSA) as labeled by the U.S. Office of Management and Budget.

Additionally, the EB-5 project must not be on the outskirts of a town or city that has a population of 20,000 or more residents as determined by the most recent decennial U.S. Census. If an EB-5 project location qualifies as a rural area at the time of the EB-5 investor's I-526 submission to USCIS, then the location will be recognized by USCIS as an official TEA.

Important note: Unlike the high unemployment TEA designation, rural areas have no official TEA designation letter. For an EB-5 project location to qualify as a rural TEA, the EB-5 investor's I-526 petition must include documentation that demonstrates that the EB-5 project location qualifies as a rural TEA as set forth by USCIS and described above.

Using Census Blocks to Form TEAs

In general, TEAs are designated by state agencies, but it is possible to request special TEA designation letters based upon combined census tracts. When census tracts cannot be combined to form a TEA, however, an alternative in some states is to use smaller geographic areas known as census blocks to create census block groups that qualify for TEA designation.

Like census tracts, census blocks are geographic areas defined by American Community Survey (ACS) data. Census block data is released by ACS at regular intervals. Currently, only a handful of states accept the use of census block data in issuing special TEA designation letters. The following states have indicated they allow or intend to allow census block groups when determining TEAs:

- Kansas
- New Mexico
- Oregon
- Texas (select cities and counties)
- Vermont
- Washington

Each state has different policies regarding whether they accept census block groups and, if so, how census blocks are treated. If this information is not available at the state's TEA website, a call to the designating authority may be required to obtain it.

The advantage to using census blocks rather than census tracts is that blocks are smaller areas that allow for a more flexible census-share calculation. In other words, when calculating whether an area qualifies as a TEA, a group of contiguous census blocks can more easily be combined to form a TEA—even when that area would otherwise be ineligible for TEA designation based upon census tract data.

For example, consider a project located in a census tract with an unemployment rate that disqualifies it from TEA designation. The first step would be to use the census-share methodology to determine if a group of contiguous census tracts might qualify for TEA designation. When no combination of census tracts results in a TEA, however, a combination of census blocks might.

However, both the national average unemployment rate and the unemployment rate of any given area change over time. These changes tend to carry more dramatic effects when the labor force of a TEA is smaller. As a result, census block groups are more greatly affected by changes to unemployment—and this sensitivity makes these smaller areas more susceptible to losing their TEA designation. Despite this disadvantage, census blocks do provide an alternative way to obtain special TEA designation letters from those states that allow this method of calculating unemployment.

USCIS Approval of TEA Designations

TEA designations are reviewed by USCIS as part of each individual investor's I-526 application process. TEAs are also reviewed as part of the I-924 project "exemplar" process for EB-5 projects in TEAs seeking pre-approval from USCIS. The EB-5 visa applicant or EB-5 project sponsor must provide sufficient evidence that the EB-5 project in question is located within a rural or high unemployment TEA by submitting third-party evidence. Several forms of evidence can be used to justify that an EB-5 project and associated investments will occur within a TEA.

The following are acceptable forms of evidence for TEA designation by USCIS:

1. Geographic and population data from the U.S. Office of Management and Budget that demonstrate an area qualifies as a rural TEA

2. Current unemployment data and statistics from the U.S. Bureau of Labor Statistic's Local Area Unemployment Statistics (LAUS) office that justify a high unemployment TEA

3. Other statistical documentation on the local area unemployment situation and population that justifies a high unemployment TEA

Important note: If an EB-5 project chooses to pursue the higher, non-TEA EB-5 investment amount (currently $1,000,000), the TEA designation process is unnecessary. Evidence of a qualifying TEA is only required by USCIS for EB-5 investors and EB-5 projects when seeking the lower TEA EB-5 investment amount (currently $500,000).

Key Takeaways on TEA Designations

TEA designations can be obtained in two distinct ways:

1. TEA designation by an authorized state agency: An EB-5 project or investor can submit a TEA designation letter from an authorized state agency or government body stating that the location of the EB-5 project in question has been formally designated as a high unemployment TEA. This is the easier approach for most EB-5 projects.

2. TEA designation by USCIS: Direct designation by USCIS requires that the EB-5 project or investor submit evidence (see the three bulleted examples above) that the location of the EB-5 project in question is within an area that has an average unemployment rate of 150% of the national average.

How to Manage EB-5 Project Disclosures

EB-5 investments are typically structured as private securities offerings relying on one or more exemptions from registration with the U.S. Securities and Exchange Commission (SEC). As a result, a project sponsor must be careful and engage proper counsel when preparing offering documents in order to remain in compliance with federal and state securities laws. In particular, at a minimum, an offering of securities needs to provide sufficient disclosure with respect to the project for a potential investor to make an informed investment decision. Such disclosures are often complicated in EB-5 offerings—and seldom uniform from project to project. As a result, care must be taken to ensure that a project is properly analyzed and that its disclosures are independently verified.

Following is a thorough—but not necessarily complete—examination of the key risk factors that every EB-5 offering should address.

Regional Center Role

The role a regional center plays may vary from project to project, and so it is vital that for any given transaction, the regional center's role is clearly delineated. For instance, a regional center may simply sponsor a project, but it might also serve as a manager or general partner in the NCE. Regional centers may also be involved in marketing a project to potential investors. As a general matter, the primary role of the regional center is to promote economic activity under the EB-5 program and therefore, to sponsor projects meeting USCIS requirements and file and report the appropriate information, documents and data to USCIS. However, since the principals of the regional center often play multiple roles in an EB-5 transaction, industry practitioners often use the term regional center to refer to multiple roles including fund administration, loan tracking, fund raising and other roles. For purposes of this section, the term "Regional Center" will refer to the purely administrative role that regional centers are designed to play with respect to USCIS. Other roles will be defined separately below.

Sponsoring a project

The primary function of a Regional Center is to sponsor EB-5 projects. For the Regional Center, this means ensuring that each such EB-5 project complies with all of the requirements of the EB-5 Program. For the EB-5 project, regional center sponsorship typically means having the ability to include a larger number of EB-5 investors utilizing the ability to count direct, indirect, and induced job creation toward the EB-5 Program's employment creation requirement—a distinct marketing advantage when seeking EB-5 investors, and the reason most EB-5 projects are sponsored through regional centers. A description of the relationship between the Regional Center and the sponsored EB-5 project is often included in the project disclosure documents. The disclosures should also include how the Regional Center will conduct its due diligence and perform its administrative responsibilities, as well as whether or not the Regional Center will employ any third-party professionals to fulfill these duties.

Serving as manager or general partner

In certain cases, some or all of the principals of the Regional Center may also serve as the manager or general partner of the NCE. We will use the term "Fund Administrator" to refer to this role in this section. In the past, the Regional Center entity itself served as the manager or general partner of the NCE, but this practice is less common today. Instead, a fund management entity is specially formed for the administration of the NCE, typically by the principals of the Regional Center. The offering documents should clearly indicate the role of the Fund Administrator and its principals regarding EB-5 Program compliance, reporting requirements, and the administration/operation of the NCE.

Marketing the project

Another key role is the "Fund Raiser", which involves marketing an EB-5 project to potential investors. The Fund Raiser is usually also the Fund Administrator as the issuer of the securities related to the EB-5 project, and is responsible for sourcing the EB-5 investment capital with respect to the Project. In the event that the principals of the Regional Center are also the Fund Administrator, they would also act in this capacity.

Since most EB-5 securities offerings are structured as private placements of securities, they must rely one or more exemptions from registration with the SEC. For example, reliance on Regulation D will require, among other things, that investor suitability is determined prior to accepting the investment.

Another pertinent issue is how investors are sourced and whether any transaction-based compensation is paid, and to whom. Compliance in this regard will almost certainly involve issues related to broker-dealer registration (Securities Exchange Act of 1934), investment adviser registration (Investment Advisers Act of 1940), and investment company registration (Investment Company Act of 1940).

These issues will be discussed in greater detail in another section.

Avoiding conflicts of interest

In addition to the roles the Regional Center plays in the EB-5 project, the Regional Center's relationships with the other parties involved in the offering must be fully disclosed, such as the project owner or developer. Historically, due to the small scale of EB-5 program and lack of third party Regional Centers, project owners and developers often had to apply for and run the Regional Center themselves, and also act as Fund Administrator and Fund Raiser.

However, this type of relationship presents inherent conflicts of interest and should be avoided. For example, if the project owner or developer has structured the investment as a debt investment into his or her project, and is also acting as the Regional Center, the Fund Administrator and the Fund Raiser, then all of the documents for the transaction have not been negotiated on an arm's length basis, most notably the terms of the loan. In essence, the project owner would be acting as both the borrower (on behalf of the EB-5 investors) and the lender (on behalf of itself). In this scenario a clear conflict of interest exists which must be disclosed in the project offering documents. In such cases, an independent party could administer the loan to prevent the conflict.

Disclosure of the relationships between the Regional Center, the Fund Administrator, the Fund Raiser, the project owner or developer and the other parties serves to protect the investors and demonstrates proper oversight.

Escrow Arrangement Options

Nowhere does EB-5 law require that investor funds go into escrow—such arrangements are, in effect, the result of the tension between EB-5 Program requirements and investor expectations. The EB-5 Program requires that an investor's capital be fully committed to an EB-5 project at the time the I-526 petition is filed. Investors, however, desire some way to limit their financial risk. Placing investor funds in escrow satisfies the EB-5 Program's requirements while helping limit investors' financial risk.

Whether an escrow arrangement exists—and if so, how it is structured—must be fully disclosed in the offering documents.

No escrow

Some regional centers offer no form of escrow arrangement, and investor funds are placed directly into the NCE. In an arrangement like this, the regional center may offer refunds to investors whose I-526 petitions are denied. Offering documents should clearly disclose all procedures and risks related to any such refund.

Specific elements that should be addressed include the extent of the guarantee and the source of the refund—or the collateral used to ensure sufficient funds will be available to cover any such refund.

Escrow released upon I-526 filing

Some regional centers use an escrow arrangement that allows for the release of investor funds once an investor's I-526 petition is filed. In this way, the investor has some assurance that, at the very least, his or her attorney received the information needed to file the I-526 petition and it was successfully submitted to USCIS.

Variations of this arrangement exist in which the funds are released from escrow upon filing, but only when at least one I-526 petition has received approval—or only if the project has gained exemplar status. Such arrangements substantially reduce the risk for investors since their funds will only be released from escrow pending the approval of the project. In such cases, I-526 petition denials are still possible, but these are generally the result of problems with an investor's personal information, source of funds, or other deficiencies in the investor's application.

Escrow released upon I-526 approval

Another escrow arrangement used by regional centers is to release investor funds from escrow only upon I-526 petition approval. This arrangement provides the least amount of risk for investors since their money will not be used until their EB-5 petition has been approved. However, given USCIS processing times of over a year, this type of escrow arrangement is typically impractical for most projects.

Other escrow and refund arrangements

One possible escrow arrangement involves a partial holdback of funds that ensures that at least some of an investor's funds will be available if his or her I-526 petition is denied. Other potential components of escrow and refund arrangements might involve substituting another investor for an investor whose I-526 is denied, minimum escrow amounts, developer guarantees, or further contributions from the developer. In any case, such arrangements, policies, and assurances should be adequately disclosed in the offering documents.

Project-Specific Risks

Any project, regardless of its nature, has generic risks—but offering documents must also take into account the risk factors that relate specifically to an individual project. These unique risks are related to the project's industry category, the project's capital stack and source of funds, and a number of other elements.

- Industry category: Certain risks are unique to each industry, and so every project should be analyzed in light of its industry to determine the related risks.
- Capital stack: The makeup of the capital stack must be fully disclosed in offering documents. Capital sources will likely include developer equity, senior debt, EB-5 funds, and may even involve incentives such as government and tax credits, grants, etc. All funding sources should be identified, and each source's funds should be given as a percent of the total capital stack. Development cannot commence until all funding sources are identified.
- Senior debt: A detailed disclosure must be provided regarding the project's senior debt, if any, including all terms and conditions. The more senior debt taken on by a project, the larger the risk of default and foreclosure. Due to this risk, an intercreditor agreement should be in place to help protect the NCE's interests by enabling it to take on the position of the developer in the event the developer defaults on this debt. To that end, a regional center might have its own due diligence team and specific internal controls—or it might

engage the services of other professionals—to increase investor protection. Any intercreditor agreement or other safeguard would need to be clearly disclosed as well.

- Capital/equity stake of the developer: Offering documents should disclose how much capital and equity are being provided by the developer. Doing so enables a better assessment of the risk the developer is taking on relative to other stakeholders.

- EB-5 capital: The amount of EB-5 capital being sought should be clearly disclosed, as should any risks associated with failing to raise the desired amount of EB-5 funds. The offering documents should demonstrate whether the project's completion depends on EB-5 capital and should describe how the project will be financed in the event the project fails to raise the entire EB-5 capital amount. For instance, offering documents should disclose whether additional capital will be raised as necessary by taking on additional senior debt, equity, or mezzanine financing.

- EB-5 loan collateral: The project's collateral should be analyzed to determine how much surplus equity might exist to protect the EB-5 loan. Disclosures should be made regarding the loan-to-cost ratio, loan-to-value ratio, and loan-to-stabilized-value ratio.

- Expected employment creation: The economic analysis should clearly demonstrate how jobs will be generated and should indicate any associated risks.

- Potential for cost overruns: Every project should anticipate the potential for cost overruns, and the mechanisms put in place to fund such overruns should be clearly described.

- Securities compliance: While every EB-5 project has certain risks related to securities—by nature, an EB-5 project is a securities offering—each project is unique and its securities risks will depend on a number of factors, including the offering's structure, size, and marketing strategy.

NCEs Using a Loan Model

When an NCE is created specifically to loan pooled EB-5 investors' funds to the JCE, the SEC may consider the NCE an "investment company" requiring registration under the Investment Company Act of 1940.

In order for the NCE to be exempt from registration under the Investment Company Act, two exemptions are often sought: the C-1 exemption, which limits the EB-5 project's offering to no more than 100 investors, and the C-5 exemption, which requires the NCE's transaction to involve real estate collateral or mezzanine financing that qualifies as mortgage-backed collateral.

The offering documents should disclose whether the NCE is bound by the Investment Company Act of 1940 and whether the offering requires one or both exemptions.

Marketing through Broker-Dealers

If the EB-5 offering involves any kind of marketing activity within the United States, only registered broker-dealers may be compensated for such services. Paying finder's fees to unregistered agents operating within the United States without an exemption would potentially be a violation of securities laws and would allow investors to invoke the right of rescission.

Offering documents should disclose how the offering will be marketed and whether any exemptions apply. Also, potential compensation—and a description of who might be compensated—should be fully disclosed.

Marketing through Investment Advisors

As with broker-dealers, any investment advisor who offers investment advice pertaining to securities must be registered under the Investment Advisers Act of 1940. This securities issue should be addressed in offering documents much the same way that the presence of broker-dealers is addressed.

Relying Upon Exemptions

The two exemptions from registration relied upon by most private offerings of securities in the EB-5 context are: Regulation D, which relates to private placements of domestic securities, and Regulation S, which relates to offshore (non-U.S.) offerings. In addition to disclosures relating to the exemption(s) relied upon by those conducting the securities offering, steps must be taken to ensure a proper process is employed to ensure the offering remains in compliance throughout the duration of the offering period.

Properly Structuring EB-5 Loan Agreements

In an effort to comply with the requirements of the EB-5 Program and U.S. securities laws, regional centers often defer finalizing loan agreements until the amount and timing of the EB-5 investment is certain. While this caution is reasonable, financial documents protect both investors and the project by allowing parties to agree on the loan structure and terms, and EB-5 project teams must therefore plan thoroughly when executing these agreements after an offer has been made. Similarly, an investor must review the loan agreement in detail to ensure it does not materially affect his or her interests.

This section explores the structure of a typical EB-5 loan agreement involving a regional center and other actors as well as additional financing documents and their importance for EB-5 investors and project teams.

Flow of Funds in an EB-5 Loan

In a regional center arrangement, the transfer of investment funds will typically follow the steps outlined below.

1. The Fund Raiser will work with various sourcing channels to attract and secure foreign investors for the EB-5 project. The Fund Administrator, acting as the manager of the NCE, and who often is also the Fund Raiser, will coordinate with the Regional Center to conduct due diligence and ensure that the loan complies with the requirements of the EB-5 Program as well as U.S. and foreign laws.

2. The EB-5 investor will make the minimum investment necessary into the NCE as required by the EB-5 Program (currently $1,000,000 for non-TEA and $500,000 for TEA investments). This amount is placed into escrow, if applicable, until it is released to the borrower, the NCE. Along with the investment amount, the investor will typically pay a subscription or administrative fee to cover administrative costs.

3. The Fund Administrator will administer the loan of the investment amount to the JCE, which will draw on the funds as necessary according to the project business plan. The Fund Administrator, acting on behalf of the NCE, and the JCE will agree on the terms of the loan, such as the maturity date, interest rate, and prepayment restrictions or requirements. Documentation related to this lending transaction may include, among other things, a loan agreement, promissory note and loan security and collateral documents, among others detailed in the sections below. As part of these agreements, the JCE may grant the NCE a security interest in its assets or may make a guarantee of completion or repayment in the event of an I-526 denial or other agreed circumstances, and these guarantees must also be reflected in the project documentation.

4. If necessary, the JCE may obtain interim or bridge financing to begin development of the project prior to receipt of the EB-5 capital from escrow in accordance with the agreed terms. As such, repayment of the EB-5 investment may be subordinated to payment to other senior lenders in the project as

outlined in any intercreditor and subordination agreements. Using the above funding sources, the JCE will complete the EB-5 project and repay the loaned investment amount at maturity using revenue from operations, the sale of the business, or other sources.

Structuring an EB-5 Loan

The loan agreement is meant to finalize terms between the NCE, acting as lender on behalf of the EB-5 investors and the JCE, the borrower and end-user of the EB-5 capital. The NCE and potential investors need to be mindful of two key things: (1) whether the JCE will create the 10 full-time jobs required under the EB-5 Program and (2) whether the JCE will provide enough revenue to repay the loan amount upon maturity along with any interest as agreed throughout the loan term. Additionally, the JCE must be able to provide the investor with any financial documents required by USCIS to demonstrate job creation as required by the investors' I-829 petition to remove the conditions of permanent residence.

The JCE will have its own concerns when entering into a loan agreement. Chief among these is the flexibility of the loan terms in that they must not restrict the ability of the JCE to run the business and must not conflict with terms agreed upon with other financing partners and senior lenders. The JCE may therefore wish to introduce a materiality threshold to account for unexpected events during construction or operations and may additionally request a grace period in the event of a default.

As discussed previously, the EB-5 investment loan may be subordinate to other loans and may or may not be guaranteed by other parties. Regardless of the unique structure of an EB-5 loan agreement, and aside from standard boilerplate provisions included with each agreement to comply with regulatory requirements, the loan agreement will likely contain the following key terms:

Borrowing Terms

1. The amount of the loan.
2. The interest rate on the loan.
3. The procedure for disbursement.
4. The maturity date and term of the loan, which is typically set to mature following the adjudication of investors' I-829 petitions by USCIS.
5. Terms for repayment of the principal and accrued interest on a monthly, quarterly, or annual basis.
6. Terms for prepayment of the loan, which typically is subject to an investors' I-829 petition being fully adjudicated by USCIS.
7. Any options for the JCE to exercise an extension in return for an increased interest rate or other extension fee.
8. Disclosure of any fees related to the loan, including any origination fees, which covers the cost of processing the loan.

In cases where the NCE has sought out multiple investors, disbursements of the loan may occur over a period of time according to specific milestones. To protect the interests of the EB-5 investors, the NCE should negotiate a binding agreement that outlines when the JCE may draw down on the loan. As the Fund Administrator will have incurred substantial costs to raise the investment funds and as the investors must rely on the JCE to use the full amount of the principal for job creation as required by the EB-5 Program, it is important to ensure that the capital is deployed properly into the JCE with sufficient protection measures in place to ensure that funds are not misused.

Closing Conditions

A typical loan agreement will provide clear guidelines on when closings on the loan may occur, specifically, which initial conditions need to be satisfied before the first advance of the loan and any conditions applying to subsequent advances. These conditions are meant to protect the NCE and the EB-5 investors, and the JCE must therefore meet these conditions to draw on the loan.

Conditions for closing may include the requirement that the JCE produce any statements related to its business and its capital stack, such as corporate authorization certificates, ancillary loan documents including intercreditor and subordination agreements, and proof that the JCE has secured any necessary funding to commence the project prior to drawing on the loan amount. These other sources of funding may include government grants or senior loans, as discussed above.

The JCE must also provide due diligence documents regarding the project, such as lien and title searches in the case of a real estate development, as well as proof that any security interests are properly perfected, guarding against claims by third parties. The Fund Administrator acting on behalf of the NCE must thoroughly review these documents to ensure the interests of the NCE and investors are protected before funding the JCE through disbursement of the loan.

Covenants, Representations and Warranties

The loan agreement will also contain representations and warranties made by the JCE to minimize risks for the NCE and investors. These representations and warranties allow the lenders to conduct due diligence on the borrower by gathering material information about its assets and operations as well as monitoring its business throughout the term of the loan, and they additionally allow the lenders to hold the JCE liable if any information provided is proven to be false. The JCE must review this section of the document carefully and may, as mentioned, request the inclusion of materiality thresholds and other mitigation agreements to protect its own interests.

Similarly, the loan agreement may also include covenants to protect the investment and the lenders by requiring the JCE to fulfill certain conditions or refrain from taking certain actions. As with representations and warranties, the borrower wishes to limit interference in its business, but the regional center is obligated to work in the interests of the EB-5 investors by monitoring operations and ensuring the loan is used as agreed. A breach of covenant triggers a default on the loan, so the parties to the agreement must ensure they understand and agree on these terms. The following two types of covenants are typically included in EB-5 loan agreements:

- Affirmative covenants obligate the JCE to provide unaudited financial statements, to notify the lenders of any material change to the business, to pay taxes and maintain insurance as necessary, and to fulfill the job creation and other requirements of the EB-5 Program. They also require that the borrower disclose financial information such as net worth, leverage ratio, and other pertinent details.
- Negative covenants prohibit the borrower from taking certain actions without the written agreement of the lenders. These actions may include selling assets, obtaining additional loans or other forms of debt or otherwise entering into material agreements, and changing the business plan or the scope of the project.

Default
The loan agreement must also include a discussion of the circumstances under which the loan will default. These include nonpayment or breach of covenant, as mentioned above, and such situations allow the lenders to act to protect the investment amount as agreed. If the NCE is subordinate to a senior lender, the NCE may be limited in remediation, but remedies include accelerating repayment of the loan and pursuing guarantors or security interests as outlined in the loan agreement.

Other Considerations for EB-5 Investors, Project Sponsors, and Regional Centers

Aside from the loan agreement itself and the provisions outlined above, EB-5 loan documents often include a promissory note signed by the borrower, security documents covering any assets to be recouped in the event of a default, a construction draw schedule to determine when disbursements will be made, any guarantees, and any subordination or intercreditor agreements applicable if the project will draw on multiple sources of funding.

Of most interest to EB-5 investors and regional centers is the use of collateral to secure the loan. In a complex EB-5 scenario involving multiple lenders, perfection of securities is crucial, so lenders must work with knowledgeable representatives to ensure any assets are protected according to U.S. laws. Additional documents may be necessary to prove that the borrower owns these assets and that they are secured against claims by a third party, as in the case of a property lien, for example. The lenders may wish to review lien waivers from any contractors involved with the project, mortgage agreements and title searches, and an appraisal of the assets in question.

While regional centers are experienced in preparing business plans, economic impact reports, and other documents required by USCIS to foster the successful adjudication of I-526 and I-829 petitions, the loan agreement is often overlooked despite its key role in protecting the interests of EB-5 immigrant investors and regional centers themselves. Investors and regional centers must work with experienced brokers and attorneys to ensure that these agreements are acceptable and that they minimize the risks inherent to the EB-5 Program by securing the loan amount and obligating the JCE to meet the agreed economic and job creation targets.

Trends in EB-5 Escrow Agreements

Escrow accounts play a key role in the movement of funds in the EB-5 regional center model, traditionally facilitating the release of funds to a project upon adjudication of an investor's I-526 petition for conditional permanent residence. These escrow accounts typically hold the entire EB-5 investment pool, and capital contributions are credited to investors once their I-526 petitions are approved. However, recent increases in wait times for adjudication, especially for mainland Chinese investors, who make up the vast majority of applicants under the EB-5 Program, have encouraged regional centers to explore other escrow models and legal mechanisms to allow for projects to receive essential funding while still making a refund of the investment possible in the event that an I-526 petition is denied.

Changing trends in the structure of escrow agreements reflect two conflicting viewpoints: while investors prefer to maintain a conservative fund release agreement to guard against the possibility of petition denial, project developers seek to access the investment capital and move forward with projects as soon as possible using more aggressive release terms. Regional centers have adopted more dynamic escrow agreements in an effort to accommodate the latter, resulting in a new escrow landscape for investors. This section discusses recent trends in this regard and details strategies regional centers can implement when negotiating escrow agreements to take into account the concerns of all parties.

Changing Demands in the EB-5 Market

The move away from escrow agreements conditioned on the approval of I-526 petitions is an attempt by regional centers to adapt to changing demands in the EB-5 market. More complex fund release mechanisms allow projects to move forward on schedule, reducing the possibility for the advent of contingencies which would otherwise affect the viability of the project and therefore approval of investors' I-526 petitions. This possibility is illustrated through the example scenario of a regional center that has raised all capital necessary for the construction and operation of a hotel but must wait for adjudication of the investors' petitions before moving forward with the project.

In this case, multiple aspects of the project might hinge on the release of escrow funds. For example, the purchase of the hotel property still needs to be finalized, as do contracts with local service providers. The potential for changes in the local real estate and business markets to affect project costs rises the longer funds are held in escrow, risking the success of the project. In this scenario, the purpose of the escrow account is to safeguard funds in the event of a petition denial, but the withholding of funds itself may very well result in the failure of the project and a denial of all associated I-526 petitions.

A regional center finding itself in such a situation may request that investors amend the existing escrow agreement to allow for an earlier release of the investment funds. However, such an ad hoc approach may not be well received by investors, who wish to safeguard the investment funds until such time as approval of the I-526 petition is assured. Additionally, because USCIS evaluates project documents during the I-526 approval stage to ensure investors will be able to meet the requirements of the EB-5 Program with the proposed project, investors may be hesitant to move forward unless this question has been answered. As such, regional centers may find that investors are unwilling to agree to early release amendments, or such a proposition may raise red flags and cause investors to withdraw their funding altogether.

The solution to this dilemma may lie in presenting investors at the outset with escrow agreements that account for the early release of funds without assurance of I-526 approval if necessary. While approval of the I-526 petition may be included as a trigger, new escrow agreements also include other conditions under which investment funds would be released to the project. These might include USCIS approval of an exemplar petition for the project or of a certain number of initial I-526 petitions, both of which would signify a likelihood that additional petitions associated with the project will be approved. Nonetheless, such agreements are riskier for investors than the traditional model is.

Strategies for Regional Centers

The role of escrow has evolved, meaning investors must now review and negotiate the terms of their investments carefully. As described above, escrow agreements may no longer safeguard the investment funds by default until approval of the I-526 petition and may instead provide for a more pragmatic release of funds to the project as needed to maintain the schedule in the project offering. In a scenario where release is triggered by USCIS approval of a certain number of petitions associated with the project, later investors would thus submit their investments to escrow with the release condition already having been met, meaning there would in effect be no escrow period for such investors despite the signing of an escrow agreement. For this reason and others, the changing escrow landscape should encourage investors to carefully review all project documents with the assistance of a qualified professional.

The following are three strategies regional centers have adopted to facilitate the early release of funds from escrow.

1. Release funds upon filing of the I-526 petition

Rather than conditioning fund release upon acceptance of the petition, some regional centers have opted to use filing as the trigger condition. This shortens the escrow period from its original length, beginning from the time funds are wired to the regional center and ending when USCIS approves the I-526 petition, to the earlier date on which the investor simply files the petition. This poses a significant risk to investors, as denial of the I-526 petition would potentially occur months or years after funds have been released.

2. Seek replacement investors in the event of an I-526 denial

In an effort to facilitate the transfer of funds to projects while assuring investors of a refund in the event that an I-526 petition is denied, regional centers have begun to include in escrow agreements the provision that in the event of a petition denial, the center will make reasonable efforts to source replacement funds and thereby allow a refund of the investment amount to the denied investor. Some projects and NCEs have additionally attempted to keep a certain amount of funds in escrow to refund denied investors, though centers adopting this strategy must ensure, as always, that each investor's full investment amount, when released, is applied to job creation rather than to refunding other investors.

3. Hold funds in overseas escrow accounts

USCIS has not prohibited the use of overseas escrow accounts for EB-5 projects on the condition that funds are transferred to the new commercial enterprise in the United States once the investor is granted permanent residence. The opportunity for an investor to work with an escrow account in his or her country of origin may ease concerns, though U.S. escrow accounts pose fewer problems in terms of exchange rates and potential restrictions on the export of capital.

Regional centers have increasingly adopted more complex escrow models in response to changing conditions within the EB-5 Program, namely lengthier wait times for approval of I-526 petitions. However, these agreements do create more risks for investors, who must consequently ensure they review escrow terms thoroughly with the assistance of qualified financial and legal professionals.

Combining EB-5 Financing with Tax Credits

In addition to inexpensive mezzanine financing or preferred equity deals through EB-5 capital, developers can take advantage of tax credit financing to generate greater returns or even make an otherwise insufficiently funded project feasible. A number of federal tax credit programs are available, some of which pair exceptionally well with EB-5 financing, and these programs can generally be used in combination with each other and EB-5 financing on the same EB-5 project.

Three Primary Types of Tax Credits

The low-income housing tax credit (LIHTC), the new market tax credit (NMTC), and the historic tax credit all fit well with the EB-5 Program since these credits and the program share a common objective of revitalizing economically depressed communities. Below is a more detailed discussion of these three credits.

1. Low-Income Housing Tax Credit (LIHTC)

Created to help finance the development of low-income housing, the LIHTC encourages private investors to pursue federal tax incentives that spur economic development and the development of affordable housing. The credit applies to both new construction and renovations.

Tax credits are allocated to applicants by designated state agencies, and these tax credits are then sold to private investors. Third-party investors or project partners are able to subsidize eligible costs incurred in the development of low-income rental housing units by either 30% using the "4% credit" or 70% using the "9% credit."

The 4% credit does not carry annual limits but is limited by a set number of private activity bonds, which must represent 50% or more of total development costs. The 9% credit, on the other hand, does carry an annual limit, and the number of credits allocated to each state is determined by population.

The taxpayer claims the LIHTC over a 10-year period.

2. New Market Tax Credit (NMTC)

The purpose of the NMTC program is similar to that of the EB-5 Program: to spur community development, stimulate the economy, and create jobs in economically depressed areas. Also like the EB-5 Program, this credit requires evidence of employment creation and other benefits to the community.

Created to promote private investment in low-income areas, the NMTC is awarded based upon the amount of equity committed by qualified investors. Typically, the NMTC is allocated to projects that involve the construction or renovation of cultural and education centers (e.g., art centers, charter schools, college campuses, etc.), emergency housing and related services (e.g., homeless shelters, transitional housing, education facilities for homeless people, etc.), and commercial property (e.g., shopping centers, technology facilities, hospitals, hotels, office spaces, etc.).

When structured efficiently, the NMTC can amount to 15%–25% of the total costs of a project.

3. Historic Tax Credit

The federal government offers a rehabilitation tax credit of up to 20% for qualified expenditures incurred during the renovation of certified historic buildings built before 1936. Most often, the owners of the historic building under renovation syndicate the tax credit to a third-party corporate investor. When the historic tax credit is used in conjunction with EB-5 funding, the EB-5 capital is employed as permanent (or replacement) financing.

Other Tax Incentives

Tax-increment financing (TIF) and tax abatements are additional tools used by municipalities to promote economic development. These incentives and other forms of public financing can be effective options in combination with EB-5 capital.

Financial Reporting Strategies in EB-5 Regional Center Projects

Under the EB-5 Program, foreign investors make significant outlays to new commercial enterprises in the United States and must not accept repayment of the investment funds until their I-829 petitions have been adjudicated. As the required investment sum is large, investors typically consult with experienced counsel and financial advisors to conduct due diligence on securities issuers and EB-5 projects.

However, investors frequently neglect to monitor a project's financial activity following the initial offering, which is based solely on projections and may not be carried out entirely as specified. This has caused concern in recent years with widely publicized SEC actions focusing on EB-5 projects. In 2015, for example, the SEC alleged that investors in a Seattle project managed by Path America Regional Center had fallen victim to fraud, and the developer had misappropriated nearly $18,000,000 of investor funds for personal use.

Given that one of the requirements of the EB-5 Program is that the entire investment amount be put toward job creation, investors have understandably sought more transparent reporting on the part of new commercial enterprises to monitor fund use and thereby safeguard their chances for successful visa adjudication through the program. Similarly, project developers must assure investors that their funds are being disbursed as planned according to U.S. securities law and EB-5 Program requirements. This section discusses several areas of focus in financial reporting for investors and project developers within the EB-5 regional center context.

Financial Reporting Goals and Requirements

Current EB-5 issuers conduct a range of financial reporting on an annual audited or quarterly unaudited basis, from reports to full financial statements including balance sheets. Investors must decide before committing funds whether the level of reporting a new enterprise will perform is sufficient for their purposes. In reviewing any financial reports provided, EB-5 investors generally aim to answer three central questions:

- Are the investment funds being put toward job creation as required?
- Will the project sustain the required number of jobs?
- Will investors receive a return on their investments?

While most projects are structured as limited partnerships or limited liability companies and therefore are not legally obligated to conduct any financial reporting in most states, entities taxed as partnerships are required to provide an annual statement on investors' shares of income, losses, deductions, and credits. However, such statements do not answer the above central three questions.

Although project developers may not be obligated to provide ongoing financial information to investors except when investors must vote based on such information, projects can benefit from thorough financial reporting procedures. Developers must aim to reassure investors that funds are being disbursed as agreed in the EB-5 business plan and that investors are receiving appropriate distributions. Additionally, financial reports can indicate to investors whether the project is on track to meet the projections on which the offering was based and whether it will be able to create the required number of jobs and provide a return on investment. Most importantly, comprehensive financial reports and auditing procedures can serve to deter fraud by all parties involved in a project.

Investors should nonetheless acknowledge that fraud is possible even in projects that provide regular reports, as a developer committing fraud would likely have the foresight to falsify financial statements in that case. Nonetheless, investors can remain vigilant in reviewing this information and can notify the SEC and pursue legal action to safeguard their investments in cases where fraud is uncovered.

Fund Disbursement Structures

In the regional center model, foreign investors contribute to an NCE, which in turn invests those funds in the JCE that operates the project and thereby creates the required number of jobs per investor. As such, investors should seek out projects that provide financial reports on the activities of both the NCE and the JCE. Projects working with lending institutions will likely be required to provide quarterly reports as well as annual audited reports to that institution, which should in turn be provided to EB-5 investors.

The regional center model also allows for investment in a "troubled business," one that has been in operation for at least two years and has sustained a loss of more than 20% of its net worth over the one to two years preceding the filing of an investor's I-526 petition for conditional permanent residence. In this scenario, a detailed audited financial statement would be necessary at the time of investment to establish to USCIS that the business is indeed troubled and that an EB-5 investment could preserve the required number of jobs.

In addition to seeking out projects that will provide sufficient financial reports, investors may wish to negotiate additional safeguards into their loan agreements to provide for the unique requirements of the EB-5 Program. For example, because early repayment of a loan to the NCE by the JCE would break the conditions of the program in that the investment amount would no longer be at risk, investors may wish to specify that funds must be redeployed into another JCE immediately upon repayment to avoid this issue. Counsel and financial advisors experienced with the program can advise investors on how the loan agreements should thus be structured.

An additional safeguard is for the project to appoint a disbursing agent, who will apply the funding as needed for each stage of the project. This provides an extra level of security in ensuring the investment amount is applied as specified in the business plan according to EB-5 requirements.

Auditing Procedures

Auditing requires that a certified public accountant review company records to verify that financial statements are accurate and correct according to the chosen reporting framework, typically the standard generally accepted accounting principles (GAAP). In addition to providing an opinion on the annual financial statements, the auditor will typically review the other quarterly statements as well without performing a formal audit. Despite the greater assurance provided by an audit, auditing procedures place a burden on companies both financially and in terms of the need to prepare financial statements on a deadline. As such, investors may agree that auditing is unnecessary, and audits are not often conducted for EB-5 projects.

The recent focus on discouraging fraud and misappropriation in the EB-5 market may require projects to commit to more regular audits of their financial statements. While projects already required to provide statements for lenders and senior investors should be able to provide these same reports to EB-5 investors with little inconvenience, other projects may be able to reduce costs by providing audited statements for the NCE, which typically has few operations and assets, and unaudited information about the JCE. This type of information combined with other oversight in the disbursement of funds would create a more transparent and reassuring environment for investors, but investors must again be aware that if financial statements have been falsified, misappropriation might remain undetected even through an audit.

Reporting Checklist for Investors

The limited partnership or operating agreement for the NCE should clearly outline the financial reporting regime and state which reports the enterprise is required to provide investors. In cases where the organizing document does not mention financial reporting, an EB-5 investor may not be provided with financial information until such time as he or she files the I-829 petition for removal of the conditions of permanent residence, which requires USCIS to evaluate the project financials to ensure the investor has fulfilled EB-5 requirements. However, investors are more commonly provided with an annual or quarterly report.

The following checklist includes questions investors should ask when reviewing project documents to evaluate the level of financial reporting to be provided:

- Will the NCE provide financial statements to investors?
- When and how often will these statements be provided?
- What financial information will these statements include?
- Will statements be prepared according to an accepted accounting framework?

- Will the statements be audited?
- Will the NCE also provide investors with financial information about the JCE?

In regional center projects involving multiple lenders, where job calculations are based on indirect job creation through the JCE as well as induced jobs created by the infusion of investment funds into the local economy, financial reporting is especially crucial in verifying that funds have been deployed as required. Investor funds must be applied only for job creation, and documentation of the appropriate movement of funds is essential for the I-829 petition.

Given the recent concerns with fraud and misappropriation of funds in EB-5 projects, securities issuers might consider providing more detailed financial information to investors regularly throughout the lifespan of the project to assure them of the proper and effective use of investment funds. Before committing to a project, investors must carefully evaluate the level of reporting promised in light of the unique circumstances of each project. With diligence, all parties can work to discourage fraud within EB-5 projects and increase the chances of success for new enterprises.

Securities Law

Anticorruption Strategies for EB-5 Securities Issuers

The international financial transactions inherent to the EB-5 Program have encouraged practitioners and governments alike to adopt stricter safeguards against corruption in recent years—especially in China, from which the majority of EB-5 applicants originate. In the United States, the Foreign Corruption Practices Act (FCPA) prohibits entities from bribing foreign officials, whereas Chinese laws further prohibit bribery in China by foreign and domestic entities. To guard against the possibility of engaging in bribery, even unintentionally, EB-5 practitioners must fully understand the compliance issues all parties face.

Chinese president Xi Jinping has recently stressed that China will prosecute all those involved in corruption, both Chinese and foreign, including government officials. Most recently, in 2014, in its largest anticorruption action ever, the Chinese government levied almost $500,000,000 in criminal penalties against pharmaceutical giant GlaxoSmithKline and sentenced multiple executives to suspended prison terms for altering financial statements and bribing medical professionals.

The U.S. Department of Justice has likewise recently cracked down on corruption and FCPA violations on a global scale. Actors within the EB-5 Program, which must operate within SEC guidelines with respect to the private placement of securities as well USCIS, should be aware of potential FCPA issues given the need for cooperation between the U.S. and foreign parties.

This section outlines current anticorruption laws and their relevance for EB-5 investors, regional centers, and other practitioners as well as several strategies these parties can use to safeguard against corruption.

International Anticorruption Laws

The United States was one of the first countries to attempt to tackle corruption abroad with the passage of the FCPA in 1977. Since then, multiple countries including China have passed similar laws. Most notable among these is the United Kingdom's Bribery Act 2010, the strict measures of which have served to establish a global benchmark for anticorruption practices. In the EB-5 context, the factor with the most potential to cause compliance issues is the payment of commissions, as outlined below.

U.S. regional centers and other securities issuers within the EB-5 system often make significant commission payments to offshore migration agents in an effort to compete in that market. However, different cultural conditions and potential translation issues mean EB-5 practitioners sometimes make such payments without full awareness of their purpose, leaving them vulnerable to corruption investigations under the laws of either or both countries. This is especially the case because certain Chinese migration agents acting under government purview may potentially be considered foreign officials within the context of the FCPA, meaning a commission could be considered an improper bribe worthy of prosecution. China additionally may consider such a payment to be bribery.

Even if the migration agent is not deemed a foreign official in and of itself, if such migration agent in turn bribes other Chinese officials using payments or gifts, both that agent, the original securities issuer, and even the investor can be held accountable for violation of both Chinese and U.S. anticorruption laws. The risk of unintentionally committing such a violation is especially high given the Chinese tradition of presenting monetary red envelope gifts to colleagues on special occasions to maintain good working relationships. As declining to participate in such traditions makes it difficult for agents to network and conduct business in China, ensuring such payments do not violate the laws of either country is especially crucial.

EB-5 Anticorruption Strategies

As both the United States and China have ramped up their efforts to fight corruption and prosecute those engaging in bribery both domestically and overseas, regional centers and other securities issuers working within the EB-5 Program must similarly adopt strategies to ensure they abide by the laws of both countries. The following are three such strategies regional centers can implement to mitigate the risk of running afoul of anticorruption laws.

1. Conduct due diligence on foreign and domestic partners

The U.S. Department of Commerce offers to warn securities issuers about potential legal issues which could arise from foreign transactions. To avoid implication in an FCPA investigation, it is prudent for regional centers and other issuers to avoid associating with persons identified on such lists. This is especially the case because even if the issuer does not engage in bribery directly, the actions of an agent paid by the issuer can result in legal liability for both parties. Regional centers can also take advantage of private screening tools to evaluate potential foreign partners as well as businesses and their employees both on first contact and periodically throughout the working relationship.

An additional step is to distribute an anticorruption questionnaire to potential foreign partners to gauge their knowledge of U.S. and Chinese laws and their willingness to identify potential corruption issues and limit legal liability for all involved. Having an attorney review these questionnaires can highlight any problem areas and allow partners to adequately address them. Hesitation to fulfill this request can thus serve to alert issuers to a party's lack of anticorruption practices, whereas a legitimate agent would not hesitate to assure a potential partner of his or her compliance with all relevant laws.

2. Create and enforce a comprehensive anticorruption policy

To protect the company and its employees, management must implement a policy which outlines compliance obligations and daily procedures for all parties and also must institute a comprehensive anticorruption training program for all staff and partners. This signifies a clear commitment from the top, which the Department of Justice has suggested is a key factor in compliance with

U.S. and international laws. In this regard, the United Kingdom's Bribery Act 2010, mentioned above, can form an excellent basis for company policies, as it sets the global standard for anticorruption practices and satisfies both U.S. and Chinese requirements, preventing the need for separate policies for each country.

Regional centers and issuers may additionally appoint a compliance officer, who can serve to highlight potential issues before they cause liability. Establishing a reporting mechanism also encourages employees to speak up in confidence about problematic practices, allowing management to address them immediately and effectively.

When operating in the multicultural EB-5 environment, training in the languages and business practices of foreign partners is essential. Within the Chinese market, a regional center may need to institute a clear policy regarding an appropriate value for gifts. Because anticorruption laws do not clarify what might be considered a bribe in this context, issuers may wish to remain conservative in their gifting policies to avoid such concerns altogether. Requiring that foreign partners additionally understand and be trained in these anticorruption policies is a crucial strategy in preventing the actions of such partners from creating a legal liability for the regional center.

3. Document all compliance policies and financial transactions

In the event of an FCPA investigation, written records of the above anticorruption program and all due diligence efforts will support that the issuer has proactively attempted to safeguard against corruption. Complete and accurate records of all financial transactions will additionally signal diligence on the part of the issuer and will allow for periodic internal audits to monitor for potential violations. These will play a key role in the argument that the issuer has made every reasonable effort to prevent bribery and corruption by employees and foreign partners.

Consulting with experienced counsel to periodically adjust company procedures and account for new risks and areas of weakness is a crucial step in complying with U.S. and Chinese anticorruption laws. By continually revisiting its anticorruption policies and maintaining awareness of international anticorruption obligations, issuers can avoid legal liability and maintain the transparency of the EB-5 Program for investors and practitioners alike.

The Effects of FINRA Rule 2040 on the EB-5 Market

As of August 24, 2015, the Financial Industry Regulation Authority (FINRA) has implemented Rule 2040, which prohibits members from making payments to unregistered broker-dealers within the United States. This poses several consequences for the EB-5 market, most notably increased oversight and further transparency regarding the payment of fees. However, the consensus is split among practitioners as to whether this rule represents a shift toward best practices. This section outlines potential ramifications of Rule 2040 for investors and investment professionals working in the EB-5 market.

Commissions and Securities Laws

Federal and state securities laws prohibit paying a commission to anyone not registered as a broker-dealer in the United States except under certain circumstances in reliance on an exemption from such registration. A commonly relied upon exemption is the finder exemption, a gray area that allows payment of fees to finders who merely connect potential investors with companies seeking capital. Companies and their directors who otherwise violate securities laws leave themselves open to sanctions.

The finder exemption covers a limited range of activities, such as cases where an agent of a commercial enterprise seeking capital, the securities issuer, introduces an investor to that enterprise. The finder must be a director or employee of the enterprise with duties other than raising capital, and his or her role in the transaction must be limited to making an introduction. For example, the finder must not take part in any negotiations between the two parties or in the sale of securities, and he or she must not be involved in the transfer of the investment amount such as by holding the funds in escrow for either party. The fee paid must additionally not be based on the success of the fundraising effort, only on the act of the initial introduction.

If a finder is found to have been involved in any of the above activities, both the finder and the securities issuer may face sanctions or other legal action. Those working with foreign investors through the EB-5 Program must also consider the laws of the investors' countries of origin, which may also require that the issuer work through a registered intermediary.

Changes with FINRA Rule 2040

This rule applies to FINRA members, these being registered broker-dealers conducting transactions in the United States. While members were previously able to take advantage of the finder exemption detailed above, Rule 2040 prohibits them from paying any commissions or other fees to unregistered U.S. broker-dealers. However, of most interest to EB-5 practitioners is subsection 2040(c), which does allow members to pay commissions to a foreign finder provided his or her only involvement in the transaction is the initial introduction between parties, these being the foreign investor and the securities issuer.

To adhere to this regulation while paying a commission to a foreign finder, member firms must additionally ensure the following:

- Neither the finder nor the investor is a U.S. citizen, and the finder is not otherwise required to be registered as a broker-dealer in the United States.
- The payment does not violate relevant foreign laws, meaning the laws of the investor's country of origin.
- The broker-dealer must agree in writing with the finder on the nature of their working relationship and the payment of fees, and the broker-dealer must document payments made to the finder and provide these records for inspection if necessary.
- The amount of commission or fees to be paid to the finder must be disclosed to the investor in writing, and he or she must acknowledge this arrangement in writing to the broker-dealer.

Under this rule, broker-dealers are thus allowed to pay foreign finders without violating U.S. securities laws or FINRA regulations.

Consequences for the EB-5 Market

Adhering to Rule 2040 fosters a market in which foreign finders refer investors to U.S. broker-dealers, and finders are paid according to terms disclosed to and agreed upon by investors. Such a market poses several benefits for EB-5 practitioners and investors alike.

Broker-dealers will be in compliance with national and international regulations

EB-5 broker-dealers who have previously taken advantage of the Regulation S exemption, which allows for the sale or offer of securities outside the United States without registration, may have been in violation of the laws of the investor's country of origin, creating a liability for both the securities issuer and the investor. Selling the security within the United States with the assistance of a foreign finder allows a broker-dealer to comply with U.S. securities regulations and avoid this issue.

As the EB-5 Program requires that the investment be made to a U.S. company to create jobs within the United States, selling the relevant securities in the United States under the guidelines of U.S. securities law is a reasonable step in that it allows investors to more easily document the legal sourcing and path of investment funds, of which proof is necessary when applying for the I-526 and I-829 residence petitions.

Investors will face less risk and be made aware of fees associated with the investment

The EB-5 Program poses a substantial risk to investors even without taking into consideration the possibility of unethical practitioners. As permanent residence is not guaranteed under the program and the investment amount is required to be at risk throughout the application process, EB-5 investors face a considerable loss in the case of a denied application and must therefore conduct due diligence on their investment opportunities and work with experienced securities and immigration attorneys to ensure they comply with program requirements as well as legal guidelines.

The opportunity to work with experienced U.S. financial advisors in lieu of conducting an offshore transaction is a significant benefit for foreign investors, who might otherwise take unnecessary risks on the advice of salespeople in their own countries of origin, who often work for high fee incentives. Disclosure of all commissions for finders will further allow investors to make educated decisions and will therefore foster a more ethical and transparent EB-5 market overall.

Increased competition will result in better deals and fewer cases of fraud

EB-5 investors often pay high brokerage fees, among the highest in the U.S. securities industry, without being made aware of the services received in return for those fees. This is a result of several factors, including communication barriers and unfamiliarity with U.S. legal and financial systems. Of interest to this discussion, however, is the current lack of transparency among broker-dealers working with foreign investors. Greater transparency as a result of compliance with Rule 2040 will create more competition in the market, as it will encourage investors to choose to work with proven professionals.

An improvement in service quality will result in an equal improvement in the quality of deals and investments in the EB-5 market, and allowing investors to conduct due diligence with full disclosure of any fees and commissions reduces the chances of fraud within this sector.

Although Rule 2040 applies only to FINRA members, it encourages a trend toward best practices in the EB-5 market. Further oversight of EB-5 transactions additionally creates a climate of transparency and a willingness to comply with both national and international regulations, decreasing liability for both securities issuers and investors. Rule 2040 represents an increasing desire to combat fraud and unethical behavior in the EB-5 market, and practitioners should take note of these changes as they strive to better serve investors and the EB-5 Program itself.

SEC Investigation Procedures for EB-5 Projects

The SEC is the government body responsible for enforcing U.S. securities law and investigating complaints of fraud or misrepresentation to investors. Under U.S. law, a security is defined as any investment contract or evidence of indebtedness such that a monetary investment has been made in a common enterprise and that the investor expects profits from the efforts of a third party. Most EB-5 projects likely fall under this definition and thus under the investigatory purview of the SEC.

The SEC has recently demonstrated its vigilance in pursuing charges of fraud in connection with the EB-5 Program, with a trend of rising enforcement in this regard. Sellers of securities, such as EB-5 developers and marketing teams, must therefore take every precaution to ensure they comply with SEC regulations and avoid the legal and financial strain of an investigation. The SEC provides a crucial service to both investors and securities sellers, protecting their interests by maintaining the legitimacy of the EB-5 Program. Sellers can therefore benefit from understanding how the SEC conducts its investigations and taking proactive steps to protect themselves and their investors.

Reasons for an SEC Investigation

The SEC may choose to investigate an EB-5 project for either or both of two reasons: the first is an investor complaint, and the second is a tip from another government agency such as USCIS, which administers the EB-5 Program. In either scenario, the SEC will use the provided information to launch its own investigation of the project in question.

In a case where an investor feels the nature of an investment has been misrepresented, the SEC will review the private placement memorandum (PPM) provided to investors by the project. While misrepresentations can be caused by translation issues and other language barriers facing foreign investors, project developers and marketers should take care not to offer investors any guarantees or unrealistically high returns, which the SEC will view as an indicator of potential fraud.

The PPM must clearly and accurately outline the objectives and terms of the investment as well as its risks. This serves the dual purpose of providing investors the information they need to make informed decisions and protecting the securities seller from liability through full disclosure of material risks. Sellers should disclose all intended uses of the investment, including any fees paid to brokers or other agents. Funds must be used exactly as disclosed to investors, as any other use may be considered by the SEC to be a material deviation worthy of investigation.

SEC Investigation Procedures

The first step in an SEC investigation is to speak with any EB-5 investors involved with the project in question. The SEC will use these conversations to form a picture of what investors have been told about a project and what documents they have been provided. The SEC may additionally seek to speak with any brokers of the EB-5 project and may subpoena project developers and marketers to collect any communications with investors, corporate documents and financials, and agreements between investors and the project. This subpoena is often the first sign project developers will receive of an SEC investigation.

At this stage, those who have been subpoenaed must seek the assistance of an attorney experienced in dealing with the SEC. Those who have received a subpoena will generally also be called in for additional individual testimony, during which they will be asked questions under oath about the project and about materials provided to investors, and it is crucial for the project that an attorney be present during testimony. Even in cases where no fraud has occurred, an attorney can work with the SEC to clear up any concerns and prevent the investigation from evolving into a federal suit.

SEC Enforcement of U.S. Securities Law

If the SEC determines after reviewing the subpoenaed documents and testimony that enough evidence of fraud or any other cause of action exists, it may choose to file a federal or civil suit against those responsible for the EB-5 project. Two recent cases stand out in this regard, both involving investors misled under the guise of an EB-5 project.

The 2013 judgement in *SEC v. A Chicago Convention Center* stands as a significant victory against fraud within the EB-5 Program. In its suit, the SEC alleged that the project promised to return any administrative fees to the nearly 300 investors involved in the event their EB-5 visa applications were denied. However, the $11,000,000 in question was spent on luxury items before the investors had the chance to even submit their petitions. Anshoo Sethi, a developer in the project and one of the defendants, has since pled guilty to charges of wire fraud and making false statements, and he faces up to 20 years in prison as well as repayment of all administrative fees collected.

The second case is that of *SEC v. Marco A. Ramirez et al.*, in which the SEC alleges that a Texas couple defrauded foreign investors of $5,000,000 under the guise of an EB-5 project. While the defendants guaranteed the investors a 5% return as well as an EB-5 visa, the corporation had yet to be designated as a regional center under the program, and the couple spent investor money on personal items and repayments to other investors rather than holding it in escrow as promised. EB-5 professionals are waiting with interest for a judgment in this case, which is still pending.

The EB-5 Program creates a prime opportunity for misrepresentation when project developers and marketers neglect to properly inform investors of the terms and risks of their investments. The SEC, often working on tips from investors who have fallen victim to fraudulent actions on the part of such developers, has recently focused its efforts on ensuring transparency within the program by rigorously investigating all complaints. These investigations often involve a deep examination of corporate documents as well as testimony by those involved, so project developers and marketers must ensure they comply with U.S. securities law to proactively prevent the need for an investigation. The counsel of an experienced SEC defense attorney is also invaluable in clearing up misunderstandings as they arise and protecting the integrity of the project.

By informing themselves of SEC procedures as well as the requirements of U.S. securities law, project developers can work with the SEC to ensure transparent and legal application of the EB-5 Program.

Redeployment Issues with EB-5 Investments

Recent wait times in I-526 and I-829 petition adjudication have created hurdles for regional centers, which must ensure investment funds are at risk throughout the conditional permanent residence period. This is especially the case for Chinese investors, who face estimated wait times of up to six years. Loan transaction structures in which the investment amount is set to be repaid to the NCE by the JCE prior to adjudication of the investor's I-829 petition thus pose a problem for all parties.

As the conditions of the EB-5 Program require that the investment remain at risk throughout the conditional permanent residence period, regional centers have made an attempt to avoid the issue by providing for the redeployment of any investment funds repaid during that time, meaning the funds are reinvested and thus remain at risk. Because USCIS has provided little clarification on which sorts of investments are considered to be at risk, though, most regional centers have adopted the strategy of investing these repaid funds into a new JCE to remain in line with the EB-5 requirements.

Of foremost concern, however, is that redeployment strategies additionally bring up several issues with U.S. securities laws that regional centers and investors must take into account.

The Securities Act of 1933

The SEC has provided some guidance relevant to the redeployment of EB-5 investments regarding the distinction of whether a new securities offering is made through such a redeployment. According to the Securities Act of 1933 (the Securities Act), all new securities offerings must be registered with the SEC, and any unregistered securities must fall under an exemption. This carries implications for redeployment because under certain circumstances, the redeployment of investment funds may be considered a new offering.

Area of relevance for EB-5 practitioners are registered blind pool offerings and asset-backed financings, most often used for real estate projects. For such loan structures, where the usage parameters for an investment are not identified until after the investment has been made, redeployment is not considered a new offering of securities provided the redeployed investment is made within the parameters of the offering documents for the original investment. However, such arrangements exclude investors from control over where their investment funds are deployed and are thus not typically a beneficial arrangement from the investor's point of view.

Similarly, investors who pay mandatory assessments arising as a result of the original investment decision are determined not to have been offered new securities under the Securities Act. Mandatory assessment may arise where more funds are needed to complete a project. However, voluntary assessments are considered by the SEC to be a new investment decision and therefore a new securities offering.

Certain redeployments do raise Securities Act concerns, such as situations in which the loan structure provides for a decision by investors to either dissolve the NCE and receive the repayment proceeds or approve their redeployment into a new JCE so the investment funds will remain at risk. Regional centers and investors thus must consider structuring any loans of the investment to account for redeployment in light of these new securities offering requirements.

In cases where a new securities offering would be determined to have been made, regional centers may be able to claim an exemption under Regulation D, Regulation S, or Regulation A+. However, these exemptions depend on the circumstances of the redeployment. Regulation D allows certain smaller companies to avoid registering their securities by filing Form D after first selling those securities, and this option should therefore be considered early in structuring the loan.

Regulation S allows for a safe harbor in which securities offered overseas do not need to be registered. However, this would likely not apply given that investors would be in the United States as part of the conditional residence at the time the new securities were offered. Regulation A+ similarly applies to smaller companies and can be investigated as a possibility.

The Investment Company Act of 1940

The Investment Company Act provides several securities registration exemptions. As such, new commercial enterprises that originally relied upon any such exemptions must ensure continued compliance during the time of the new securities offering. Three such exemptions under this act are detailed in §3(c)(1), §3(c)(5), and §3(c)(7), of which the first two are most relevant for EB-5 projects. The first concerns private funds owned by no more than 100 shareholders, and the second concerns funds engaged in the purchase of real estate.

To apply for redeployments determined to be new offerings, these exemptions must be structured into the initial investment.

The Investment Advisers Act of 1940

Redeployment may potentially create issues under the Investment Advisers Act, as well, depending on the number of clients being advised, as the act exempts an adviser from registration if he or she has fewer than 15 clients in the year preceding the redeployment. Certain state adviser laws may also come into play depending on the circumstances under which the redeployment takes place and the value of the assets involved. As these differ depending on the project location, each regional center must be aware of its state adviser requirements.

For EB-5 projects, the number of clients counted under this act is up for debate. If the threshold of 15 clients is reached, the adviser must register. However, the SEC has provided little guidance on whether the new commercial enterprise represents one or multiple clients. In the former case, the NCE itself would be considered one client, whereas in the latter each partner or member of the NCE would be considered an individual client.

The act holds that an NCE is considered one client if the adviser provides investment advice based on the needs of the NCE rather than the individual needs of the partners. For redeployments, the SEC has previously granted no-action relief in cases where advisers did not make any recommendations regarding redeployment options. However, the SEC has taken action in cases where advisers provided advice to individual members of an LP or LLC regarding investments and tax issues. As this could conceivably be the case for advisers of an EB-5 project involving multiple partners and members, regional centers must take Investment Advisers Act compliance into consideration when structuring a redeployment situation.

Conclusion

To avoid unforeseen securities law concerns in the event that an investment must be redeployed to maintain its at-risk status, new commercial enterprises should take this possibility into consideration while structuring the original securities offering. One strategy is to grant the general partner or managing member leeway through the original offering document by including only general parameters for the use of the investment and providing that actor the right to determine how repaid funds will be redeployed without the need for an investor vote, which would allow the SEC to consider the redeployment a new investment decision.

Regional centers may also be able to take advantage of exemptions under the three acts outlined above, but continued exemption is conditional upon the same requirements being met at the time of the redeployment. In some cases, as with a Regulation S exemption, this would be unlikely. Regional centers and investors alike must therefore carefully consider the structure of a loan to ensure the possibility of redeployment is accounted for in any cases where an exemption is sought for the original investment.

USCIS has yet to clarify how it will address the issue of funds repaid prior to adjudication of I-829 petitions because of increased wait times. In its draft memo of August 10, 2015, USCIS clarified that investments must be sustained and at risk, which has been interpreted to mean that simply holding any repaid funds in the NCE will not suffice to meet the requirements.

As EB-5 practitioners become aware of increased wait times and adapt to these challenges, the need for redeployment can be avoided altogether by providing for a longer loan term or otherwise preventing funds from being repaid to the NCE until the I-829 petition has been adjudicated.

Redeployment additionally presents challenges of its own concerning the timing of investments and the availability of a job-creating project at that crucial juncture. Investors and regional centers must therefore carefully consider how they will address the liquidation of a loan prior to the I-829 adjudication and therefore the end of the conditional residence period.

As with all decisions concerning an EB-5 investment, practitioners benefit from consulting with a qualified securities attorney to identify potential areas of concern and ensure the loan is structured in such a manner so as to protect investors while complying with U.S. securities laws.

USCIS Implementation of EB-5 Law

The EB-5 Immigrant Investor Program was created by Congress in 1990 in order to generate job-creating foreign investment in the United States. The program was enacted through the Immigration and Nationality Act, sections 203(b)(5) and 216A, and pertinent EB-5 regulations are located within the Code of Federal Regulations (C.F.R.) in Title 8, sections 204.6 and 216.6.

In general, this law and its related regulations are vague. As a result, what the law seems to say can differ from how USCIS implements EB-5 law.

Following are several elements of the EB-5 Program, each of which is explained both through the lens of the law and through a practical examination of how USCIS actually implements these provisions.

Establishing a New Commercial Enterprise

An NCE is defined in 8 CFR 204.6 as a "for-profit activity formed for the ongoing conduct of lawful business" after November 29, 1990. This may entail (a) creating an "original business" or (b) purchasing a business and then restructuring it "such that a new commercial enterprise results." This can also mean (c) expanding an existing business "so that a substantial change [40% increase] in the net worth or number of employees results."

While a business established after November 29, 1990, is clearly an NCE, the regulation is less clear concerning restructured and expanded businesses. How USCIS interprets these provisions is also unclear, and as a result, they are rarely used.

Investing the Required Capital

According to 8 CFR 204.6, each EB-5 investor must invest $1,000,000 unless the job-creating entity is located in a TEA, in which case the required investment is $500,000. According to the regulation, a TEA is "an area which, at the time of investment, is a rural area [population less than 20,000] or an area which has experienced unemployment of at least 150 percent of the national average."

In practice, USCIS typically expects state-issued TEA designation letters with rational support for the designation.

Furthermore, 8 CFR 204.6 requires each investor to invest or be "actively in the process of investing" the appropriate amount of capital.

USCIS requires that investors make their entire investment upfront or that their capital be irrevocably committed to the NCE.

Proving Lawful Source of Funds for EB-5

According to 8 CFR 204.6, the capital invested must be "obtained through lawful means."

USCIS requires extensive documentation regarding source of funds. Rather than requiring the standard preponderance of the evidence, USCIS expects investors to prove beyond reasonable doubt that their capital was obtained lawfully.

This expectation requires investors to trace their capital from its source to the EB-5 project, and in some cases, it may require them to demonstrate multiple layers of lawful source of funds. For example, if invested capital was obtained as a gift, USCIS requires documentation that proves the money given to the investor was obtained lawfully.

Creating Jobs

According to 8 C.F.R. 204.6, an EB-5 investment must create "full-time positions for not fewer than 10 persons either directly or indirectly." This employment creation must be demonstrated by "reasonable methodologies" that include "economically or statistically valid forecasting tools."

Over time, what USCIS has accepted as "reasonable methodologies" has changed. For example, USCIS originally accepted the tenant occupancy model. Then, for a time, this model was not accepted. Now, USCIS may accept it with sufficient evidence.

Title 8 section 204.6 also calls for investors to submit a "comprehensive business plan showing...the need for not fewer than 10 (10) qualifying employees."

USCIS requires the comprehensive business plan to be credible and feasible and treats it as more than just a prediction—the likelihood that the business plan will successfully result in the creation of the necessary number of jobs must be clearly demonstrated.

An EB-5 investment may also be made in a troubled business (i.e., one which has incurred a net loss of 20% or more in the past 12 or 24 months), and in such cases, the regulation stipulates that the number of existing employees must "be maintained at no less than the pre-investment level for a period of at least two years."

In practice, because EB-5 investments in troubled businesses are rare, little information is available regarding how USCIS addresses such petitions.

Managing the Enterprise

According to 8 C.F.R. 204.6, an EB-5 investor must be engaged in managing the NCE, either through "day-to-day managerial control or through policy formulation." The investor cannot maintain a "purely passive role." For NCEs structured as limited partnerships, if the investor is a limited partner with all the rights, duties, and powers typical of that role, such an investor will be regarded as "sufficiently engaged" in managing the NCE.

This section of the regulation is fairly clear, and USCIS adheres to it closely.

Removing the Conditions to Resident Status

The requirements that must be met to remove the conditional basis of the EB-5 investor's permanent resident status are outlined in 8 C.F.R. 216.6. Form I-829 must be filed within the last 90 days of the two-year conditional status, and supporting documents must demonstrate the following:

- An NCE was created
- The required capital was invested in the NCE
- The NCE and investment were sustained for the two-year conditional period
- The employment creation requirement was met

USCIS will not approve Form I-829 if it is materially different from Form I-526.

Business Plans and Job Creation

Avoiding Common Issues in EB-5 Business Plans

When a USCIS adjudicator believes a visa application lacks sufficient information to justify an approval, he or she may issue the candidate an RFE to ask for further detail on any aspect of the application. For investors and regional centers working within the EB-5 Program, these requests often focus on the business plan element of the application and can significantly delay the final approval as well as any funding contingent on the issuance of an EB-5 visa.

Here we will discuss common reasons for RFEs and outlines strategies investors and regional centers can use to more effectively structure their business plans and avoid raising questions as to their businesses' economic or legal legitimacy. While USCIS adjudicators are responsible for ensuring that a visa application meets all the requirements of the EB-5 Program, they are not experts in every industry, and it therefore falls upon the investor or regional center to provide a comprehensive explanation of the investment project that allows the adjudicator to efficiently find the information he or she needs to make a decision on the matter of the EB-5 visa.

The following three strategies can be used proactively to prevent the need for an RFE.

1. Consult with Experienced EB-5 Professionals

Many problems resulting in a request for evidence can be avoided if a regional center or investor consults with an attorney experienced in creating EB-5 business plans. In this vein, the person or group of people tasked with putting together the business plan must combine their entrepreneurial passion for the new commercial enterprise itself with a detailed knowledge of the finer points of the EB-5 Program.

Consulting with an expert will allow the project to create a business plan that conveys the unique potential of the enterprise in question while also adhering to EB-5 requirements. The plan should outline the concept for the enterprise in detail such that USCIS adjudicators will understand how it will succeed in its target market, and it must demonstrate compliance with EB-5 requirements, as well, in that the enterprise must be new, jobs must be created according to the program timeline, and the investment must be at risk for the duration.

The plan should be compliant with not only the letter but the spirit of the *Matter of Ho* guidelines, with each section containing relevant and meaningful information collected with regard to the enterprise in question. Regional centers and investors should carefully vet their chosen attorneys to ensure they are knowledgeable about the enterprise and its industry as well as the EB-5 Program, as the business plan must thoroughly address both these elements.

2. Structure the EB-5 Business Plan Effectively

The business plan should provide enough detail that the adjudicator will be able to find answers to any questions regarding the economic and job creation prospects of the business as well as the legitimacy of the investment funds. If an adjudicator is unable to easily find the answers to his or her questions or if necessary information is missing entirely, the investor will be issued an RFE and may be required to completely restructure the business plan to address multiple deficiencies. This is often the case for applicants' whose business plans lack detail in several respects or raise significant concerns for USCIS regarding particular facets of the application, for example, the source of the EB-5 investment funds.

Below are some key tips for creating an effective business plan.

Use Matter of Ho as a reference

The ruling in the *Matter of Ho* case, which concerned the RFE issued for an EB-5 petition in 1998, provides an outline for all components necessary in an EB-5 business plan. This can serve as an excellent starting point for business plan creation, but investors should keep in mind that several recommendations have been issued since *Matter of Ho* to further clarify the standards by which USCIS evaluates applications. Working with experienced regional centers and attorneys will allow investors to draw on a wealth of knowledge to ensure all necessary elements of the business plan are addressed.

Avoid contentious practices

The job creation and economic impact prospects of a project are key elements of its legitimacy as an EB-5 investment target. Because of this, investors must be able to clearly present economic projections and job creation targets, both direct and indirect. While proving the creation of direct jobs is fairly straightforward, some projects rely on indirect jobs, such as those created by tenants of a real estate development, to meet their EB-5 targets. Some projects may also attempt to incorporate guest expenditures, as in a hotel, into the economic impact of the project. These figures are difficult to substantiate and may call the project's prospects into question, so investors should avoid these practices if possible to ensure a smooth application.

Give summaries as well as details

A detailed application will lessen the chances of an RFE, as adjudicators should be able to find all relevant information within the submitted business plan. However, investors should also include summaries where necessary to point out any key details for reference by the adjudicator. A good organizational structure and logical use of headings and subheadings will allow an adjudicator to quickly and easily find any information necessary.

3. Provide Comprehensive Justification (Third-Party Data/Evidence) for All Financial Projections

Any financial projections given in the business plan, as for revenue and expenses, should be supported thoroughly with relevant research and data. The following strategies used alone or in combination can help an investor or regional center make a convincing case for the prospects of a business venture.

Commission an independent analysis

Feasibility studies and other analyses from unbiased third parties can prove invaluable in justifying financial projections, as they examine the target market, including supply and demand, as well as any competition. Such studies, when conducted by professionals with proven industry experience, will present their own opinions on the feasibility of businesses and will provide sufficient detail to answer an adjudicator's questions.

Refer to historical performance and industry benchmarks

Business plans focusing on subsidiaries or expansions of existing entities may be able to refer to historical performance as a benchmark for financial projections. In such cases, any differences between the new venture and the existing business should be explained and any similarities highlighted to justify the use of historical data, and all figures should be backed up by relevant financial statements.

Similarly, some businesses may be able to rely on the existence of standards established by independent associations or consultants to justify their projected costs and expenses. Investors should keep in mind, however, that new businesses may not necessarily be able to meet standards for established ones, so financial projections should be adjusted accordingly with explanations.

Use team members' industry experience

Regional centers often recruit teams experienced in their respective industries to ensure that an investment project runs smoothly. While USCIS generally considers members of the investment team and the business in question to be biased because they aim, as employees of the business, to make a strong case for its financial prospects, team knowledge and industry experience can prove a vital resource when gathering data to justify financial projections. If citing team expertise in the business plan, investors should take care to detail those team members' industry backgrounds to legitimize their points.

The strategies above are meant to provide a foundation upon which investors, working with regional centers and knowledgeable immigration attorneys, can create effective business plans to support their EB-5 applications. While USCIS adjudicators will issue RFEs in cases where business plans lack detail or raise questions as to the prospects of an investment venture, investors can proactively address these concerns by referring to industry standards and existing USCIS recommendations as well as consulting with professional third parties to create comprehensive business plans.

Strategies Based on RFEs Trends for EB-5 Projects

Changes in USCIS policy over the previous few years have resulted in increased scrutiny of EB-5 business plans in an effort to ensure projects fulfill the goals of the program and protect investors from potentially fraudulent actors working within it. A significant example of these changes is the memorandum published on May 30, 2013, highlighting the intention for USCIS adjudicators to review business plans more thoroughly according to the standard of a "preponderance of evidence."

Whereas regional centers and investors previously considered business plans an afterthought when filing I-526 petitions, the May 30 memo brought about sweeping changes in the way business plans were structured and the strategies project developers used to verify the economic and job creation potential of new commercial enterprises funded by foreign investors as part of the EB-5 Program. Much of these changes were based on guidelines provided by USCIS in RFEs following the publication of the memo.

As such, RFEs can prove a valuable resource for investors and regional centers developing business plans to support new projects. We will cover recent trends in RFEs as well as strategies regional centers and other practitioners can take to proactively address any concerns USCIS adjudicators might pinpoint during the evaluation of investors' I-526 petitions for conditional permanent residence.

Trends Following the May 30, 2013 Memo

Immediately following the publication of the May 30, 2013 memo, USCIS adjudicators began scrutinizing the calculations used to determine the job creation potential of new commercial enterprises, namely with regard to construction and tenant occupancy jobs. Additional areas of focus were a lack of market analyses and the use of accurate and industry-relevant data to support projects' financial projections. In response, many regional centers abandoned the practice of relying on tenant occupancy jobs to meet the EB-5 job creation requirement and began commissioning third parties to provide credible data based on each project's unique regional and industry outlook.

The following year brought further intense oversight of financial projections and hiring timelines as well as the need for projects to provide proof of proper licensing and permits. As a result, practitioners continued to make use of third-party data to support the claims in their business plans and began providing USCIS with sufficient documentation of all permits and licenses associated with their projects.

More recently, in an effort to increase transparency and protect investors, USCIS has issued RFEs focusing on the ability of new commercial enterprises to compete with existing businesses in the United States. Business plans now must include a comprehensive marketing strategy, and developers have begun conducting SWOT analyses to better identify areas in which improvements can be made before submitting the I-526 materials.

These trends illustrate increased demands on investors and regional centers to demonstrate how their projects meet the EB-5 requirements. However, they have also resulted in a more robust adjudication process meant to strengthen the ability of the program to create jobs in the United States and thereby fulfill its original purpose.

Third-Party Data and RFEs

Recent RFEs have indicated that USCIS adjudicators are now reviewing financial projections more carefully in an effort to further protect investors by allowing only legitimately viable businesses to proceed in the EB-5 Program. This increased level of oversight has encouraged projects to make more diligent use of third-party data to support their financial and job creation claims.

EB-5 project developers must ensure new commercial enterprises are built on a solid foundation by incorporating relevant and accurate data during the planning stages. In this regard, regional centers have begun commissioning feasibility studies to illustrate projects' economic prospects based on credible regional and industry data. This data can serve as a valuable basis for financial projections and any calculations used to determine the job creation prospects of an enterprise.

In addition to proactively preventing the need for an RFE by providing USCIS adjudicators with all the information they will need to make informed decisions, EB-5 investors and regional centers can use third-party data to successfully combat an RFE if necessary. Such was the case with regional centers making use of tenant occupancy jobs following the publication of the May 30 memo and the change in USCIS adjudication standards. With reliable data backed by historical trends and current industry projections, regional centers were able to illustrate to USCIS the legitimacy of such tenant jobs and therefore the ability of their projects to meet the EB-5 job creation requirement.

RFEs as a Resource for EB-5 Practitioners

Any changes introduced to USCIS adjudication criteria will result in RFEs that can serve as a valuable resource for practitioners aiming to develop strategies to move forward and better address concerns with the program. Changes in the requirements for business plans illustrate this principle, as investors and regional centers have adapted to new requirements by overhauling their documentation strategies.

The current rash of regional center closures serves as a reminder that the primary goal of the EB-5 Program is to create jobs, and actors not fulfilling that goal risk not only investors' funds and U.S. residence prospects but also the future of the EB-5 Program itself. Practitioners have an obligation to learn from RFEs and apply those guidelines in their own business plans, as better use of data allows developers to identify problem areas and rectify them during the planning stages rather than once the project is underway and funds are at risk.

USCIS has provided significant guidelines over the years through memos and other publications, but RFEs serve to illustrate these guidelines more practically. To prepare for potential changes to the program and to create better business plans and more accountable projects in the present, EB-5 practitioners can learn from USCIS decisions and develop proactive strategies for their own enterprises. RFEs provide a continuing view into the adjudication process and a significant learning tool within the EB-5 market.

Calculating EB-5 Job Creation

The main purpose for the EB-5 Program is to encourage foreign investment in U.S. enterprises in order to create jobs. As a result, the primary requirement for the program is that each investment generate no fewer than 10 permanent, full-time jobs for U.S. workers.

The way these jobs are calculated depends on how the investment is made: for direct investments, only direct jobs can be counted; for investments made through regional centers, direct, indirect, and induced jobs can be counted.

Direct, Indirect, and Induced Jobs

Direct jobs are those actually created by the new commercial enterprise receiving the investment. These tend to be the ongoing operational jobs of the new business itself but may include direct construction jobs if the construction period lasts two or more years. Again, for foreign nationals who invest directly in an enterprise, only direct jobs may be counted toward the job creation requirement of the program.

Indirect jobs are those created as a result of the EB-5 project's spending on goods and services from local companies. Goods may include construction materials, equipment needed for operations, or other locally produced supplies. Services range from building maintenance to legal counsel—any professional service a business may pay a local company to provide.

Unlike direct and indirect jobs, which are created through the payroll and spending of the project itself, induced jobs are those created as a result of employees spending their wages. As the jobs created by the new enterprise provide income for employees, these employees spend some of that income on local goods and services—which further stimulates the local economy.

While any project can count eligible direct jobs, in order for indirect and induced jobs to be counted as EB-5 jobs, a regional center must be affiliated with the project. A project developer can opt to apply for regional center designation or rent an existing regional center with the necessary geographic scope. Because regional centers can include indirect and induced jobs in a project's job creation count, sponsoring a project through a regional center almost always produces favorable job creation numbers. For some projects, only indirect and induced jobs can be counted—in such cases, the project must be sponsored through a regional center.

How to Calculate EB-5 Job Creation

Calculating the number of jobs created by an EB-5 project generally requires the assistance of an economist, who generates a report using accepted economic or statistical methodologies. The two most common models used in this process are RIMS II, provided by the U.S. Department of Commerce and IMPLAN, provided by MIG, Inc.

Both RIMS II and IMPLAN are input/output models that consider the relationships between industries in order to estimate the overall economic impact the project will have in the region. The models generate a final demand multiplier, which is applied to expenditures to determine job creation.

The primary purpose of this economic report is to demonstrate to USCIS that the project will create the necessary number of jobs if the business plan and budget are followed. When an investor files his or her I-526 petition, this report serves as evidence that the employment creation requirement of the EB-5 Program will be met. Two years later, when the investor files Form I-829, this report is used in conjunction with documentation of actual expenditures to prove the necessary number of jobs were, in fact, created.

Most projects generate jobs from construction as well as operations, and these two job types are calculated differently. Construction jobs are calculated based upon expenditures, not the actual number of people involved in the project's construction. On the other hand, operations jobs are calculated based upon the actual number of people put to work full time, which can also be calculated based upon revenue.

EB-5 Job Creation: Construction and Operations

EB-5 Construction Jobs

Construction jobs are calculated by applying the final demand multiplier to construction expenses. The final demand multiplier represents the number of jobs created per million dollars. For most projects, this multiplier is between 12 and 14.

When calculating how many jobs will be created during construction, several additional factors should be considered.

Construction duration

If the construction period of the project takes less than two years to complete, only indirect and induced jobs may be counted; however, if the project takes more than two years to complete, direct jobs may be counted as well.

Digging is often considered the start of construction, but demolition may be considered the start as long as construction commences without delay after demolition is complete. The safest way to measure start time, however, is from the onset of vertical construction.

Construction ends either when the certificate of occupancy is issued or, in the case of manufacturing facilities, when the building begins to be used.

Different expense types

A project's hard costs, soft costs, as well as any furniture, fixtures, and other equipment (FF&E) are calculated separately and use different multipliers.

Some hard construction costs, such as contingencies and fees, are not EB-5 eligible. Costs associated with general conditions may also be ineligible, but this is presently a minority opinion among USCIS adjudicators.

EB-5 eligible soft costs include architectural, design, engineering, and testing fees. Many soft costs may or may not be eligible, depending on the adjudicator. These costs include building permits, building fees, utility hookup fees, insurance premiums, finance charges, taxes, and marketing.

Cost inflation

Over time, costs increase due to inflation. Input/output model coefficients and multipliers, however, often use data from previous years. As a result, current dollar values must be deflated to the values used in the input/output model in order to properly arrive at the final demand multiplier. Deflation figures are reported by the U.S. Bureau of Labor Statistics (BLS).

USCIS supporting evidence requirements

In order for an investor's I-526 petition to be approved by USCIS, the form must be supported by evidence that the project's costs are reasonable. USCIS expects to see the general contractor's detailed construction budget with costs itemized by category. This budget must also be compared to the cost per square foot of equivalent projects in the region using relevant, up-to-date data such as RSMeans data.

For construction projects expected to last more than two years, USCIS requires a monthly schedule of anticipated construction costs.

In order for an investor's I-829 petition to be approved by USCIS, the form must be accompanied by evidence the funds were spent. Such evidence includes wire transfers, canceled checks, vouchers, etc.

EB-5 Operations Jobs

Operations jobs can be calculated in two ways, by direct count and by revenue—both of which should yield the same result.

For the first method, direct jobs are counted and then multiplied by the employment multiplier. For the second method, revenue from the pro-forma income statement is used to calculate EB-5 job creation by deflating the revenue to the values used in the economic analysis and then multiplying these deflated dollars by the final demand multiplier. If the two methods don't produce similar results, USCIS may deny any investor petitions that rely on these operations jobs.

For example, a new hotel project might anticipate $3,000,000 in annual revenue from accommodation. In order to calculate EB-5 job creation from this revenue, the economic analysis must first deflate this figure appropriately—in this case, by 8.6%—which yields a deflated value of $2,760,000. Next, the hotel's accommodation revenue is multiplied by the final demand multiplier of 16.9. This means that a total of 46 operations jobs will be created by the hotel's accommodation revenue. To calculate the number of direct jobs created, the total number of jobs (which includes indirect and induced jobs) must be divided by the employment multiplier—in this case, 1.7. So, of the 46 operations jobs created, 27 would be direct jobs; the rest would be indirect and induced.

The scenario above provides a basic example of how operations jobs are calculated. A number of other factors, however, must be considered when determining how many operations jobs can be counted toward the employment creation requirement of the EB-5 Program.

EB-5 Job Requirements

In order for jobs to be counted toward the employment creation requirement, they must be full-time positions for qualified U.S. workers.

Full-time positions are those in which the employee works an average of 35 or more hours per week year round. As a result, seasonal positions cannot be counted as direct jobs.

A full-time position may be filled by two half-time workers as long as the position itself is a single job. For instance, a full-time chef position filled by two separate employees can be counted as long as the two employees work a total of 35 hours or more. Two separate part-time job positions, however, cannot be counted as one full-time job.

In addition to the requirement that these jobs be full time, the positions must be filled by qualified U.S. workers. Qualified U.S. workers are those who are authorized to work by way of citizenship or permanent resident status and include asylees, refugees, and individuals under suspension of deportation. Nonimmigrants, for example, those with H-1B visas, are not qualified employees and do not count toward EB-5 employment creation.

If USCIS determines that an illegal immigrant has been employed using false papers—whether the developer was aware of the pretense or not—the job will not be counted and investor I-829 petitions may be denied due to insufficient EB-5 job creation.

EB-5 job data

Various surveys are used in concert with the RIMS II estimates in order to calculate direct operations jobs. Depending on the job category, the EB-5 job creation metric may be based on the square footage of the building under development.

Project ownership

Currently, USCIS counts operations jobs only for projects in which the developer maintains significant ownership after construction is complete.

While USCIS has indicated the requirement for significant ownership, the agency has not defined what significant ownership entails. "Significant" does not mean a majority interest—as little as 15% ownership seems to satisfy this requirement.

EB-5 project type

USCIS tends to favor certain projects over others—though this tendency has changed over time.

The project types most likely to be approved by USCIS include restaurants, hotels, medical offices, hospitals, senior living centers, and single and multi-family residential dwellings. On the other hand, USCIS is less likely to approve office building and shopping center projects, even though these have been popular in the past.

USCIS rationale for the approval of certain project types over others seems to be directly related to the creation of operations jobs. The assumption is that for office buildings and shopping centers, no net increase in jobs occurs—revenue simply shifts to the new office spaces and retailers.

While USCIS will consider arguments that an establishment does produce a net increase in jobs, for example, due to a shortage of particular retail goods, proving that new operations jobs are actually created in the region as a result of the project can be challenging and will require an experienced EB-5 company.

USCIS Job Documentation Requirements

All of the necessary figures (e.g., revenue, deflation, final demand multiplier, etc.) must be presented and discussed in the project's economic impact analysis and business plan.

An investor's Form I-526 must show only that these figures are consistent with similar projects in the area. If, for example, the project is a hotel, the I-526 and accompanying documentation must demonstrate that the occupancy rate, average daily rate, and the number of direct jobs per room line up with other local hotels.

When an investor submits Form I-829, however, the accompanying documentation must prove that the figures and estimates of the economic analysis were realized—that the projected number of operations jobs actually exist. Proving this requires the investor to submit relevant tax forms (e.g., Form W-2, Form I-9, Form 941, etc.).

Economic Analysis for EB-5 Regional Center Projects

The primary purpose of the EB-5 Program is to stimulate the economy through foreign investment, particularly in rural areas or areas of high unemployment known as TEAs. As a result, USCIS requires ample evidence that a project will indeed produce the necessary economic impact—specifically, that 10 full-time jobs will be created for each EB-5 investor involved in the project.

For direct investments by a foreign investor into a new commercial enterprise, only direct job creation is counted. Direct jobs are those created by the new commercial enterprise itself.

But for a project sponsored by an EB-5 regional center, the broader economic impact can be counted, which involves direct job creation as well as the creation of indirect and induced jobs. Indirect jobs are created through the EB-5 project's spending on goods and services, and induced jobs are those created as employees spend the wages they've earned.

In order to calculate this broader economic impact, an economic analysis is necessary.

Basics of Economic Analysis for EB-5 Regional Center Projects

The overall purpose of the economic analysis is to prove to USCIS that the project produced the necessary 10 full-time jobs per EB-5 investor. The EB-5 Program specifically requires a project's economic impact analysis to use reasonable economic or statistical methodologies to estimate employment creation.

This economic analysis, however, is not limited to the project capital derived from EB-5 investments—the entire project is considered for the sake of its economic impact. In other words, all full-time direct, indirect, and induced jobs for U.S. workers created by the project will count toward the EB-5 employment creation requirement.

Projects in which EB-5 financing is a smaller percentage of the capital stack tend to have a higher ratio of jobs per EB-5 investor, which makes it easier for each investor to prove he or she has met the employment creation requirement of the program.

Types of EB-5 Economic Analysis

Typically, the economic analysis used with an EB-5 project is an input/output model, which can be loosely defined as a quantitative economic model that takes into consideration the relationships between the various industries in an economy. By considering these relationships, this type of analysis can be used to determine the broader economic impact of the project.

While other input/output models can be used, the two that are most common for EB-5 projects are IMPLAN and RIMS II. IMPLAN is provided by MIG, Inc., while RIMS II is provided by the U.S. Department of Commerce through its Bureau of Economic Analysis. EB5 Affiliate Network strongly recommends the use of RIMS II since it is an official government database and the job creation calculations tend to be more favorable for EB-5 regional center projects.

Factors That Affect EB-5 Economic Analysis

A number of factors affect job creation analysis, but the two most important factors are geographic location and industry.

Geographic location
The geographic location of a project affects its economic impact multipliers within input/output modeling. Generally speaking, the larger the area or higher the population, the larger the multiplier—which indicates greater job creation.

The project's location and impact area are determined by where the project's goods and services are purchased and where its employees live.

Industry
The industry classification of a project is determined using the North American Industry Classification System (NAICS). The project's NAICS code affects its economic impact multipliers because some industries, such as manufacturing, have larger multipliers, while others, such as retail, have smaller multipliers. The business activity of a project will determine its NAICS classification.

Economic (Job) Multipliers for EB-5 Projects

One challenge of estimating the economic impact of an EB-5 project is calculating potential indirect and induced effects in the local economy. In this arena, economic multipliers are a way of quantifying the total effects of an economic stimulus, in this case the EB-5 project, across all economic levels in the employment area. While the initial investment and project, for example, the operation of a restaurant, creates a direct effect in the form of jobs created, it also has indirect and induced effects, which are detailed below.

Local Economic Impact: Indirect and Induced Jobs

Indirect effects refer to the economic impact within local industries. For example, the operation of the restaurant mentioned above may require the purchasing of materials from local companies. Induced effects refer to the economic impact of any spending of labor income associated with the project. For example, a contractor hired to make improvements to the restaurant may spend part of his or her income in the local economy, creating an induced economic impact.

The economic multiplier of a project represents all indirect and induced economic activity created by that project within the employment area. This figure is calculated based on the amount spent locally for the project as well as payments to local employees. As such, the multiplier is unique for each project and can vary by industry and region. For example, a regional employment area may have a smaller multiplier than a state employment area for the reason that employees may spend more throughout a state than in one region. Multipliers may also vary based on regional and industry wage standards.

Within the EB-5 market, economic multipliers are based on a figure known as the response coefficient, referring to the number of jobs created per dollar of investment. This is in contrast to a multiplier based on the number of jobs created per direct job. The response coefficient is calculated by summing all economic inputs spurred by the initial stimulus of the direct investment, as illustrated below.

In the case of the EB-5 restaurant project mentioned above, the initial investment is $1,500,000, resulting in 25 jobs. Part of this amount goes toward purchasing materials from local suppliers, generating additional jobs in the first round of indirect effects. Part of the investment is also used to pay employees. While a portion of this goes toward taxes and another portion may leave the employment area, some of this amount will be spent locally and will generate additional jobs in the first round of induced effects. Second rounds of indirect and induced effects follow, as well: the materials purchased in the first round include appliances from a local manufacturer, which must itself purchase material locally to fulfill the order and thereby creates additional indirect jobs. Similarly, an employee who purchases household goods from a local grocer also creates additional jobs.

Subsequent rounds are accounted for using this logic, with each round growing smaller as money goes toward taxes, savings, and extra-regional spending. The total economic impact of a project based on each dollar of investment yields the multiplier for that project, which can be used to calculate indirect and induced jobs toward the required total of 10 full-time jobs per investor under the EB-5 Program.

Multipliers are calculated based on several economic models, chief among which are Impact Analysis for Planning (IMPLAN), Regional Economic Models Inc. (REMI), and Regional Input–Output Modeling System (RIMS-II). Each provides multipliers for economic impact assessment by region, but investors and regional centers in the EB-5 Program must keep in mind that these estimates include not only full-time but also seasonal and part-time jobs. Each project can use a unique multiplier based on these models to calculate its economic impact in the employment region.

Regional Center Geographic Scope

Regional centers typically involve a narrowly defined area in which the new commercial enterprise will be started—usually a handful of contiguous counties. Sometimes larger regional centers are formed, such as the 36-county area that comprise the New York City combined statistical area, the 43-county area known as the Texas Triangle, and the state of Florida.

Generally speaking, the larger the region, the larger the EB-5 economic multiplier. So a regional center spanning three counties will have a smaller multiplier than that of an entire state, which in turn has a smaller EB-5 economic multiplier than several states combined together. While these larger EB-5 economic multipliers have been used in past economic analyses—and have been accepted by USCIS—this method of using larger multipliers has become more difficult.

The stance of USCIS is that every case will be adjudicated according to its own merit, but in practice, larger areas are harder to get approved. There are no guarantees for the approval of a larger area, but the best approach is to ensure that the proposed EB-5 business is well documented and presents a credible operation plan across the entire proposed geographic area. Furthermore, for large geographic areas, another level of economic analysis combining multiple county clusters together, known as an "Economic Spillover Report", can also be completed to increase the likelihood of un-challenged approval by the USCIS.

Basic Job Calculation

For the example restaurant above, if the employment multiplier in the region for that industry is 12.5 and the total direct investment was $5,000,000, then the total economic impact estimate would be 12.5 × 5(Million) = 62.5 jobs.

As is the case with all calculations submitted as part of an economic impact report, investors and regional centers must work with financial and legal representatives familiar with the requirements of the EB-5 Program to ensure the business has the potential to create the required number of jobs as well as to ensure investors are provided with accurate information about the viability of a new commercial enterprise. USCIS evaluates any figures provided carefully, and thus all financial projections must be based on sound information so as to ensure a smooth visa adjudication process for investors.

Real Estate Developments, Hotels, and Restaurants

Real Estate Development and the EB-5 Program

The EB-5 Program was established to facilitate job creation in the United States. While real estate developments have historically been limited in their ability to create the requisite number of jobs per investor as a result of regulatory limitations, these developments currently comprise a large number of EB-5 investment projects. We will examine trends in EB-5 real estate projects and break down some of the benefits and drawbacks of these projects for investors and developers.

How EB-5 Financing Suits Real Estate Projects

The financial crisis of 2008 was devastating for real estate development, with the result that projects were unable to obtain conventional financing, particularly construction loans. Prior to this time, EB-5 job creation regulations had been unclear on the potential for construction jobs to fulfill the required job creation quota per investor, and EB-5 investors avoided real estate projects because of this uncertainty.

During the crisis, however, the EB-5 Program relaxed these regulations in an effort to encourage real estate investment. In late 2008, Senator John Cornyn requested that USCIS revisit the job creation regulations as they related to regional centers and the construction industry, and USCIS replied with a memo the following year to clarify that induced or indirect construction jobs could count toward the EB-5 job creation requirements.

This clarification brought about a change in the real estate landscape, as regional centers could now recruit investors for large developments. These foreign investors brought with them an influx of financing as well as a number of new mechanisms for project developers, among them unsecured short-term low-interest loans, which allow developers to save millions over conventional financing. Additionally, recent 2013 guidelines have specified that EB-5 investments can be used as bridge financing and that projects can be credited for jobs even after construction has commenced.

For EB-5 investors, real estate projects offer real collateral as well as the promise of a return on investment, as opposed to manufacturing projects, for example, where returns may not follow within an acceptable timeframe. Some EB-5 investors also prefer real estate as a tangible investment which they can physically inspect, unlike intangible investments such as stocks and bonds. Real estate investments have traditionally proven a good inflation hedge to protect against a loss in the U.S. dollar, as well. Additionally, investors appreciate the opportunity to conduct their due diligence on a project using background checks and appraisals.

The new flexible regulations and real need for investment among real estate developers has created an excellent conduit for EB-5 investors.

Considerations for Developers and Investors

Recent events surrounding the Chicago Convention Center (CCC) project and the fallout from that scandal have encouraged caution on the part of both investors and developers. In that case, the SEC pursued securities fraud charges against the CCC developers for misrepresenting the legitimacy of the real estate project to hundreds of EB-5 applicants. For example, the developers falsely claimed that all necessary permits for the projects had already been obtained. Additionally, Illinois Governor Patrick Quinn, who was immune from liability in the resulting fraud trial, had spoken highly of the project, lending it credibility and encouraging investors to drop their guard.

The results of that case slowed the EB-5 market in China significantly, and investors and immigration agents have since adopted a more cautious outlook about real estate projects. Where the involvement of a politician or government official in a project would once have implied to investors that the project bore no risk of fraud, investors are now wary of such developments. Additionally, investors generally conduct extensive due diligence before committing to a project, as marketing material containing misinformation is still endemic in China today.

Investors should additionally keep in mind that local regime changes can affect the real estate climate in prime EB-5 investment targets such as New York, where the current mayor, Bill De Blasio, has adopted a stance favoring affordable housing. This means developers of hotels and other luxury real estate may face hurdles regarding construction permits and government financing. As always, investors and their representatives must take the time to thoroughly research potential investments and take into account such factors before committing any funds.

More positively, the SEC has recently made efforts to prevent misrepresentations by developers marketing projects to potential EB-5 investors. Developers are forbidden from intentional false statements, reckless material misrepresentation, and omission of material information, meaning any marketing materials must not be misleading to investors. Nonetheless, misinformation remains a problem, especially in the Chinese market.

Frequently Asked Questions about EB-5 Real Estate Projects

Can a developer use EB-5 investment funds to buy real estate?

While no USCIS guidelines prohibit a developer from using EB-5 funds to purchase real estate, those funds generally cannot be considered part of the economic impact of the development project. The *Matter of Izummi* ruling has clarified that any investment funds must be used by the business responsible for the job creation on which the EB-5 petition is based, meaning that a developer might legitimately use some funds to buy a parcel of land and some to create and operate a business on that land. While the real estate purchase itself cannot be considered to have created jobs, the resulting business operations would, therefore justifying the initial EB-5 investment. This and any other use of EB-5 funds must be detailed in the business plan for a project.

On the other hand, an EB-5 candidate cannot simply buy real estate in the United States to qualify for the program. USCIS requires that the investment capital be placed at risk, such as through the creation of an enterprise, and funds must result in the creation of 10 full-time jobs per investor.

Do tenant jobs count toward the job creation requirement?

Because the goal of the EB-5 Program is to create jobs, USCIS requires that any tenant jobs counting toward the job creation requirement meet certain criteria to prove that the tenant would not have been able to operate in the region prior to the development project. This means any tenant jobs must be newly created rather than transferred from another location of a business.

The following are examples of evidence that should be provided with an EB-5 application to justify the counting of tenant jobs:

- A marketing plan and description of the regional prospects of the business
- A breakdown of historical or industry trends and financial projections
- Proof of limited or no vacancy in existing commercial space in the region
- Proof of a lack of suitable space for the business in question
- Signed documents from a government official attesting to the lack of space
- A description of the services to be provided by the business

The creation of tenant jobs is difficult to prove. If a developer is unsure as to whether those jobs would meet USCIS criteria, the best option is to remove them from the job creation total to avoid the issue entirely and decrease the chances of being issued an RFE.

How do debt, equity, and preferred equity differ for EB-5 projects?

EB-5 real estate projects may be structured as any portion of the capital stack, provided that the project generates sufficient jobs to support the investors' EB-5 petitions. However, they are typically structured as a debt investment or loan to be returned to an investor when his or her permanent residence has been approved. In certain circumstances, it may also be structured as a traditional equity investment, meaning they investor will hold shares in the equity of the project and receive dividends or distributions based on the performance of the new commercial enterprise enterprise.

A third category is to categorize the EB-5 funds as preferred equity, meaning an investor will have a priority claim on the assets and earnings of the new enterprise, and as such he or she would earn dividends to be paid out before dividends to owners of common stock. However, investors holding preferred equity generally do not have voting rights in the new enterprise, as would common stock owners. Because this sort of agreement can be interpreted as a redemption agreement if not structured correctly, and redemption agreements are not allowed under EB-5 rules, investors and developers should proceed with caution when using this model for an EB-5 real estate project.

The number of EB-5 real estate projects has tripled over the past five years, and real estate projects are among the most successful for EB-5 investors and developers. Real estate developments are attractive investment opportunities for EB-5 investors because of their potential for returns and job creation and their security against inflation of the U.S. dollar. For developers, EB-5 funds provide alternative sources of financing as well as significant savings over conventional loans. Despite recent legal SEC investigations in this field, investors and developers willing to conduct their due diligence can benefit from the opportunities of EB-5 real estate projects.

Evaluating EB-5 Capital for Real Estate Projects

What makes EB-5 capital a particularly attractive source of mezzanine financing for real estate developers is the lower interest rates coupled with potentially more beneficial loan terms. While any real estate project can meet the requirements of the EB-5 Program, some projects are particularly suited to this source of financing. It should also be noted that preferred equity deals are becoming more popular as an alternative to mezzanine financing. How well a project matches the EB-5 Program will depend largely on the geographic location of the project and the employment opportunities it creates.

Geographic Location of the Project

The EB-5 Program has an investment threshold of $1,000,000 (as of the date of this book) unless the project is located within an area of particularly high unemployment (150% of the national average) or that meets certain population requirements. These areas are known as TEAs, and their investment threshold is only $500,000 (as of the date of this book).

TEAs are determined by designated state agencies and are subject to change as unemployment rates and population change. For example, in 2015, the national unemployment rate dropped to 5.3%, and so for an area to qualify as a TEA based on unemployment, it must now have an unemployment rate of 8.0% or higher.

For any developer interested in adding EB-5 financing to its capital stack, project location is a vital consideration. While projects located outside TEAs can receive EB-5 capital, few projects do. For EB-5 investors, investing in a project not located within a TEA means risking twice the capital with no upside. Since EB-5 investors are seeking U.S. permanent resident status and not strong returns, they will seek projects with the lowest financial risk.

Project located outside TEAs can still draw EB-5 capital, but such success is typically based upon relationships, unique project appeal, or a higher rate of return.

Expected Employment Creation of the Project

The EB-5 Program requires that each investment produce at least 10 eligible full-time jobs. These jobs must be created within two years following the approval of the EB-5 investor's immigration petition (Form I-526) by USCIS.

The way employment creation is calculated depends on the way the project is receiving EB-5 capital. If the project is receiving EB-5 capital directly from a foreign investor, only jobs created directly by the new commercial enterprise can be counted. For projects sponsored by a USCIS-designated regional center, however, indirect and induced jobs may be counted in addition to direct jobs.

Direct, Indirect, and Induced Jobs

Direct jobs are those created directly by the project. These jobs must be full-time, permanent positions filled by U.S. workers—also, they cannot be filled by EB-5 investors or their dependent family members. Construction jobs may be counted toward the EB-5 employment creation requirement as long as the real estate construction period is 24 months or longer.

Indirect jobs are those created as a result of the project's needs. These ancillary jobs are created through the spending of project funds on materials, supplies, and any necessary services from real estate brokers, engineers, architects, etc.

Induced jobs are those created by the project's economic impact within the region as people employed by the project (directly) and those employed because of the project (indirectly) spend their money.

While direct jobs can be demonstrated fairly easily, indirect and induced jobs must be calculated using accepted statistical or economic forecasting methodologies and demonstrated in a credible economic report, typically prepared by an economist.

Project Job Cushion and Investor Immigration Risk

Developers who affiliate with a regional center have a distinct marketing advantage since their projects can more easily meet EB-5 requirements by counting direct, indirect, and induced jobs. While the EB-5 Program requires only 10 job positions per investor, having a greater number of job positions that can be counted toward an investor's employment requirement lessens the immigration risk by creating job cushion.

The real estate projects most likely to successfully raise EB-5 capital are those with little-to-no immigration risk. EB-5 investors will be drawn to projects that will create the necessary job cushion through construction expenditures alone. Projects with construction underway may even create the necessary number of jobs through construction expenditures before ever receiving any EB-5 capital—and if an EB-5 investors were to invest in such a project, his or her immigration risk would be effectively eliminated, which is very attractive.

On the other hand, because of the constraints of the EB-5 Program, any funding or construction delays can have serious impacts on EB-5 investors. Projects with higher risks of delays, shortfalls, or overruns—and especially those that are reliant on a certain level of EB-5 capital for completion—will be less attractive to potential EB-5 investors.

Employment creation is at the core of the EB-5 Program, and so real estate projects that will create (or have created) the necessary employment—and thereby have low immigration risk—are likely excellent candidates for the inexpensive mezzanine financing or preferred equity deals available through EB-5 investment.

EB-5 Investments in Distressed Properties

While the typical EB-5 real estate project involves the construction of new commercial property, distressed properties can also be purchased as part of an EB-5 project. Such properties can be enticing due to low acquisition costs (as low as 25% of former value) and substantial profits through rental income and resale.

Whether investing in new construction or an existing property, however, the primary requirement of the EB-5 Program remains job creation. So, as long as a distressed property can be utilized in such a way that the necessary number of jobs are created, such an investment is feasible.

Selecting the Right EB-5 Investment Property

For every EB-5 investor involved in a project, 10 permanent, full-time U.S. jobs must be created, and so the best properties will be vacant since they have the highest potential for creating jobs where none exist.

Properties with tenants may work for an EB-5 investment if the property has enough vacant space to accommodate the necessary job creation. Also, an investor may be able to count existing jobs if the investment is in a troubled business and prevents jobs from being lost—but proving such circumstances to USCIS is difficult.

In general, vacant industrial, office, and retail spaces selling at one third to one quarter their previously assessed values make the best candidates.

Creating a Suitable EB-5 Business Plan

Aside from gaining permanent resident status for each EB-5 investor involved, the basic goal of this type of EB-5 investment is to purchase inexpensive property, draw in new tenants, and then make substantial profits through rent collection and resale within five years.

Unlike the construction projects more typical of the EB-5 Program, a project that involves the purchase of a distressed property poses certain challenges for creating a business plan since the property is being paid for, at least in part, by EB-5 capital. This is problematic because the capital necessary for purchasing the distressed property is unavailable until the business plan is approved by USCIS, but the business plan and support documentation (e.g., economic report) must be specific to the property.

The solution is to submit a sample, real project to USCIS that fits the kind of distressed properties being considered. Once approved, EB-5 financing will be available, and any changes to the business plan based on the specific property being purchased can be incorporated (after the project has been completed) into the investor's I-829 filing to prove that the 10 required jobs were actually created. The key here is that the USCIS recognizes that project details can change during the development/implementation phase and so as long as the required 10 jobs per investor have been met at the I-829 stage, the investor's I-829 petition will be approved.

EB-5 Job Creation for Real Estate Developments

Job creation is the aim of the EB-5 Program, so investors and developers must come to understand how USCIS evaluates the job creation potential of EB-5 investments. For real estate developments, jobs are typically broken into two categories: construction and operations. Which jobs fall under each, as well as other topics relevant for EB-5 investors and regional centers, are outlined below.

EB-5 Jobs: Construction versus Operations

Construction jobs are those resulting from the building project, and these can include both direct and indirect or induced jobs. As USCIS only allows direct construction jobs to count toward the total EB-5 requirement for projects lasting more than two years, the job creation report must outline which jobs are direct and which are indirect.

The business plan and job creation report must also provide a timeline for all construction tasks and any costs associated with each. Additionally, projects expected to run longer than two years must be supported by statements from a third party to provide a basis for that timeline. If investors fail to provide sufficient support, USCIS has the discretion to reduce the recognized number of jobs created per investor based on the given information.

Operations jobs are those resulting from businesses owned by the developer and by tenant businesses leasing space in the development. While developer jobs can be credited to EB-5 investors, USCIS places significant restrictions on when tenant jobs can be included in the total number of jobs created. For example, USCIS requires proof that tenant jobs are completely new positions, meaning an operations job transferred from an old location to the new development would not count toward the job creation total.

As proving the creation of tenant jobs is difficult, EB-5 investors tend not to include these jobs in their totals. However, investors choosing to do so must include in their business plans an independent analysis proving that the development area has an unmet need for the tenant's services and that the tenant jobs would not be created if not for the new development. In this case, investors must be wary of committing to projects that rely heavily on tenant jobs to meet the job creation requirement.

In both cases, construction and operations, investors must conduct their due diligence and provide sufficient supporting documents to prove their job creation numbers.

EB-5 Job Creation Requirements

The EB-5 Program requires that each investor create 10 or more full-time jobs through his or her investment. For example, a project with 10 investors would need to create one hundred or more full-time jobs to meet this standard.

However, regional centers should not max out their numbers of investors based on job creation projections, as USCIS might disagree with these estimates and thus reduce the recognized number of jobs created per investor, putting those investors' visa applications into jeopardy.

For this reason, to ensure that each investor meets the minimum EB-5 job creation requirements, projects should include an investment cushion and obtain investors accounting for only 80% to 85% of projected jobs. A project expected to create one hundred jobs should therefore seek only eight investors to account for any unexpected deviations from the projected number.

For real estate developments, construction job totals should be outlined in the job creation report and are calculated based on hard and soft construction costs as well as the cost of furniture, fixtures, and equipment (FF&E):

- Hard construction costs are the cost of building the development, such as materials and labor.
- Soft construction costs include fees for architects and engineers, permit filing, financing, and attorneys.
- FF&E comprise any furniture, fixtures, and equipment within the development, including those not permanently connected to it.

While most hard construction and FF&E costs can be included when estimating the number of jobs to be created by a development, USCIS generally will not consider soft costs such as taxes, permit filing fees, insurance, and financing to result in the creation of new jobs, and as such investors should carefully consider which costs to include in the job creation report, as errors could incorrectly inflate the estimate of legitimate jobs created by the development and thus affect investors' EB-5 applications.

The EB-5 Job Creation Timeline

USCIS has mandated that the required 10 jobs be created within two and a half years of the date an investor files his or her I-526 application and before the I-829 application is due. The I-526 application is an investor's petition to immigrate to the United States under the EB-5 Program, whereas the I-829 application is an investor's petition to remove the conditions of his or her permanent residence. While it is unlikely that an investor will be required to submit an I-829 petition within two and a half years of his or her I-526 application, investors should nonetheless keep this timeline in mind.

For projects where construction lasts less than two years, the job creation timeline is fairly straightforward, as investors must simply ensure that they submit their I-526 petitions within two and a half years prior to the projected construction completion date. For construction projects lasting longer than two years, it may be necessary for regional centers to carefully time job creation to ensure each investor files his or her petition by the correct date and is credited with the required number of jobs.

The economic impact report for each project should therefore outline the number of jobs created over time as well as the appropriate filing date for each investor's I-526 petition. Regional centers must ensure that construction costs can support the number of investors who will need to file I-526 petitions, while investors themselves may occasionally need to postpone filing their petitions until assured the jobs required to meet the EB-5 standard will be created within two and a half years of their filing dates.

Similarly, the job creation report should carefully outline any operations jobs to be created within the appropriate timeframe.

Successful application for an EB-5 visa requires that investors understand the job creation potential of their projects. For real estate developments, this means diligently calculating both construction and operations jobs supported by the project and ensuring that those fall within the required timeline. USCIS expects that the business plan and job creation report will include full documentation and independent analysis to support any figures claimed, which places a burden on investors and regional centers to carefully plan their projects to meet these stringent requirements.

By breaking down how many jobs can be expected through construction and operations and building an adequate cushion into the number of investors for each project, regional centers can ensure each investor meets the required 10 full-time jobs within two and a half years of his or her I-526 filing date.

8 Reasons to Consider EB-5 Hotel Projects

1. Operations Job Creation

A new hotel project is an excellent source of job creation. A daily operations staff, housekeeping, and ongoing guest services mean that an EB-5 investment in a hotel project has a higher chance of creating more than the requisite 10 jobs.

2. Direct Job Creation

If the project's construction phase lasts longer than 24 months, USCIS regional center guidelines allow EB-5 investors to count the construction jobs as direct, permanent jobs. This crucial window of 24 months allows investors to count more jobs than those projects with construction lasting under 24 months.

3. Full Capital Stack Counts toward Job Creation

No matter what percentage the EB-5 capital represents of the total capital needed to complete the project, all money raised counts toward the EB-5 investor's job creation requirements. This principle is not unique to hotel projects, but due to the large up-front construction expenditures related to the building of new hotels, if EB-5 is used in the mezzanine position of the capital stack, the EB-5 investors will enjoy a significant job cushion.

4. Job Cushion

USCIS requires 10 jobs to be created per EB-5 investor. Job cushion refers to any number of jobs over the required 10 jobs that each EB-5 investor can count. Projects that create direct, indirect, and induced jobs have a greater likelihood of creating more than 10 jobs per investor, which allows for greater job cushion. For example, if the EB-5 hotel project costs $200 million to build and creates 800 permanent jobs, if 12.5% of the money came from 50 EB-5 investors investing at $500,000 each, the total pro-rated amount of jobs created that USCIS would allocate to each EB-5 investor would be 16 jobs.

5. Better Chances of Permanent Residence Status

Investors who choose projects with a high job cushion increase the probability of having their conditional permanent visas become fully permanent at the I-829 stage. Hotel projects that succeed may create a substantial number of permanent jobs for a relatively low percentage of EB-5 capital investment.

6. Investment Safety

The marketplace recognizes new hotel investments as relatively safe for a return on capital due to the presence of collateral and if run by an experienced operator. The risk is especially low when compared with other potential EB-5 investment opportunities.

7. Project Structure

Foreign investors find the structure of EB-5 hotel projects easy to understand. For first-time investors, the revenue models of hotels are often perceived as more straightforward than those of other projects. For instance, one of the greatest keys to a hotel's success is a smart choice of location, something most investors can determine with little more than a map.

8. Trusted Brands

Through hotel projects, EB-5 investors have an opportunity to work with trusted international hotel chains that have experience creating and sustaining successful hotels, which maximizes your opportunity for investment return and qualified projections of permanent job creation.

EB-5 Document Preparation for Hotel Developers

Developers have historically benefited from using EB-5 investment funds for hotel projects in the United States. With its opportunity to offer significant savings over conventional loan arrangements, EB-5 financing can prove an excellent alternative for developers in the hospitality industry. Here we will review some of the key documents to be submitted with an EB-5 petition and discuss several factors affecting hotel projects and the adjudication of hotel EB-5 cases.

The Business Plan

USCIS has laid out clear guidelines for EB-5 business plans in the *Matter of Ho* ruling. Firstly, any hotel business plan must specify the location of the hotel and discuss the details of the business, including the number of rooms and any amenities the hotel will offer. Additionally, the business plan must include a marketing plan as well as an analysis of competing hotels in the region.

A budget should also be included with the business plan. This must break down when each portion of financing will enter the project. A financial statement discussing the calculations and any assumptions used to determine the revenue per available room (RevPAR), the average daily rate (ADR), and the occupancy rate should also be provided, as well. This section of the plan should also include the construction budget used to calculate any construction jobs to be counted toward the EB-5 job creation requirement.

Lastly, the business plan should include an examination of the hotel brand and any relevant material agreements. Both franchise and management agreements should generally be executed before an investor files his or her EB-5 petition, but, if not, the business plan should specify a timeline for finalizing these agreements and include letters of intent from franchisors and managers.

The above guidelines are general, and EB-5 investors and developers are, of course, encouraged to review the *Matter of Ho* ruling to determine the best course of action for their unique projects.

The Economic Impact Report

The EB-5 Program is meant to facilitate job creation, so the economic impact report is considered the most important document in an EB-5 application, as it calculates the number of jobs to be created by a hotel development project through construction and operations.

Calculation of construction jobs is fairly straightforward based on eligible hard and soft costs, whereas operations jobs are generally calculated using projected hotel revenue as specified in the financial statements included with the business plan. Revenue is generally calculated by multiplying the ADR by the occupancy rate, resulting in the RevPAR. All these figures should be included with the business plan, as well.

The following three issues concerning job creation may affect hotel projects:

- Tenant jobs. USCIS is strict on which jobs may count toward the job creation total. Jobs created by tenants of a development, such as restaurants or bars within the hotel but not owned by it, might not count toward this total and might therefore need to be excluded from the job creation projections.
- Operations jobs. If hotel construction lasts longer than expected, operations jobs may not count toward the job creation total, as USCIS has specified that jobs must be created within two and a half years of the approval of an investor's I-526 petition. Developers must therefore time the EB-5 investment so as to ensure that the requisite 10 full-time jobs are created within that timeframe. For example, if construction is slated to begin when the EB-5 funds enter the project and is projected to take three years, only construction jobs from the first 30 months of the project can be used to fill the quota.
- Visitor spending. If the hotel will be operational within the timeframe specified above, visitor spending revenues can be used to calculate additional job creation in the region caused by the presence of the hotel. However, because USCIS requires the hotel to demonstrate that it will attract visitors to the region rather than simply capitalizing on an existing market of visitors, visitor spending is very difficult to prove in an EB-5 context. Each project should consider this facet of the economic impact model carefully based on its individual circumstances.

The Feasibility Study

The EB-5 petition should include a study using independent data to validate the financial projections from the business plan and economic impact report. This means the RevPAR, ADR, and occupancy rates used to calculate job creation as specified in those documents should be backed up by historical and industry data on the performance of comparable businesses within two and a half years of the stage at which the EB-5 investment would enter the project. The business plan, economic impact report, and feasibility study must be interconnected in that the calculations used in the first two documents should be based on figures from the feasibility study.

By following USCIS guidelines regarding these three documents, developers can take advantage of the opportunities offered by the EB-5 Program.

EB-5 Direct and Regional Center Investments in Restaurants

Quick service restaurants (QSRs) encompass not only fast food franchises but other fast casual dining options, such as cafes and bars. Historically, QSRs have provided consistent opportunities for direct investment under the EB-5 Program. The QSR model aligns with the goals of certain investors who which to take on a more active role in their EB-5 investment and want to own and directly operate a business in the United States.

However, recent delays in visa processing times have not only frustrated investors but also eaten into the job creation window of two and a half years and made it more difficult for investors in QSRs to meet the requirements of the EB-5 Program. As such, regional centers have emerged as the primary method for investors hoping to use the QSR model as a successful channel for their EB-5 petitions. Here we will discuss both models, direct investments and regional centers, as well as their benefits and drawbacks for EB-5 investors.

Direct Investment in a QSR

The direct investment model offers several points of interest for potential EB-5 investors:

- The cost of opening a QSR can range between $350,000 and $2,000,000, and the initial EB-5 investment will cover a large portion of this, including the franchise fee, any construction or improvement costs, insurance, marketing, payroll, and furniture, fixtures, and equipment (FF&E) required to get the business off the ground. A $500,000 investment in a TEA or a $1 million investment otherwise (depending on the location) can therefore meet the new business requirement of the EB-5 Program.

- A QSR can easily meet the job creation requirements of the program, as well. Most QSRs are open every day for at least 12 hours, and each can support three work shifts and 18 to 24 full-time jobs, well above the minimum threshold of 10. This offers the opportunity for a location to attract more than one investor, meaning two investors with limited funds could potentially work together to open a QSR under the program.

- Investors in a regional center have the right to vote on policy but otherwise take on a passive role in the business in which they are invested, which is ideal for investors who wish to continue to work in their current capacity while waiting for their EB-5 petition to be approved. In a direct investment QSR model, however, the investor will generally take on daily management responsibilities and shall be responsible for the financials, reporting, and related information related to the investment, including keeping proper books and records related to job creation.

Investment in a Regional Center QSR

USCIS has yet to address the issue of long wait times for visa applicants, particularly mainland Chinese investors under the EB-5 Program. Current wait times are between 10 and 24 months, and this delay introduces several difficulties that make regional centers a more practical option for some EB-5 investors.

- Prior to the approval of his or her I-526 petition, which allows the investor to live in the United States, a foreign investor will be unable to manage the daily operations of the QSR. This means the investor will have to rely on hired staff to manage the business in his or her absence for as long as it takes for USCIS to approve the I-526 petition. This possibility is unacceptable to investors who would prefer to be on site to ensure the successful operation of the business, and such investors may prefer instead to take a back seat on management altogether by working with a regional center when faced with this reality.
- Similarly, investors hoping to take a less direct approach to management regardless can also benefit from working with a regional center. While regional center investors are expected to demonstrate management by exercising their right to vote on matters of policy, they will rarely take part in the daily operations of a QSR, which are instead entrusted to project managers experienced in this industry and vetted by the regional center. Such investors will also therefore avoid the need to hire managers and other competent interim staff on their own.
- Investors have two years following the approval of the I-526 petition and before the filing of the I-829 petition, which removes the conditions to permanent residence, to create the 10 full-time jobs required by the EB-5 Program. However, delays in the processing of these petitions mean that an investor may be several years into operations by the time the I-526 petition is approved. For a QSR or any business to survive beyond its first year is an accomplishment, and an investor thus runs the risk of losing his or her investment and all created jobs, and thus approval of the I-829 petition, if the QSR fails before the I-829 petition can be filed. Regional centers can take advantage of broader job creation requirements, as detailed below, to avoid this risk.
- A regional center investment allows for direct, indirect, and induced job creation as determined based on construction jobs, tenant jobs, and operations jobs, with the created jobs credited to the investor upon completion of the construction project or building purchase. Regional centers can thus plan a project to ensure that each investor is credited with the required number of jobs within two years of his or her I-526 petition filing date. Investors who would otherwise have had to ensure the continued successful operation

of a business for several years can instead take advantage of this option.

Recent delays in the processing of visa petitions, especially those filed by Chinese investors, who make up the majority of investors under the EB-5 Program, have encouraged investors to look into regional centers as an alternative to traditional direct investment in a QSR. As detailed above, regional centers offer several advantages to investors facing long delays, such as the ability to count indirect and induced jobs toward the job creation total and the opportunity to adopt a meaningful managerial role without concern for daily operations and hiring decisions while still overseas.

Direct investment and regional centers offer their own benefits and drawbacks, but a potential EB-5 investor can become educated on these and choose the investment model that best suits his or her needs.

EB-5 Investor Markets

EB-5 Investment from India

One of the most popular paths to U.S. employment for foreign nationals is the H-1B visa. Under the Bush administration in 2003, the H-1B visa cap was reduced from 195,000 to 65,000. The H-1B Visa Reform Act of 2004 increased this cap by 20,000 for candidates who earned a master's or PhD from a U.S. institution. The resulting 85,000 cap for H-1B visa recipients has remained unchanged until now. President Donald Trump's Buy American and Hire American Executive Order, signed in April 2017, imposed additional restrictions for those applying for H-1B visas. This executive order and the reduced visa cap has made the EB-5 visa program a popular route for Indian investors seeking to obtain permanent residence in the U.S. while avoiding the work visa application and renewal process entirely.

With a population of more than 1.3 billion, India receives the largest number of H-1B visas, making up 75.6% of approved H-1B visas in fiscal year 2017. Indian workers participating in the H-1B program tend to be strong in information technology, which has led to benefits within the U.S. tech industry. However, Indian interest in H-1B visas has declined over the last several years, leaving many U.S. tech jobs unfilled. This effect has been exacerbated through President Trump's recent executive order. For Indian citizens especially, the EB-5 visa has become a strong second option.

Wealth and Economy

In the last several years, the level of wealth in India has increased significantly. As of 2017, India contained more than 260,000 millionaires with a combined wealth of over $1 trillion, ranking it in eleventh place behind countries like the U.S. and China. Income inequality in India is expected to continue growing, with the richest 1% owning more than 50% of the country's wealth.

Political Landscape

As a former colony of the British Empire, India's parliamentary democracy is designed after that of the U.K. The executive branch, headed by a president and prime minister, is answerable to the bicameral legislative branch. Like the U.S. judiciary, the Indian judicial branch has multiple levels and is independent. One major difference between India's and America's democracies, however, is India's continued dependence on the caste system. Although past efforts were made to prevent discrimination based on caste, the caste system in India remains strong today and plays a large part in Indian politics and society. As a result, social mobility is still difficult for individuals born into lower castes.

Crime and Safety

While India's crime rate of 379 crimes per 100,000 people in 2018 was lower than the crime rate in the United States, the number of rapes, homicides, kidnappings, and dowry deaths has been increasing. India has been ranked as one of the most dangerous countries for female travelers, and bank fraud and cyber attacks are on the rise as well. The Indian police force suffers from a shortage in personnel and vehicles, issues with infrastructure and communication, lack of proper training and weapons, and problems with political corruption. This environment has encouraged wealthy Indians to consider emigrating.

Environmental Conditions

As with many quickly developing countries, the lack of strong factory regulations in India has led to a dangerous increase in pollution, especially in cities. The top 10 most polluted cities in the world are contained in northern India, far surpassing China. This trend has been accompanied by a rise in rates of cardiovascular and respiratory diseases, which have decreased India's overall life expectancy. The stricter air and water regulations and cleaner living standards in the U.S. present a more appealing alternative for Indian EB-5 investors and their families.

Educational Quality

Improvements in India's educational system and its large university network have played a large part in the country's recent economic growth. However, while India has made efforts to boost the quality of its public education and increase enrollment in primary schools, its high school graduation rates hovered at only 42% as of 2015. With teacher shortages, problems in school infrastructure, and poor quality of learning, many Indian families turn to American schools and universities to better educate their children.

EB-5 Project Selection Preferences

Indian EB-5 investors tend to favor smaller projects that require more personal involvement and active participation. Instead of putting money into a larger project, these EB-5 investors often prefer to start their own enterprises with local Indian partners or to select a project being developed by an Indian developer or sponsor. Indian EB-5 investors are also strong negotiators when it comes to the terms of investment and any extraneous costs, including administrative and immigration attorney fees. EB5 Affiliate Network (EB5AN) regularly works with Indian project developers and sponsors to assemble the required project documentation through an I-526 template. EB5AN also provides regional center sponsorship under one of its 15 USCIS-approved regional centers for projects seeking Indian EB-5 investors.

Capital Flow and Other Challenges with the EB-5 Process

Current laws allow Indian individuals to move $250,000 to other countries, which means two partners can transfer the required $500,000 for an EB-5 investment with relative ease. However, the main issue for EB-5 investors from India is providing official documentation that the funds originate from a legal source and have been properly taxed. The prevalence in India of money that is earned legally but not reported to the Indian government can complicate the EB-5 application process. Prospective Indian EB-5 investors must therefore hire skilled immigration attorneys and source of funds consultants to verify that their documentation is sufficient and satisfies USCIS requirements.

Marketing Channels for Investors

Unlike China's EB-5 market, where a majority of EB-5 investors flow through a select few large immigration brokers, India's EB-5 market is highly fragmented with only a handful of established and experienced agents. The majority of Indian investors to date are sourced through networks of small companies that tangentially touch wealthy Indian EB-5 investors. Common examples are chartered accountants, travel agencies, real estate brokers, and wealth managers. Additionally, many Indian EB-5 investors are sourced directly by regional centers and project sponsors through in-person seminars in India. These entities also target Indian investors already located in the U.S. who are on alternative visas, such as H-1B or F-1 visas.

EB-5 Investment from Vietnam

Over the last 30 years, Vietnam has developed from one of the poorest nations in the world into one of the fastest-growing economies. This increase in wealth and the search for better opportunities have led to a rise in wealthy Vietnamese investors.

Wealth and Economy

The number of millionaires in Vietnam has skyrocketed by more than 400% in a decade, totaling more than 14,000 in 2016 and surpassing the total number in neighboring countries such as the Philippines. Centimillionaires—those worth at least $100 million—are also multiplying. Vietnam's wealth growth rate surpassed even that of China from 2007 to 2017.

Political Landscape

As in China, Vietnam's government is run by a communist party that closely monitors the movement of its people and assets. This gives the government the ability to seize possessions and property as it sees fit. So far, however, this has not deterred Vietnam's numerous foreign investors from doing business in the country.

Crime and Safety

Crime against foreigners in Vietnam is generally limited to petty theft but has been increasing in recent years. Vietnam also has become a hotspot for cybercrime targeting governments, businesses, and bank accounts. Because bribery and corruption are common in the country, affluent Vietnamese often look to emigrate to the U.S.

Environmental Conditions

Like India and China, Vietnam is notorious for bad air and water quality that is only worsening as its economy grows. Low energy prices and underfunded public transportation systems have compounded the crisis, with mopeds and cars clogging the city streets. Other contributors are deforestation, weak emissions regulations, and substandard waste treatment. The Vietnamese government is making efforts to combat these issues before they intensify, but many wealthy Vietnamese are looking elsewhere for cleaner living situations.

Educational Quality

Vietnam's state-run school system continues to struggle with inequality and ineffective teaching methods, although the government is working to revamp the system. In recent years, the English requirement in most schools has greatly increased English literacy. School curricula, however, still focus on rote memorization over writing, extracurriculars, and critical thinking.

EB-5 Project Selection Preferences

As with Chinese investors, Vietnamese investors tend to favor large, conspicuous projects sporting established brand names. Vietnamese EB-5 investors often prefer to start their own enterprise with local Vietnamese partners or to select a project being developed by a Vietnamese developer or sponsor. EB5 Affiliate Network regularly works with Vietnamese project developers and sponsors to assemble the required project documents using an I-526 template. EB5AN also provides regional center sponsorship under one of its 15 USCIS-approved regional centers for projects seeking Vietnamese EB-5 investors.

Capital Flow and Other Challenges with the EB-5 Process

Because of its communist ideology, the government in Hanoi exercises tight control over money flowing in and out of the country. Consequently, it can be challenging for Vietnamese EB-5 investors to funnel money out of Vietnam and into projects in the U.S.

Marketing Channels for Investors

Immigration brokers in Vietnam tend to be more concentrated than in India, with a few experienced agents dominating the EB-5 market. The Vietnamese market, however, is not quite as monopolistic as in China, leaving Vietnamese EB-5 investors with a few more options to choose from.

EB-5 Investment from Saudi Arabia

Although the United States surpassed Saudi Arabia and Russia in 2018 to become the world's largest producer of crude oil, Saudi Arabia has amassed great wealth over the last half century with its own plentiful oil reserves. This has enabled it to maintain a large presence on the world stage, and the nation is home to an abundance of moneyed residents. Nonetheless, the recent crackdowns by the Saudi government against dissenters and perceived corruption have led to increased interest in EB-5 investing among wealthy Saudis.

Wealth and Economy

As a result of its large oil reserves, Saudi Arabia is known for containing some of the world's richest people, especially among the royal family and its associates. The nation is currently home to more millionaires than any other Middle Eastern country, totaling 176,000 in 2017. Saudi Crown Prince Mohammed bin Salman (MBS) has also launched an ambitious plan called Vision 2030 to diversify the Saudi economy, reduce its dependence on oil, and expand public service sectors throughout the country.

Political Landscape

MBS has been seen by many as a reformer for the Saudi people, purging corruption within the government and royal family and ushering new changes into the kingdom. The most publicized reform has been the repeal of a long-held ban on female drivers. Saudi activists, however, are still commonly detained and tortured for expressing dissent, and the Crown Prince has been heavily criticized for his country's role in the humanitarian crisis in Yemen. MBS has also been embroiled in the scandal surrounding the 2018 murder of Washington Post columnist Jamal Khashoggi in the Saudi consulate in Turkey. Political instability in Saudi Arabia has prompted many potential EB-5 investors to seek safety in a more liberal environment.

Crime and Safety

Crime rates among the Saudi population are low, but this is likely due to the extreme punishments given to criminals or those who dare to speak out against the government. Penalties include lashings, torture, amputations, excessive prison sentences, and public beheadings. Another issue of concern in Saudi Arabia since 2015 is the ballistic missiles being launched across the border by Houthi rebels in Yemen. Such attacks are in response to Saudi Arabia's continued military presence in Yemen. The country also has an increased risk of terrorist attacks, though the Saudi government has strengthened its security forces in response to the threat. Still, many wealthy Saudis prefer to move their families to a more stable location.

Environmental Conditions

As the home of the largest desert on Earth, Saudi Arabia's frequent sandstorms compound the air pollution already emitted by factories and vehicles in its cities. The Saudi capital of Riyadh is now one of the most polluted cities in the world, with current pollution levels shortening the average Saudi's life by 1.5 years. Agricultural practices and city expansion risk threatening the country's rich biodiversity as well. Other large risks are oil spills, desertification, and shrinking underground reservoirs of water. The Saudi government is making some effort to transform the country's economy into something more environmentally friendly, but sustainability is not yet a popular concept among the Saudi public.

Educational Quality

Elementary through high school education is free for all Saudis, with a slightly lower enrollment rate for girls than boys. Saudi Arabia is also creating more than 150 vocational training centers across the country to decrease its economic dependence on oil. Each year, thousands of Saudi students are sent to American universities, with the total reaching nearly 60,000 in 2018. The vast majority of these students are sponsored by the Saudi government with the intention that they will use their newfound knowledge to benefit the kingdom upon their return.

EB-5 Project Selection Preferences

As in Vietnam, Saudi EB-5 investors prefer large, flashy projects boasting established brand names. EB5 Affiliate Network frequently works with Saudi project developers and sponsors to assemble the required project documentation for EB-5 Form I-526. EB5AN also provides sponsorship through its 15 USCIS-approved regional centers for projects seeking Saudi EB-5 investors.

Capital Flow and Other Challenges with the EB-5 Process

The Saudi government imposes no limits on how much money can be moved out of the country, assuming the money is earned legally. Saudi EB-5 investors and foreigners working in Saudi Arabia must ensure that the money they try to transfer matches their earnings on paper, otherwise the government has the authority to open an investigation into the funds.

Marketing Channels for Investors

As in India, the Saudi EB-5 market consists of only a few experienced agents. Most Saudi EB-5 investors are sourced through small entities such as travel agencies, chartered accountants, wealth managers, and real estate brokers. Additionally, regional centers and project sponsors target many Saudis directly through in-person seminars in Saudi Arabia itself. Saudis already in the U.S. on visas such as the H-1B or F-1 are also targeted.

EB-5 Investment from Turkey

Despite social and political upheaval, Turkey's economy has continued to grow rapidly over the last few years and is still seen as a strong force in the region. Turkey now boasts the eighteenth highest GDP in the world, but rising debt makes this continued pace of growth uncertain. Turkey also faces increasing inflation that hit a 15-year high of 25.2% in October 2018. The Turkish lira is now trading at a rate of 5.5 lira per U.S. dollar, providing incentive for potential Turkish EB-5 investors to leave the country.

Wealth and Economy

In the last few years, Turkey has seen the highest emigration rate of wealthy citizens of any major economy, with a full 12% of its millionaires leaving the country in 2017. This mass departure can be attributed to high inflation, intensifying security and economic issues, and President Recep Tayyip Erdogan's clampdown on his political opponents.

Political Landscape

Turkey was founded as a secular republic in the early 1900s and has made strides toward becoming a full democracy. President Erdogan, however, has been accused of attempting to establish an autocracy, and he has gained notoriety for limiting dissent and free press. A failed coup in 2016 resulted in the arrest of thousands of soldiers and professionals seen as threatening to Erdogan's government, and hundreds of journalists have been detained for criticizing his administration. Nevertheless, a 2017 referendum switched Turkey's government to a presidential system, giving Erdogan significantly more power. Additionally, Turkey's attempts to join the EU have been held back by its dubious human rights record, including the oppression of Kurds, who make up a fifth of the nation's population.

Crime and Safety

Turkey's crime rate over the last two decades has increased significantly, even when taking into account its growth in population. Its number of prisoners almost quadrupled, with a 400% rise in robberies, homicides, and drug-related offenses. Armed violence also increased by 61% from 2015 to 2017, leading affluent residents to search for safer places to live and raise their families.

Environmental Conditions

Turkey's rapid industrialization has led to unsafe levels of air pollution for at least 97% of Turkish city-dwellers, with the country quickly becoming one of the world's largest producers of greenhouse gases. Coupled with water pollution and overfishing, Turkey's abundant biodiversity is in jeopardy. The Turkish government has, however, already begun plans to adopt more sustainable energy sources, including wind, solar, and hydropower.

Educational Quality

Primary school is free for all Turkish citizens, and 12 years of education are required for both boys and girls. However, as in Vietnam, Turkish education tends to emphasize memorization over critical thinking. Furthermore, curricula and educational materials are determined by the government's education ministry, and in 2017, the decision was made to remove evolution from all high school biology textbooks. Many critics accuse the Turkish government of trying to influence Turkey's youth with religious ideology, which was compounded by the firing of 33,000 teachers after the failed coup in 2016. Therefore, many wealthy Turkish parents are looking elsewhere for more secular educational opportunities for their children.

EB-5 Project Selection Preferences

Turkish EB-5 investors are wary of their country's high inflation rate and the current political crisis. With the clock ticking, wealthy Turks are most concerned with getting their money out of the country and into the U.S. as soon as possible. As a result, EB-5 investors from Turkey tend to favor EB-5 projects that can move quickly, with returns on investments being a lower priority.

Capital Flow and Other Challenges with the EB-5 Process

Foreign exchange brokers can be found in most Turkish cities and can help facilitate money transfers into and out of the country. Potential Turkish EB-5 investors, however, must be particularly prepared to answer questions about the source and destination of their funds since the Turkish government is trying to crack down on the financing of terrorist organizations. EB-5 investors from Turkey can transfer up to $50,000 before their bank has to notify the Turkish Central Bank of the exchange.

Marketing Channels for Investors

The Turkish EB-5 market tends to be scattered, with only a handful of established immigration brokers. The majority of Turkish investors are connected through networks of small companies, such as chartered accountants, travel agencies, real estate brokers, and wealth managers. Additionally, many Turkish EB-5 investors are sourced directly by regional centers and project sponsors through in-person seminars in Turkey. These groups also target Turkish investors who are already in the U.S. on alternative visas.

EB-5 Investment from Iran

Iran is home to the world's fourth-largest reserve of oil and second-largest reserve of natural gas, and it is within the top 10 world producers of both of these natural resources. As such, it has become the second largest economy in the MENA region behind Saudi Arabia. However, Iran has been the subject of increased international sanctions due to its interference in neighboring countries' affairs as well as skepticism over the promised discontinuation of its nuclear program.

Wealth and Economy

Sanctions lifted in Iran in early 2016 led to a dramatic increase of overseas Iranian spending on real estate in London and other European locations. Iran contains 1,300 individuals with at least $10 million in assets, and the number of millionaires after the initial removal of sanctions was expected to reach 55,000 by 2025. Some analysts at the time predicted a total of $8.5 billion would be spent on overseas property within 10 years of the sanctions being lifted. All of this predicted growth, however, has been thrown into doubt now that the U.S. has reinstated international sanctions. Iran could now be headed for a recession, pushing wealthy Iranians to leave the country.

Political Landscape

Iran is an Islamic theocracy headed by a president and a supreme leader. Political instability in Iran has driven many residents to seek other countries in which to live, including America. Tensions with the U.S. have intensified over the last two years, however, culminating in President Trump pulling the U.S. out of the Joint Comprehensive Plan of Action, known commonly as the Iran nuclear deal, in May 2018. Iran is also one of seven countries included in the current U.S. travel ban, rendering it highly improbable that Iranian EB-5 investors could earn an EB-5 visa even if their applications were approved.

Crime and Safety

Iran is considered very safe for foreign tourists, and its rate of violent crimes is quite low. Iran does, however, have one of the largest prison populations in the world and is a hotspot for narcotics and human trafficking. Hundreds of people are incarcerated for political reasons, and executions are common. As in Turkey, the Iranian government regulates freedom of expression and often penalizes journalists and activists for speaking out against the regime.

Environmental Conditions

Frequent dust storms, water contamination, and high air pollution are all present in Iran, leading to burgeoning health costs for its population. Tehran in particular faces some of the world's highest levels of air pollution due to a combination of outdated vehicles, power plants and factories, and the city's higher altitude. Iran's government took action by passing the Clean Air Law in 2017, which has slowly implemented changes to reduce pollution and prevent premature deaths.

Educational Quality

Primary education in Iran is required for all children, although schools are separated by sex. The country has a high literacy rate, and schools are quite competitive, involving multiple entrance exams and heavy parental participation. English is a compulsory second language throughout high school, and women make up the majority of college students. Because Iran has a larger college-educated population than its economy can accommodate, it has a very high youth unemployment rate and one of the highest rates of brain drain in the world. This dilemma has led to widespread social unrest among young people in Iran.

EB-5 Project Selection Preferences

The vast majority of Iranian EB-5 investors prefer to work through regional centers, although significant barriers prevent most regional centers from accepting Iranian money. Iranian EB-5 investors in particular must prove that their funds come from a legal source. EB5AN works with Iranian EB-5 investors to assemble the proper I-526 documentation and can provide regional center sponsorship under its 15 USCIS-approved regional centers.

Capital Flow and Other Challenges with the EB-5 Process

As described above, Iranian investors were eager to start moving their money out of Iran as soon as sanctions against the country were lifted in January 2016. Matters have since been complicated by the sanctions' reinstatement in addition to the existing U.S. sanctions related to Iran's human rights abuses and missile program. Navigating this complicated field of regulations and associated compliance costs has discouraged many U.S. banks from accepting Iranian money despite its legality.

Marketing Channels for Investors

As with the Saudi Arabian market, the Iranian EB-5 market consists of a limited number of established and experienced agents. The majority of Iranian

EB-5 investors are culled through networks of small companies that work with investors, including real estate brokers, travel agencies, and wealth managers. Iranian EB-5 investors are also targeted through seminars within Iran held by regional centers and project sponsors. Wealthy Iranians already living in America on other visas are targeted as well.

EB-5 Investment from Brazil

With a population of nearly 212 million, Brazil now makes up the third-largest EB-5 market behind China and Vietnam, with the advantage of not yet having faced visa retrogression. Brazil's interest in EB-5 visas is likely attributable to the country's recent economic downturn, its high crime and corruption rates, and its poor quality of education.

Wealth and Economy

Despite having the seventh-largest economy in the world only a decade ago, a recession spanning 2015 and 2016 shrank Brazil's GDP by 8%, and the country is now facing high inflation and unemployment rates. Approximately 2,000 millionaires fled the country in 2017, continuing a trend seen over the last several years. Nevertheless, the number of Brazilian millionaires is expected to rise from the current 164,000 to 296,000 in 2022.

Political Landscape

Brazil has been rocked in recent years by major corruption scandals that even led to the impeachment of the nation's president. Bribery and fraud are commonplace in Brazil's politics, tax management, and judicial system. The current president, Jair Bolsonaro, has authoritarian leanings and is an apologist for Brazil's previous military regime. These factors provide a major incentive for wealthy Brazilians to leave the country.

Crime and Safety

Crime rates in Brazil have reached record highs, with a staggering 30.8 murders per 100,000 people in 2018. Organized crime, drug gang rivalries, and an under-resourced yet violent police force are all contributors. Fear of crime has dampened Brazil's nightlife, with soldiers and tanks often appearing to keep the peace. Over 15,000 armored cars were sold in 2017 alone. A promise to curtail crime, loosen gun laws, and protect ordinary Brazilians was a large part of President Bolsonaro's public appeal. A full 62% of young Brazilians surveyed said they would leave the country if they could, and many affluent Brazilians are trying to find a way out.

Environmental Conditions

One of the biggest environmental challenges for Brazil at the moment is deforestation. Brazil is home to the Amazon rainforest, the world's largest tropical rainforest and a massive source of biodiversity and oxygen production. President Bolsonaro has already made moves to increase deforestation to facilitate higher agricultural production, worrying many environmental groups and activists. High pollution plagues large Brazilian cities such as São Paulo, and the country is experiencing a major waste management crisis. On the other hand, the Brazilian government has been investing heavily in wind power for the last decade, and it is promoting international green building codes around the country.

Educational Quality

Brazilian schools have fallen far behind the recommended average in reading and math scores, exacerbating the current economic crisis. The country's education system is troubled by inefficient spending, inadequate investment in teachers, and low-quality curricula. The nation currently has 2,600 public and private universities, and the government is making efforts to improve its vocational training. Nevertheless, many Brazilians are looking elsewhere for better academic opportunities. More than 13,000 Brazilian students are currently studying in the U.S., making it the tenth largest international student population in America.

EB-5 Project Selection Preferences

Brazilian EB-5 investors are keeping a watchful eye on the unstable political situation unfolding in their country. In order to protect their wealth, many EB-5 investors from Brazil prefer to invest in projects that can produce quick results. Like other Latin American investors, Brazilian EB-5 investors lean toward working with regional centers and investing in smaller projects with physical results. However, with the time constraints posed by the current financial crisis in Brazil, the returns from Brazilian EB-5 investments are often secondary considerations.

Capital Flow and Other Challenges with the EB-5 Process

Because of Brazil's strong trading ties with Florida, cities like Miami have become hotspots for Brazilian EB-5 investors interested in moving to the U.S. Shifting money out of Brazil, however, is costly and challenging due to bureaucratic banking known for its inefficiency. Additionally, monthly transfers out of Brazil are limited to $10,000 BRL, or about $3,000 USD.

Marketing Channels for Investors

Brazil is the world's fifth-largest country and provides a large source of potential EB-5 investors. The EB-5 market in Brazil, however, is highly fragmented, with a nominal number of EB-5-specific immigration brokers for investors to work with. As a result, most Brazilian EB-5 investors must go through smaller firms such as accountants, real estate brokers, travel agencies, and wealth managers. Many regional centers and project sponsors hold workshops within Brazil to increase awareness of the EB-5 visa process, and they also target Brazilians already in the U.S. who are concerned about their immigration status in the current political climate.

EB-5 Investment from Venezuela

Venezuela is home to the world's largest reserves of crude oil, surpassing even Saudi Arabia. While this supply led to a booming economy in the 1990s, the government's mismanagement of money and pivot to socialism have led to the impoverished nation seen today. Because of the current political upheaval and the resulting uptick in violence, many wealthy Venezuelans desire to emigrate but find it challenging to do so.

Wealth and Economy

Venezuela's spiraling economy due to falling oil prices has been gripped by hyperinflation predicted to reach 10,000,000% this year. Residents can hardly afford to buy necessities and must keep up with constantly changing prices. Shortages in food, medicine, and fuel have led to extensive looting. Affluent Venezuelans who are able to preserve their wealth are often drawn to the safety of U.S. cities such as Los Angeles and Miami.

Political Landscape

The current humanitarian crisis and violent political turmoil between President Nicolás Maduro and his rival Juan Guaidó have prompted an international response. Large groups of Venezuelans have joined caravans trekking toward the U.S., and humanitarian aid has been blocked from entering the country. Mass poverty and hunger are threatening the nation's population while Maduro favors large displays of military might. Wealthy Venezuelans have plenty of motivation to leave the country in its current state.

Crime and Safety

Venezuela holds the highest murder rate in the world, with an average of 81.4 homicides per 100,000 people in 2018. This total is slightly lower than in the previous two years, likely because some criminals have hidden among the three million Venezuelans fleeing the country since 2015. Added tensions between President Maduro and his political rival have only intensified the situation, pushing wealthy and ordinary citizens alike to leave the country.

Environmental Conditions

In an effort to combat Venezuela's worsening economic crisis, President Maduro has tried to market the country's ample mineral resources by opening up the Orinoco Mining Belt—which covers more than 12% of the country's land—to international mining. This move has already endangered the country's rich biodiversity and rainforests and led to increased deforestation and pollution. Other environmental problems in Venezuela include water shortages, sewage pollution, and soil degradation.

Educational Quality

In the ongoing economic and humanitarian crisis, education has become the least of many Venezuelan families' concerns. With hyperinflation and the current food shortage, school supplies have become unaffordable, leading to a high rate of student absenteeism. Teachers are also in short supply, with many schools asking parents to take over when teachers stop coming to class. School infrastructure is failing, and academic freedom has been jeopardized. Students themselves are often subjected to political threats and questioned about their views.

EB-5 Project Selection Preferences

Venezuelan EB-5 investors are most interested in a quick escape from the political and economic turmoil wracking their country. For this reason, EB-5 investors from Venezuela prefer to put their money in projects that can move at a faster pace. They also lean toward working with regional centers for smaller projects with visible results. With the Venezuelan humanitarian crisis only getting worse, high returns on investments are not the primary concern for Venezuelan EB-5 investors seeking safety in the U.S.

Capital Flow and Other Challenges with the EB-5 Process

Considering the near-worthlessness of the Venezuelan bolivar, it is exceedingly difficult to withdraw even a small amount of money from a Venezuelan bank. Because of this, potential Venezuelan EB-5 investors who want to transfer their wealth often have to complete the transaction from within a neighboring country.

Marketing Channels for Investors

As in Brazil, few EB-5-specific brokers are available for Venezuelan investors. The main challenge for U.S.-based brokers and agents is to simply increase awareness of the EB-5 visa program in Venezuela and other Latin American countries. They must also put in the effort to build relationships with Venezuelan tax specialists, lawyers, and wealth managers who interact regularly with the country's wealthiest citizens. Additionally, many brokers target affluent Venezuelans who already reside in America on other temporary visas who are nervous about their status given current U.S. immigration policies.

EB-5 Investment from Mexico

Mexico's GDP of $2.4 trillion has topped that of even Canada, although it has a much lower standard of living. Mexico's strong economy is largely due to being one of the biggest exporters in the world and having more trade agreements than any other country. We have yet to see how the new Canada–United States–Mexico Agreement will affect Mexico's economy once the treaty is ratified. Either way, many affluent Mexicans have personal connections in the U.S., which makes the EB-5 visa an appealing method for eventually earning a green card.

Wealth and Economy

Mexico's strong export economy has led to the creation of almost 87,000 millionaires in Mexico City alone. Although the negative rhetoric toward Mexico during Donald Trump's election impacted Mexico's economy, it quickly recovered its losses. Many Mexicans have ties to family and friends in America, and those who own property in the U.S. look to the EB-5 visa as a legal path of entry.

Current immigration laws in the U.S. have made it more difficult for Mexicans to enter or stay in the United States. Many Mexican citizens have been denied entry into the U.S. because of the fear that they may overstay their visas.

Political Landscape

Corruption has come to a head in Mexican politics, with protesters demanding transparency and the newly-elected President López Obrador vowing to crack down on underhanded officials. Bribery, embezzlement, and blackmail can be found in all levels of Mexico's government, putting wealthy residents at an increased risk of political violence.

Crime and Safety

Many Mexican families are making the perilous journey into the United States between points of entry on the southern border to escape the ruthless drug cartels and organized crime plaguing the country. Territory wars between drug traffickers have killed tens of thousands of Mexican citizens while raking in billions of dollars in annual sales. El Chapo, the notorious Mexican drug lord who already escaped from prison once and spent months on the run, has finally been indicted and faces life in prison in the U.S.

Environmental Conditions

Lax enforcement of factory regulations and an increased number of cars on the road have given Mexico some of the worst air pollution in the Americas. Harmful chemicals in the air, especially near the border with the U.S., have led to higher rates of respiratory illnesses, asthma, lung cancer, and death. In the last decade, the government has responded by promoting a biking and walking culture in its cities, including the implementation of one of the world's biggest bike-share systems. Many Mexicans in more rural areas, however, continue to suffer from uncontrolled pollution, prompting many to seek better health and cleaner air across the border.

Educational Quality

While the Catholic Church initially had a large influence on Mexican education, all of its public school education is now secular. Schooling in Mexico is mandatory until age 18, with primary school being free for all students. Nevertheless, the number of students who actually graduate is quite small, and the number of those who move on to college is even smaller. One of the reasons behind these low retention rates is a dearth in funding for proper school infrastructure in rural areas, where a large portion of the Mexican population lives. Public schools in Mexico are also known for corruption, so many Mexicans who can afford it choose instead to send their children to private schools.

EB-5 Project Selection Preferences

As in other Latin American countries, Mexican EB-5 investors tend to prefer working with regional centers on small-scale projects that yield tangible results. EB-5 investors from Mexico are not quite as concerned with fast-moving EB-5 projects as investors in Brazil or Venezuela, but the motivation to escape from Mexico's high rates of crime and corruption remains.

Capital Flow and Other Challenges with the EB-5 Process

Although different banks have various limits, moving money from Mexico to the U.S. is commonplace and generally simple for Mexican EB-5 investors. Money-transfer services are offered by many banks and transfer companies within Mexico.

Marketing Channels for Investors

Mexico was previously a significant source of EB-5 investors coming to America. The number of Mexicans applying for EB-5 visas, however, dipped significantly after the election of Donald Trump. The best option for EB-5 brokers in the U.S. is to continue trying to increase awareness of the EB-5 program in Mexico. They should also work to build relationships with lawyers, accountants, and wealth managers who regularly interact with wealthy

Mexicans. Additionally, many affluent Mexicans who already live in the U.S. are eager to participate in the EB-5 program to protect their status as legal immigrants in a shifting political climate.

Strategies and Resources

Regional Center Strategies for USCIS Site Visits

Recent efforts by USCIS to ensure regional centers are fulfilling their purposes under the EB-5 Program have led to a trend of more frequent site visits. As USCIS shuttered a significant number of regional centers from 2015 to 2018, site visits have become an increasingly relevant concern for project representatives, who must seek to satisfy any concerns brought up during these visits so as to illustrate a given project's compliance with EB-5 Program requirements.

Additionally, aiming to curb instances of fraud within the program, the Fraud Detection and National Security (FDNS) division of USCIS has similarly initiated site visits for EB-5 projects. It is therefore crucial that the regional centers, new commercial enterprises (NCEs), and job-creating entities (JCEs) involved in an EB-5 project prepare for the eventuality of a site visit and adopt practical strategies to handle these visits and appropriately address any concerns raised. Four such strategies are analyzed below.

Prepare for the Possibility of a Site Visit by Working with an EB-5 Attorney

Certain issues that might otherwise precipitate a site visit can be avoided through proper preparation of financial documents and other materials submitted to USCIS as part of the EB-5 petition. An attorney experienced in the preparation of such materials can instruct the regional center and other project partners according to USCIS guidelines and can additionally ensure all materials are suitable for auditing in the event of a site visit. If concerns are raised during the visit, a knowledgeable EB-5 attorney can likewise help the regional center respond appropriately to address and remedy those issues with USCIS and get the project back on track.

Equally important is to ensure the attorney is present during the site visit. Whereas regional center representatives might be unsure of the scope of questioning permitted of USCIS agents, an attorney will interject if an agent veers off topic and can thus help direct the site visit and keep all parties on task. An attorney will additionally be equipped to prepare representatives for the types of questions USCIS agents may ask and can provide strategies to answer these questions clearly and in a manner that will satisfy the agents.

Request Identification and Contact Information from Visiting USCIS Agents

USCIS agents are required to present identification upon entry to a project site. This ID is necessary for security purposes and verifies to representatives on the site that the agents are authorized to conduct the site visit. However, because visiting agents will also serve as a point of contact between USCIS and the project, site representatives should request to photocopy any ID presented and should additionally make note of other contact information through which the agents can be reached. For example, if a point of concern is raised during the site visit, project representatives may wish to follow up directly on that issue with the visiting agents after consulting with attorneys and other relevant parties.

Accompany the Agents on Their Inspection of the Site

The best course of action for project representatives is to guide USCIS agents to a comfortable setting where the agents can ask questions and review project documents. This allows agents and representatives to address any concerns thoroughly without distraction from construction or other site operations. However, it is likely that the agents will wish to tour the site as well, and the designated project representatives and attorneys should accompany the agents on that tour for the following reasons:

- The USCIS agents will be required to submit a report on whatever activities they witness during their inspection. If the regional center is asked to follow up on concerns after the site visit, representatives must be able to refer with clarity to whatever occurred during the inspection and thus should be present throughout.
- While certain representatives will have been walked through the site visit process by the project attorneys and therefore will have a good understanding of USCIS inspection protocols and the types of questions they may be asked, agents who tour the site unaccompanied may interview other contractors or employees at the site who are unequipped to answer such questions and may respond incorrectly or vaguely on crucial points.

Accompanying the USCIS agents allows project representatives to address concerns promptly and thoroughly and thus proactively avoid the need for further investigation.

Take Note of Any Concerns Brought Up during the Site Visit

As mentioned above, recent concerns with fraudulent actors working within the EB-5 Program have prompted USCIS to increase its oversight of projects. If any concerns or discrepancies are highlighted during a site visit, USCIS may exercise the discretion to share that information with other government agencies such as the SEC so further action can be taken as necessary to protect the interests of investors and enforce U.S. laws. Similarly, USCIS may pass along information to the Department of Labor or other relevant bodies if the need arises. For these reasons, regional centers must be prepared to respond to questions accurately and thoroughly to prevent any unnecessary escalation.

Trends in Regional Center Terminations

The role of regional centers has undergone continual adjustment over the past few years as USCIS has reevaluated the goals of the EB-5 Program. Within the last few years, the Administrative Appeals Office (AAO) began to challenge the inconsistent standards applied by USCIS to approve and deny regional center designations. The uncertainties surrounding requirements for regional centers have been further highlighted by a rash of regional center terminations, totalling 135 in 2018 alone.

Regional centers have the option to appeal these termination decisions, and one such appeal has illustrated the changing way USCIS views regional center designations. The decision in *Matter of A-L-V- LLC* reviewed the termination of a regional center based on its failure to promote economic growth under the EB-5 Program. Although the center had attempted to get multiple projects off the ground over the years and had filed its I-924A annually as required, USCIS made the decision to terminate the center, and this decision was upheld by the AAO.

A-L-V, which had been designated a regional center in 2008, countered that it had been unsuccessful in launching projects because of local economic conditions. Despite the fact that USCIS has not stated that regional centers must initiate projects within a certain timeframe or risk termination, the center had been pursuing projects throughout it designation but had prudently chosen not to move forward with projects considered unviable. This challenge was unsuccessful, and the AAO agreed with the points from the USCIS decision, namely that A-L-V had not raised any investment funds nor created any jobs, and therefore it had not promoted economic growth as required for continued designation under the EB-5 Program.

USCIS highlighted several points in its termination decision, and these are paraphrased below:

- A regional center is defined in 8 C.F.R. § 204.6(e) as an economic unit promoting economic growth through increased exports, job creation, capital investment, etc. To demonstrate that it has continued to promote such growth, a regional center must annually provide USCIS with updated information to that effect by filing its I-924A form.
- The regional center thus must have previously promoted economic growth and continue to do so to maintain its designation. USCIS considers several factors in deciding this element: the amount of capital raised, the number of jobs created or preserved, the number of industries affected, the number of enterprises established, and the quality of I-526 and I-829 petitions filed by investors working with the regional center.
- USCIS allows for flexibility in maintaining regional center designations such that regional centers can raise varying amounts of capital and invest in different types of commercial enterprises. This is meant to account for different conditions across regions and

industries, and USCIS applies flexibility at its discretion based on the unique circumstances faced by each center. For example, USCIS might show leniency in maintaining the designation of a recent regional center as opposed to an older center demonstrating no promotion of economic growth.

- USCIS additionally takes into account any progress a regional center has made in pursuing and developing projects, and a decision to terminate may be affected by the likelihood that such projects will soon promote economic growth. USCIS also takes into consideration reasonable or unforeseeable delays in project development. However, these allowances are not meant to encourage regional centers to remain inactive while exploring potential projects hypothetically.

How Does USCIS Define a Regional Center?

The A-L-V termination decision has somewhat clarified the stance USCIS means to take regarding regional center designations and terminations as the EB-5 Program evolves. It implies that a regional center must be actively engaged in raising capital and promoting projects, meaning centers with ongoing projects and those promoting projects to investors should be able to maintain their designations if they properly document those activities in their annual filing of the I-924A.

Centers which may be affected by this change are those that have applied for designation so as to be able to offer EB-5 projects to investors among other developments and have yet made no progress in doing so. It appears USCIS means for regional centers to demonstrate successful project development within a certain timeframe following designation, though this timeframe has not been made clear.

The popularity of the regional center model and subsequent expansion of the program to encompass hundreds of regional centers has created risks for investors in that USCIS is unable to directly oversee the activities of each center or verify its actors, as illustrated by recent Securities and Exchange Commission investigations into regional center projects. The aim to cut down on inactive regional centers demonstrates that USCIS is committed to maintaining the role of regional centers within the EB-5 Program, but practitioners must remain diligent in ensuring centers verifiably fulfill the program's economic goals.

Strategies for Regional Centers Facing an NOIT

Each EB-5 regional center is required to submit an annual Form I-924A to USCIS to justify its designation as a regional center by demonstrating that it has fulfilled the goals of the EB-5 Program, such as job creation and economic growth in TEAs. While filing the I-924A has historically been a required but fairly inconsequential event for regional centers, USCIS has recently adopted a stricter stance in ensuring regional centers achieve their purpose.

Previously, termination was only a possibility for regional centers involved in illegal acts such as fraud or misrepresentation to investors. However, with the number of regional centers now nearing 800, USCIS has begun seriously monitoring information provided with the I-924A and has terminated regional centers unable to uphold their EB-5 commitments. In these cases, USCIS will issue a notice of intent to terminate (NOIT) to the regional center in question, which gives the center the opportunity to respond to any concerns and reinforce its economic necessity under the EB-5 Program.

In the last decade, USCIS terminated 291 regional centers, and almost half of these terminations occurred in 2018 alone. These statistics illustrate the recent trend of increased enforcement with regard to regional centers and their ability to perform as required under the EB-5 Program. Regional centers will typically be issued a NOIT for any of the following three reasons relating to the previous few fiscal years:

- The regional center has been unable to attract capital investment or prove any job creation.
- No investors under the EB-5 Program have filed I-526 or I-829 petitions proving investment in that regional center.
- The regional center has not conducted any activity to serve the purposes of the EB-5 Program.
- This section discusses each of these reasons in detail and outlines strategies each regional center can use to proactively avoid a NOIT or to reaffirm its status as a regional center upon receipt of a NOIT from USCIS.

Lack of Capital Investment or Job Creation

Regional centers unable to demonstrate capital investment or job creation should endeavor to prove to USCIS their ongoing efforts to achieve those objectives. A regional center can do so by proving that it has provided investment opportunities for EB-5 investors or that capital investments are planned to be made after the I-924A reporting period.

A regional center that has previously prepared project documents for EB-5 investors and conducted due diligence on a project only to discover that the project would not be viable because of unforeseeable market circumstances should be able to prove these actions to USCIS. Such responsible planning and caution in not moving forward with a potentially risky project that may

142

otherwise have failed to generate the necessary funds for completion or create the required number of jobs speaks well of the regional center, and USCIS will take these factors into consideration.

Similarly, a regional center that has refunded EB-5 investors after being unable to acquire any necessary permits or licenses or agree upon project terms with developers has exercised reasonable fiscal caution and should provide records of these actions to USCIS. The aim is to demonstrate that the regional center has taken valuable actions over the previous fiscal years that, while not resulting in a viable project to generate capital and jobs, have nonetheless supported the goals of the EB-5 Program.

A regional center in the process of planning for an upcoming project, for example, one in the process of preparing an I-924 Exemplar Application, can use this fact to affirm its continued dedication to the program. In its response to the NOIT, the regional center should include a detailed description of the upcoming project and a breakdown of how investor funds will result in job creation in the TEA. Although commencement of the project will fall outside the I-924A reporting period, the planning stage demonstrates that the regional center is capable of taking action to create capital and jobs.

Lack of Pending I-526 or I-829 Petitions

The same rationale applies to a regional center not associated with any pending I-526 or I-829 petitions from EB-5 investors. Any upcoming projects for which investors will need to file I-526 petitions should be detailed in the response to the NOIT regardless of whether the project will commence outside the I-924A reporting period. Any activity to market projects to investors or otherwise promote economic growth as required by the EB-5 Program should also be discussed.

For example, a regional center working with marketers to promote a project among foreign investors should present those marketing efforts and explain how the project in question will fulfill the EB-5 goals. Any I-526 petitions to be filed in connection with that project should be mentioned, as should how the investment capital from those investors will create economic growth and the required number of new jobs in the United States. USCIS wants to see evidence of a regional center serving its purpose, and active marketing efforts and ongoing project planning demonstrate this.

Lack of Activity Serving the Purposes of the EB-5 Program

This category encompasses a broad variety of concerns. Aside from the strategies outlined above, which demonstrate active steps the regional center is taking to commence a project, the regional center can also demonstrate its purpose in the context of the EB-5 Program by providing documentation such as financial statements and contracts to prove that it has commissioned services to get projects off the ground and thereby fulfill its role.

143

For example, the regional center may have hired business consultants, financial experts, foreign marketing firms, and immigration and securities attorneys to explore the viability of certain projects and to market them to foreign investors. Consistent expenditures for these sorts of activities alone prove that the regional center has been serving the purposes of the EB-5 Program in that it has actively been investigating projects and preparing to market them to potential investors abroad.

Regional centers can use the above strategies to respond to a NOIT and demonstrate the necessary roles they play in promoting the EB-5 Program. After responding to a NOIT, a regional center will generally remain in contact with USCIS as it conducts additional investigations to assess the regional center's progress and determine whether the facts indeed justify its continued existence. To avoid the risk of a NOIT and when responding to one, regional centers must be diligent in providing detailed information to USCIS through the I-924A and additional documentation. In applying these strategies and continuously working to fulfill the goals of the EB-5 Program, regional centers will remain a key resource for investors and the success of the program overall.

Chinese EB-5 Investor Survey

A recent independent survey of approximately three hundred wealthy Chinese investors interested in immigration programs revealed the key criteria they use to evaluate immigration opportunities. The results from the survey focused on Western countries and highlighted the most important aspects of each immigration option. The key takeaways highlight the benefits wealthy Chinese families receive from immigration far outweigh the cons. The below content illustrates the key data surrounding the top immigration destinations, reasons for immigration, key cities in China, and the various wealth levels of the surveyed individuals.

Top 10 Immigration Destinations for Chinese Investors

For Chinese nationals, the United States, the U.K., and Canada still rank as the most sought after immigration destinations according to a recent independent study of Chinese high-net-worth individuals. Australia, Singapore, and Germany followed close behind, with Hungary and Portugal coming in ninth and tenth place, respectively. Unsurprisingly, education was cited as the most heavily weighted criteria for immigration, followed by opportunity for real estate investment and complexity of immigration policy. The United States ranked highest in education, real estate investment, immigration policy, passport access, and adaptability but lower in taxes and medical treatment.

Rank	Education	Real Estate Investment	Immigration Policy	Living Expenses	Personal Tax	Medical System Efficiency	Passport Waiver	Ease of Integration	TOTAL
1 USA	10/10	10/10	10/10	9/10	6/10	6/10	10/10	10/10	9.10
2 UK	9/10	10/10	8/10	6/10	9/10	8/10	10/10	9/10	8.70
3 Canada	8/10	8/10	8/10	9/10	7/10	9/10	9/10	10/10	8.30
4 Australia	8/10	8/10	7/10	7/10	8/10	9/10	7/10	8/10	7.75
5 Singapore	8/10	7/10	5/10	6/10	10/10	10/10	8/10	8/10	7.60
6 Germany	8/10	7/10	6/10	8/10	6/10	7/10	10/10	7/10	7.40
7 New Zealand	7/10	7/10	5/10	7/10	10/10	7/10	8/10	8/10	7.15
8 Korea	6/10	6/10	7/10	8/10	7/10	9/10	9/10	7/10	7.10
9 Hungary	5/10	4/10	8/10	8/10	5/10	5/10	6/10	5/10	5.70
10 Portugal	4/10	5/10	7/10	8/10	4/10	4/10	9/10	7/10	5.65
Category Weight	25%	15%	15%	10%	10%	10%	10%	5%	

Figure 4. Immigration destinations for Chinese investors.

U.S. citizenship carries many benefits for foreign nationals. The U.S. passport, for example, provides access to more than 170 countries without the need for a visa. Immigrants can pay in-state tuition for access to public education or attend world-class public research universities like the University of California, Berkeley, or the University of California, Los Angeles.

Student Populations of the Top 10 Immigration Countries

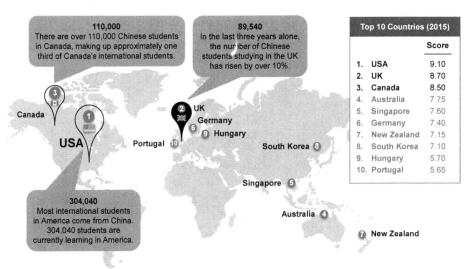

Figure 5. Student populations in the top 10 immigration destinations.

International students continue to flock to the United States, the U.K., and Canada in droves. Of the 820,000 international students currently attending U.S. colleges and universities, an estimated 300,000 come from China. The United States has the best university system in the world, boasting prestigious schools like Harvard, Princeton, Yale, and Stanford. Most foreign nationals who hope to send children abroad for better education will choose the United States. Canada is also highly attractive to immigrants seeking education for their children.

Reasons for Becoming a Global Citizen

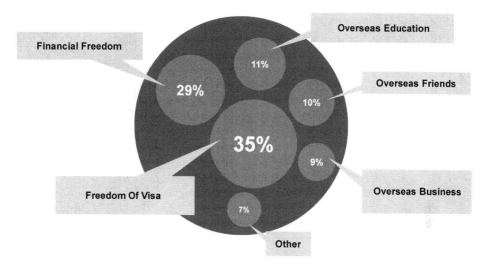

Figure 6. Reasons for immigration.

Chinese immigrants cite the passport, and the visa freedom that accompanies it, as the most important motivator for seeking foreign citizenship. The U.S. passport, for example, provides access to 174 countries visa-free. The U.K. passport also provides access to 174 countries visa-free.

Overseas education was another important factor cited in the study. The top education destinations for Chinese nationals, the United States, the U.K., and Canada, boast prestigious colleges and universities and high populations of international students.

Minimum Net Worth for Financial Stability

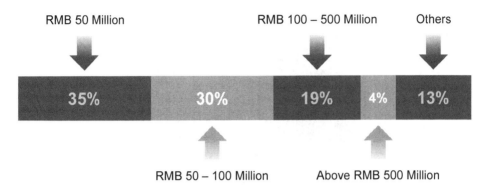

Figure 7. Beliefs on minimum net worth requirements.

A recent poll of high-net-worth individuals from China found that one-third of respondents believed a net worth of 50,000,000 RMB (~7,600,000 USD) is the minimum requirement for achieving a degree of financial stability and freedom. One-third believed somewhere between 50,000,000 and 100,000,000 RMB (7,600,000–12,200,000 USD) in net worth represents the minimum, and close to one-fifth thought 100,000,000–500,000,000 RMB (12,200,000–76,000,000 USD) is the minimum. Only 4% of the individuals surveyed believed a net worth of greater than 500,000,000 RMB (76,000,000 USD) is the minimum threshold for achieving a degree of financial stability.

While these alarmingly high estimates reflect the biases of the high-net-worth individuals surveyed, these results nevertheless showcase the enormous amount of capital available to these individuals. Put in perspective, a $500,000 EB-5 investment constitutes just 6.5% of the net worth of the lowest tier of high-net-worth individuals included in the survey.

Top 25 Destinations: Immigration and Real Estate Investment

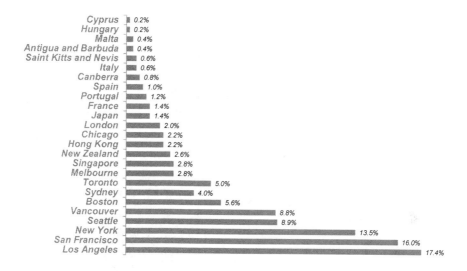

Figure 8. Destinations for real estate investment.

California, specifically Los Angeles and San Francisco, dominate the list as the top two immigration and real estate investment destinations for Chinese nationals. New York, Seattle, Vancouver, and Boston follow close behind, which means U.S. cities claim four out of the five top immigration destinations.

Los Angeles is home to large populations of high-net-worth Chinese nationals, who live in suburbs like Rowland Heights, Arcadia, and Hacienda Heights. The sunny weather, abundant space, and high density of Asian immigrants has made Los Angeles suburbs a top immigration destination for Chinese nationals and their children. The inflow of investment has driven up real estate prices and led to rapid construction of luxury homes targeted specifically at Asian buyers.

Canada and Australia also boast cities in the top 10 immigration destinations, including Vancouver, Sydney, Toronto, and Melbourne. Surprisingly, only one Asian country, Singapore, ranked in the top ten.

Top 10 Most Important Cities for Culture and Business

City	Rate	Ranking
1 Hong Kong	25%	
2 Shanghai	18%	
3 New York	17%	
4 Beijing	16%	
5 San Francisco	6%	
6 Los Angeles	5%	
7 London	4%	
8 Sydney	3%	
9 Singapore	2%	
10 Paris	2%	

Figure 9. Destinations for culture and business.

For Chinese nationals, the most well-known and important cities for culture and business were Hong Kong, Shanghai, and New York. These cities are large, influential cities with a vibrant arts & culture scene, as well as large financial centers where vast amounts of money flow through. New York City and Hong Kong are actually statistically similar in terms of population and size. NYC has a population of roughly 8.4 million people in 469 square miles of land, while Hong Kong has a population of 7.2 million in 426 square miles of land. Shanghai, however, covers almost 2700 square miles of land with a population of over 14 million inhabitants.

Beijing, San Francisco, and Los Angeles were also important cities for culture and business. Beijing is one of the most populous cities in the world with more than 21 million inhabitants and is home to offices of the central government, state owned enterprises, and historical sites. San Francisco boasts a vibrant technology and startup scene as the heart of Silicon Valley. Los Angeles attracts millions of tourists each year to visit Hollywood and its large film, entertainment, and fashion industries.

Factors Affecting Wealth and Quality of Life in China

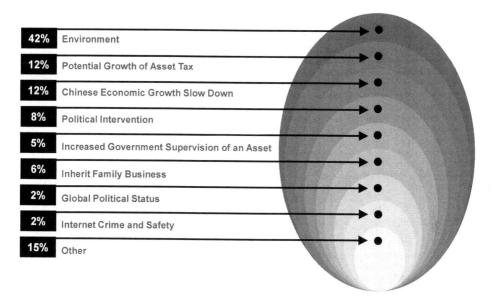

42%	Environment
12%	Potential Growth of Asset Tax
12%	Chinese Economic Growth Slow Down
8%	Political Intervention
5%	Increased Government Supervision of an Asset
6%	Inherit Family Business
2%	Global Political Status
2%	Internet Crime and Safety
15%	Other

Figure 10. Factors negatively impacting quality of life.

Chinese nationals cited a variety of serious factors that negatively impact quality of life in China. Chief among them was the environment and pollution in China's major cities. Air quality was one of the top concerns voiced by the Chinese public to politicians in this year's political elections. The inhabitants of Beijing, known for its thick smog, are forced to wear masks and stay indoors most days, which makes many outdoor activities impossible. Chinese parents, out of a desire to provide a healthier and better environment for their children, are seeking to raise their children elsewhere.

Economic considerations continue to be another major push factor for Chinese immigrants. Concerns about an economic slowdown, as well as a push for higher taxes on personal income, are pressuring high-net-worth individuals to move their capital elsewhere, despite China's restrictions on moving money outside the country.

Immigration Reasons for High-Net-Worth Individuals

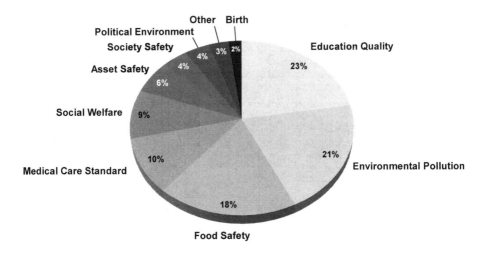

Figure 11. Reasons for immigration among high-net-worth individuals.

For high-net-worth individuals, the quality of education in the country of immigration was a chief concern. Although Chinese schools and universities are quickly gaining international recognition, many Chinese nationals still believe Western education at American and British schools is superior. The United States boasts almost two thousand public universities, including renowned universities like the University of California, Berkeley, and the University of California, Los Angeles.

Air and environmental quality was the second most important concern for high-net-worth Chinese immigrants. Beijing, Shanghai, and other metropolitan cities in China are blanketed by thick smog daily, leading Chinese families to seek cities with clean air and a better environment. Food safety, medical care, and social welfare were also important considerations. Furthermore, as the Chinese economy slows down and as taxation and asset protection remain uncertain, wealthy Chinese seek the stability of countries like the United States, Canada, and the U.K.

Benefits and Drawbacks of Immigration

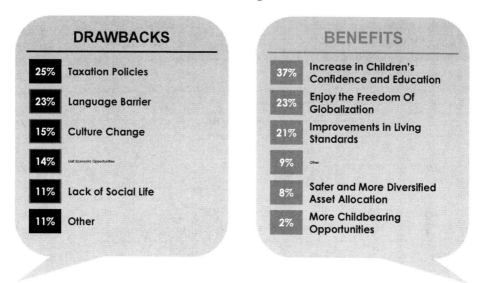

Figure 12. Benefits and drawbacks of immigration for Chinese investors.

While many Chinese immigrants look to EB-5 as a ticket to better education, health, and real estate investment opportunities, immigrating to a new country can be very daunting for foreign nationals. Cultural shock, language barriers, and alienation from friends and family can make immigration a stressful experience for foreign nationals.

This survey of high-net-worth Chinese nationals revealed that taxation policies, language, and cultural change are the biggest drawbacks of immigration. In the United States, for example, an individual's worldwide income is still subject to U.S. taxes, which can be a major drawback of U.S. citizenship. Many of the benefits, however, like quality public education for children, freedom to travel the world, and a high standard of living, can more than offset the stressors of living abroad. The United States continues to see a persistent inflow of immigrants from many countries seeking a better, healthier life.

Chinese Multimillionaire Distribution

After understanding the top destinations for immigration and real estate investment, we must look at the distribution of Chinese multimillionaires. The 2015 Hurun Fortune Report shows that there were a total of 1.21 million multimillionaires in China by May 2015. The top three cities for these multimillionaires were Beijing, Shanghai and Guangdong.

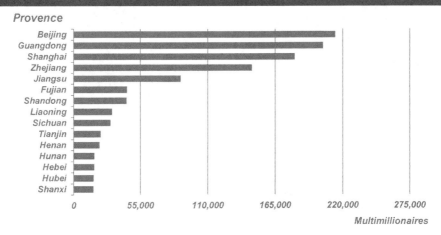

Figure 13. Distribution of multimillionaires in China.

If you are a U.S. project developer looking to source investors from China, there is a good chance at finding them in one of the following three cities: Beijing, Guangdong, and Shanghai. A 2015 report found that 1.21 million multimillionaires live in China, and these top three cities accounted for 49.5% of them. The fact that these three cities have such an accumulation of high-net-worth individuals is not surprising. Guangdong, for example, is a major international finance and trade center and the most populous province in China, with 79.1 million permanent residents.

What multimillionaires in China lack, however, is the financial stability, global freedom, and asset protection that high-net-worth individuals in Western countries enjoy. Many wealthy Chinese nationals continue to actively seek promising investment opportunities in real estate, stocks, and companies in the United States and other countries as a means to diversify and protect their assets.

Top 10 Destinations to Study Abroad

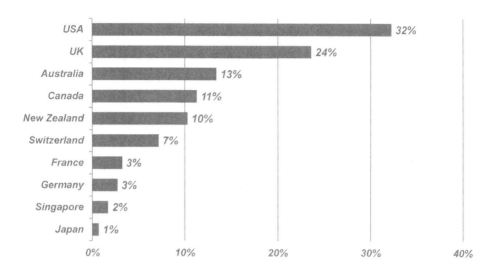

Figure 14. Top 10 destinations for study.

International students seem to overwhelmingly prefer studying abroad in the United States, followed by other English-speaking countries like the U.K., Australia, Canada, and New Zealand. Studying abroad can be an important investment made by Chinese parents on behalf of their children in order to provide them with quality education and the opportunity to learn in an unfamiliar and stimulating environment. Many companies tend to favor educational backgrounds at American institutions and resumes with experience at American companies.

Top 10 Countries for Passport Effectiveness

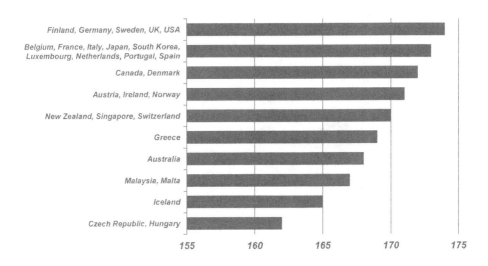

Figure 15. Most effective passports.

A huge draw for acquiring foreign citizenship in a country like Germany, Sweden, or the United States is the power of the passport. In terms of passport flexibility, the top countries are Finland, Germany, Sweden, the U.K., and the United States, all of which boast access to 174 countries visa-free (no country specific visa required for travel). Canada and Denmark follow close behind, with access to 173 countries visa-free.

Chinese citizens who have traveled abroad know the inconvenience of applying for visas to the United States or other countries. Many visa application processes can involve intense interviews and screenings as well as significant delays. Getting a visa can be exhausting and time consuming. If you are a global traveler, having access to an American or British passport can be a very valuable, long-term investment.

Immigration Investment Program

Rank	Country	Requirements of Investment	Period	Visa Waivers	Tax Advantages
★★★★★	Antigua	Donate at least $200,000 or purchase $400,000 worth of real estate; can sell in 5 years.	3 - 4 Months	130	No global tax, no heritage tax, no property tax, no capital income tax.
★★★★	Saint Kitts	Donate at least $250,000 or purchase $400,000 worth of real estate; can sell in 5 years.	12 Months	120	No individual income tax, no capital income tax, no corporate income tax for 15 years, new tax rebate in 5 years.
★★★★	Malta	Donate at least €650,000, invest €150,000 in government bonds and purchase €350,000 worth of real estate(or rental income more than €16,000 p.a.).	12 - 18 Months	160	No global tax, no heritage tax, no net wealth tax, no capital tax, no gift tax.
★★★	Cyprus	Group investment funds at least €2,500,000, buying one or more residences (more than 5 families); individual invests at least €5,000,000 in government bonds, bank deposits, business investment or similar.	3 - 4 Months	150	Lowest business income tax in Europe at just 10%.
★★★	Dominica	Donate at least $100,000 or purchase real estate worth $200,000; can sell in 5 years.	3 - 6 Months	90	No capital tax, no gift tax, no heritage tax, no overseas income tax, no capital income tax.
★★	Grenada	Invest at least $350,000 in real estate.	3 - 4 months	120	No capital tax, no gift tax, no heritage tax, no overseas income tax, no capital income tax.

Figure 16. Attractive immigrant investor programs.

The United States is not the only country to have a program similar to EB-5. Many island nations have very attractive incentives designed to attract foreign investment. Antigua, an island nation in the Caribbean, for example, offers significant tax advantages—no global tax, heritage tax, property tax, or capital income tax—for a mere $200,000 investment. Saint Kitts, another Caribbean island nation, offers significant tax advantages for a $250,000 investment.

Tax havens, however, are not always in the best interest of every investor. Many have no desire to own property or assets in the Mediterranean or Caribbean, for instance, and instead prefer to invest money where they are sending their children for college. Still, the tax advantages of these island nations continue to attract investors.

Reasons for Overseas Investments

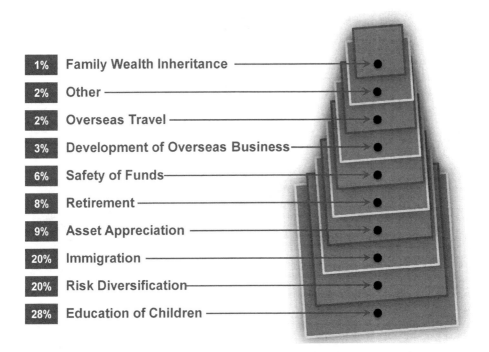

1%	Family Wealth Inheritance
2%	Other
2%	Overseas Travel
3%	Development of Overseas Business
6%	Safety of Funds
8%	Retirement
9%	Asset Appreciation
20%	Immigration
20%	Risk Diversification
28%	Education of Children

Figure 17. Main reasons for overseas investment.

As it turns out, quality education for children is the number one criteria for investing in assets overseas. More than 300,000 students from China are currently studying in the United States, and many of their parents have considered or are considering investing in properties, businesses, or other assets in the United States Many Chinese families are also concerned with diversification of risk, seek better returns on their capital, or aim to safeguard their money.

Moving capital outside of China, however, has proven to be difficult. The government, in an effort to prevent money from leaking out of the country, has a limit of transferring $50,000 abroad per year, which offers Chinese investors little choice on where to put their investments or what they can spend their money on.

Most Desirable Types of Overseas Travel

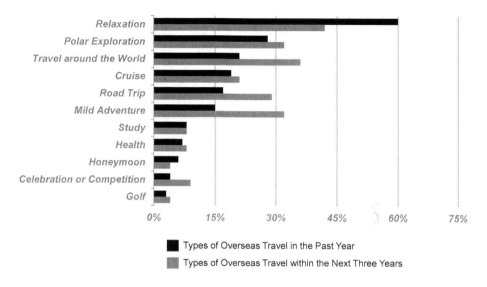

Figure 18. Common types of overseas travel.

China's richest jetsetters are increasingly searching for unique destinations and experiences as they travel off the beaten path and prioritize leisure over shopping. A 2015 report on Chinese travelers who spent $30,000 or more on travel over the past year (although the average amount spent among participants was $58,000) found that their preferences are unique from China's mass travel market.

The North and South Poles were particularly popular and became a top destination among this elite group for holiday vacations. Known for their mystical landscapes, rare wildlife, and novelty, the Poles are catering more to an experienced group of travelers who can say "been there, done that" to the destinations most popular with China's more than 100 million outbound travelers.

Overseas Travel Destinations

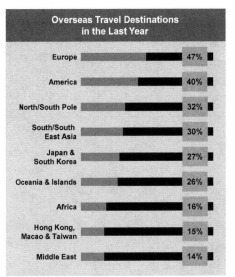
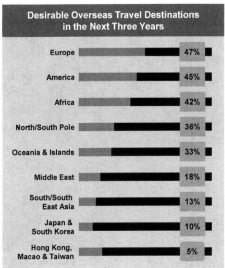

Figure 19. Top overseas travel destinations.

Since 2012, China has been the world's largest outbound tourism market, according to data from the United Nations World Tourism Organization (UNWTO). The most popular destinations included Europe, America, and surprisingly, the North and South Poles. Tourists from China spent $129 billion abroad in 2013, more than any other market in the world.

A big component of Chinese tourism is shopping and luxury goods. Chinese tourists are known as the world's biggest consumers of luxury goods. Sales to Chinese tourists in the designer outlets of Europe soared by more than 35% in 2014 and have more than quadrupled over the past four years. Over the next three years, it is predicted that Africa will become the third most popular tourism destination since many luxury travelers seek to visit unique and undiscovered locales.

Top Six Medical Travel Destinations and Reasons for Medical Travel

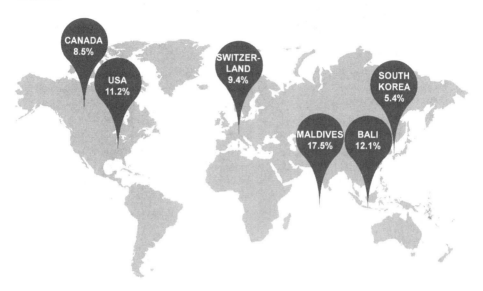

Figure 20. Destinations for medical travel.

Fed up with mainland China's crowded and noisy hospitals, a greater number of wealthy Chinese are opting to go abroad in search of better medical services. Many opt to travel in order to rest and rehabilitate from stressful jobs or to get away from the polluted air of China's cities. Others seek medical check-ups at prestigious and renowned hospitals in the United States. Some travel to countries like Korea to improve their appearance through cosmetic changes.

Top destinations for rehabilitation and medical treatment include the Maldives, Bali in Indonesia, and the United States. Many factors influence the decision to rehabilitate abroad, which include cost, distance from China, and the availability of specialized treatment.

Sport Preference by Gender

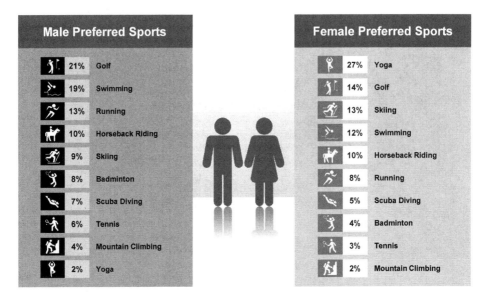

Figure 21. Chinese sport preference by gender.

Sports are becoming an increasingly important part of normal life for Chinese citizens. For males, a poll found the top three most popular sports to be golf, swimming, and running. For women, on the other hand, the top three were yoga, golf, and skiing. Many sports have not yet achieved a significant level of popularity in China, leading many Chinese nationals to travel abroad in order to do scuba diving, horseback riding, or golf while on vacation.

Furthermore, sports are becoming an increasingly important agenda for the Chinese government. In March of last year, the Chinese government announced its plan to improve the country's outlook on sports, beginning with soccer. Recently the Chinese State Council drafted a soccer reform plan in an effort to decrease corruption, increase professionalism, and develop a regulated soccer business.

Source: Chinese Investment Report by Visas Consulting & Hurun Report. Chinese Investors Surveyed = ~300.

Online Resources

For the following free guides and sample documents and for other helpful resources for project developers, please visit www.EB5AN.com.

TEA Designation Guides, Maps, and Sample Materials

TEA designation is critical for any EB-5 project in the market today. Our TEA map allows project developers to enter their project addresses to determine which census tracts the projects are located within. The map will then indicate whether those tracts automatically qualify as TEAs. We additionally offer lists of already designated TEAs by state as well as a guide with step-by-step instructions on contacting state agencies to request TEA letters. EB5AN has helped clients obtain TEA letters for regions with more than sixty combined census tracts together.

Free EB-5 Job Calculator

Understanding the total potential job creation of an EB-5 project allows a project sponsor to determine exactly how many EB-5 investors a project can support under the current 10 jobs per investor requirement from USCIS. Our free EB-5 job calculator provides instant EB-5 eligible job creation estimates for all project types in all 50 states. The job calculator is driven by a RIMS II database that takes into account the specific cost and revenue economic multipliers issued by the Bureau of Labor Statistics (BLS) to determine the projected job creation impact of a specific project based on its construction budget and timeline and operational pro-forma.

EB-5 Project Risk Assessment Tool

The EB-5 Project Risk Assessment Tool provides needed transparency and insight into project diligence and selection by giving investors a targeted list of questions that offers guidance on the key immigration and financial risk factors of potential EB-5 projects. The tool contains 36 multiple-choice questions and features a visual project risk assessment with an easy to understand immigration and financial risk chart. Jointly developed with Klasko Law, the Project Risk Assessment Tool combines the EB-5 financial and real estate development experience of EB5AN with the unparalleled EB-5 immigration law expertise of Klasko Law. The result is a highly functional, easy-to-use tool that guides investors through the initial diligence of EB-5 projects from both financial and immigration risk perspectives.

The EB-5 Project Go-to-Market Playbook

1. 100% free PDF file download
2. Best practices for marketing an EB-5 project overseas
3. Actionable steps to increase project appeal to foreign agents and investors

Marketing an EB-5 project overseas to foreign agents and investors can be a daunting task. To insure success, it is important to be prepared with all of the documentation and supporting materials that will differentiate the project and increase investor conversion.

Our EB-5 Project Go-to-Market Playbook contains a detailed outline of EB-5 project marketing best practices. The playbook contains a strategy framework with eight (8) primary topics that are applicable and helpful for all EB-5 project issuers and promoters.

The EB-5 Investor Global Markets Report

EB-5 investors come from many countries around the world. The volume of investors varies greatly between countries, and the market landscape for raising EB-5 capital is constantly changing. This report is the most comprehensive source for country-level EB-5 and economic specific information, with more than sixty pages of EB-5 data and statistics on the global EB-5 investor market.

This valuable EB-5 data is analyzed by country and by region to give EB-5 project sponsors an informative and up-to-date view on EB-5 market conditions and recent trends. (中国版本包括. Chinese version also included.)

- Country-specific EB-5 data and statistics: Mainland China, India, Brazil, Russia, Korea, Hong Kong, etc.
- Region-specific EB-5 data and statistics: Asia Pacific, South/Central Asia, the Middle East, Latin America, Europe, etc.

Sample EB-5 Project Developer Term Sheet

EB-5 project sponsors typically must negotiate a term sheet for the placement of EB-5 capital with a real estate developer or with another business entity seeking EB-5 capital. These term sheets are critical in the EB-5 process because it is important to define all of the key variables associated with the placement and timing of EB-5 capital.

Since the placement of EB-5 capital has many moving pieces and is much more complicated than a basic loan/financing term sheet from a traditional lender, EB-5 project sponsors should include as much detail around timing, loan term, and other key deal terms. Defining all variables and terms clearly at the start of the EB-5 process will help insure that an EB-5 project is marketable and has the highest likelihood of attracting EB-5 capital from accredited foreign investors.

Guide to EB-5 Subscription Agreement Automation

The subscription agreement is a critical piece of the EB-5 investment process, and as the EB-5 market becomes more and more competitive, making the subscription process as simple and straightforward as possible has become increasingly important. EB5 Affiliate Network has therefore developed an automated subscription process that allows a new investor to simply complete one page of required information electronically; this information will then automatically populate all other required forms through the remainder of the subscription agreement and its accompanying documents, appendices, exhibits, and forms. Additionally, we offer a video with step-by-step instructions how to create automated subscription agreements for EB-5 projects.

Topics for Investors

Visa Basics

Basics of U.S. Citizenship

Generally speaking, children born within the United States or its territories, except those born to foreign diplomats, are citizens by virtue of their place of birth. Children born to U.S. citizens—whether in the United States or abroad—are also natural born citizens.

Foreign nationals who desire U.S. citizenship must apply for it through United States Citizenship and Immigration Services (USCIS) and undergo the naturalization process. Upon successfully completing this process, a foreign national becomes a naturalized citizen of the United States along with any children under age 18 (called "derivation" of citizenship).

Immigrants who obtain permanent resident status through participation in the EB-5 Immigrant Investor Program are eligible to apply for citizenship five years after they were granted their initial conditional permanent resident status.

Rights and Privileges of U.S. Citizenship

United States citizenship comes with various rights and privileges:
- Citizens have the right to vote in local, state, and federal elections.
- Naturalized citizens are able to run for local, state, and federal elected offices except the offices of president and vice president.
- Children born to U.S. citizens are classified as natural born citizens regardless of where they are born.
- Citizens may obtain U.S. passports, which, in many cases, enables them to travel overseas without the need for visas.
- Citizens enjoy access to U.S. government assistance while abroad.
- Citizens enjoy better access to federal employment opportunities—most government agencies only employ citizens.
- Citizens enjoy access to top-tier higher education and may be eligible for in-state tuition when applying to public colleges and universities.
- The families of citizens often experience faster processing when immigrating to the United States.

Responsibilities of U.S. Citizenship

Along with the rights and privileges granted by U.S. citizenship, citizens accept a number of responsibilities:
- Citizens are required to pay all applicable income tax at the federal, state, and local level.
- Citizens are afforded the right to vote and run for elected office, but this is also a civic responsibility. All citizens are encouraged to vote and participate in the political process.
- Citizens may, at times, be summoned to serve as jurors.

- All male citizens from age 18 to 25 must register with Selective Service. Registration does not necessarily entail service in the U.S. Armed Forces.

Becoming a U.S. Citizen through Naturalization

Naturalization refers to the process by which an applicant obtains citizenship according to the requirements set forth in the Immigration and Nationality Act (INA).

In order to be eligible for naturalization, a foreign national must meet one of the following criteria:
- Has held permanent resident status for at least five years
- Has held permanent resident status for at least three years and is applying for naturalization as the spouse of a U.S. citizen
- Has served in the U.S. Armed Forces

Foreign nationals who meet any of the criteria above are able to apply for naturalization, which requires submitting Form N-400, Application for Naturalization, to USCIS. Within this application, they must prove they meet one of the eligibility requirements listed above and demonstrate that they possess good moral character by disclosing any criminal history.

The basic fee associated with filing Form N-400 is currently $595. An additional fee of $85 is required for biometric services that include conducting a background check as well as photographing and fingerprinting the applicant. For applicants under age 14 and over age 79, the biometrics fee is waived.

Depending on the USCIS location, processing times for N-400 applications generally range from four to six months. After an applicant's Form N-400 has been processed by USCIS, he or she will be interviewed and must pass a U.S. civics and English language test.

Upon approval, the applicant will be given a ceremony date, and during the ceremony, he or she must take the Oath of Allegiance. Through this oath, the prospective citizen swears allegiance to the United States, swears to support and defend the U.S. Constitution and the nation's laws, and swears to serve the country when necessary.

Types of U.S. Immigrant Visas

USCIS issues immigrant visas to foreign nationals who desire permanent resident status in the United States and meet certain requirements. Immigrants granted permanent resident status are issued green cards, and they are able to live and work in the United States.

Foreign nationals can apply for various kinds of immigrant visas, including immediate relative visas, family preference visas, diversity visas, and employment-based visas.

Immediate Relative Immigrant Visas

Foreign nationals with immediate relatives who are U.S. citizens are able to apply for immediate relative immigrant visas. Unlike other immigrant visas, the number of immediate relative visas issued each year is unlimited.

An immediate family member is defined as a spouse, unmarried child under age 21, or parent. The following visa types are for immediate relatives of U.S. citizens:

- IR-1: Spouse of U.S. citizen
- IR-2: Unmarried child of U.S. citizen
- IR-3: Orphan adopted abroad by U.S. citizen
- IR-4: Orphan to be adopted in the United States by U.S. citizen
- IR-5: Parent of U.S. citizen

In order to start the process of obtaining a green card for a foreign relative (the beneficiary), the immediate relative who is a U.S. citizen (the petitioner) must file Form I-130, Petition for Alien Relative, to USCIS.

Beneficiaries living in the United States under a different legal status must file Form I-485, Application to Register Permanent Residence or Adjust Status. Once the application is reviewed, the applicant may be required to appear for biometrics collection and/or an interview.

Beneficiaries living outside the United States must file for an immigrant visa through the consulate in their home country. Upon the approval of Form I-130, USCIS forwards the petition to the National Visa Center, who will review the documentation and forward it to the U.S. embassy or consulate of the beneficiary's home country. The embassy or consulate will set an interview date, and upon successfully interviewing and passing a medical exam, the beneficiary will receive his or her immigrant visa.

Family Preference Immigrant Visas

Distant relatives of U.S. citizens and specific relatives of lawful permanent residents may be able to apply for family preference visas. The relationship between the U.S. citizen or lawful permanent resident and the relative determines the family preference category. These categories, followed in parentheses by the annual limit of visas issued, are as follows:

- Family First Preference (F-1): Unmarried child of U.S. citizen and his or her minor children (23,400)
- Family Second Preference (F-2): Spouse, minor child, and unmarried child (over age 21) of lawful permanent resident (114,200)
- Family Third Preference (F-3): Married child of U.S. citizen, his or her spouse, and their minor children (23,400)
- Family Fourth Preference (F-4): Sibling of U.S. citizen, his or her spouse, and their minor children (65,000)

The process of applying for a family preference visa is the same as applying for the immediate relative visa—Form I-130 is filed with USCIS by the petitioner, and then the beneficiary either submits Form I-485 (for those living in the United States) or applies for an immigrant visa through the embassy or consulate in his or her home country (for those outside the United States).

Diversity Immigrant Visas

Through the Diversity Immigrant Visa Program, foreign nationals from countries with historically low rates of immigration to the United States can apply for permanent resident status.

The number of visas issued through this program is limited to 50,000, and applicants are selected randomly based on the number of visas available per region or country. Eligibility requirements apply, and so selection through this process does not guarantee an applicant will be granted a visa.

Employment-Based Immigrant Visas

For qualified foreign nationals, USCIS makes available approximately 140,000 employment-based visas each year. These visas are divided into five preference categories as follows:
- Employment-based First Preference (EB-1): Priority workers
- Employment-based Second Preference (EB-2): Professionals who hold advanced degrees or who possess exceptional ability
- Employment-based Third Preference (EB-3): Skilled workers, professionals, and unskilled workers
- Employment-based Fourth Preference (EB-4): Certain special immigrants
- Employment-based Fifth Preference (EB-5): Immigrant investors

Each of these employment-based preference categories has its own set of requirements that must be met before an applicant will receive his or her permanent resident status.

Types of U.S. Nonimmigrant Visas

Nonimmigrant U.S. visas allow foreign nationals to temporarily enter the United States for tourism, education, or work. The type of visa a person needs depends on the purpose of his or her visit to the United States; each visa type carries different requirements and restrictions.

Following are the most common nonimmigrant visas and some basic details about each.

Visas for Business Visitors and Tourists

Foreign nationals seeking to visit the United States for business or tourism may do so on a B-1 or B-2 visa, respectively.

- B-1 visas are for individuals traveling to the United States for business—to negotiate a contract, to meet with associates, to attend a conference, to settle an estate, etc.
- B-2 visas are for individuals traveling to the United States for vacation, tourism, or for medical care.

To apply for a B-1 or B-2 visa, a foreign national must file Form DS-160, Online Nonimmigrant Visa Application, with the U.S. Department of State. An applicant must have a current photograph and valid passport. He or she will be interviewed at the U.S. embassy or consulate in their home nation and must establish nonimmigrant intent—in other words, the applicant must prove that he or she intends to return to his or her country of origin after visiting the United States.

The maximum allowed length of stay for these visas is generally six months.

Visa Waiver Program

Through the Visa Waiver Program (VWP), foreign nationals from specific countries are permitted to enter the United States for business or tourism without B-1 or B-2 visas as long as their length of stay is no more than 90 days.

Currently, nationals from the following 37 countries are eligible for the VWP: Andorra, Australia, Austria, Belgium, Brunei, Czech Republic, Denmark, Estonia, Finland, France, Germany, Greece, Hungary, Iceland, Ireland, Italy, Japan, Latvia, Liechtenstein, Lithuania, Luxembourg, Malta, Monaco, the Netherlands, New Zealand, Norway, Portugal, San Marino, Singapore, Slovakia, Slovenia, South Korea, Spain, Sweden, Switzerland, Taiwan, and the United Kingdom.

Visas for Students and Exchange Program Participants

Foreign nationals seeking to enter the United States as students or exchange program participants may do so on F-1, M-1, or J-1 visas.

F-1 visas are for individuals who want to study in the United States at qualified institutions. Such institutions include elementary and high schools, colleges, universities, seminaries, conservatories, and language training programs as long as the institution is authorized to accept international students. Those with F-1 visas must be full-time students and must demonstrate that they will return home upon completion of their programs. Ties to home that demonstrate intent to return include employment opportunities, membership in professional organizations, and family-owned property.

M-1 visas are for individuals who want to enter the United States to participate in vocational or nonacademic programs.

J-1 visas are for individuals who wish to participate in either an educational or cultural exchange program. J-1 exchange visitors may include students, trainees, interns, research assistants, teachers, professors or scholars, specialists, au pairs, and camp counselors.

Applying for a student or exchange program visa

Before a foreign national can apply for an F-1, M-1, or J-1 visa, he or she must be accepted into a qualified program. The individual must then enroll in the Student and Exchange Visitor Information System (SEVIS), a database used to track F-1, M-1, and J-1 visitors.

As with the B-1 and B-2 visa application process, an F-1, M-1, or J-1 visa applicant must file Form DS-160, provide a current photo and valid passport, be interviewed by the U.S. embassy or consulate in his or her home country, and establish nonimmigrant intent.

In addition to these requirements, an F-1, M-1, or J-1 visa applicant must provide any necessary eligibility forms related to the specific program in which he or she will participate (e.g., diploma, SAT score, etc.) and proof of sufficient funding for all costs that will be incurred throughout the duration of his or her stay in the United States.

Generally, the length of stay allowed by these nonimmigrant visas is limited to the duration of the program in which the individual is participating, but extensions may be requested.

Visas for Temporary Workers

Foreign nationals who desire to work in the United States may be eligible for nonimmigrant, temporary worker visas. Various work visas are available, and the specific visa an individual is eligible for is determined by a number of factors.

H-1B visas are for individuals working in specialty occupations that generally require at least a bachelor's degree. Specialty occupations are diverse, and include computer programming, electronic component manufacturing, research and development in various scientific fields, and more.

L-1 visas are for intracompany transferees—staff in the specialized knowledge, management, or executive categories who transfer to a U.S. office of the same employer.

E-1 visas are for individuals who wish to enter the United States to engage in international trade. These foreign nationals must be from countries with which the United States maintains treaties of commerce and navigation. The following are E-1 treaty countries: Argentina, Australia, Austria, Belgium, Bolivia, Bosnia and Herzegovina, Brunei, Canada, Chile, China (Taiwan), Colombia, Costa Rica, Croatia, Denmark, Estonia, Ethiopia, Finland, France, Germany, Greece, Honduras, Iran, Ireland, Israel, Italy, Japan, Jordan, Korea (South), Latvia, Liberia, Luxembourg, Macedonia (FYROM), Mexico, Montenegro, Netherlands, Norway, Oman, Pakistan, Paraguay, Philippines, Poland, Serbia, Singapore, Slovenia, Spain, Suriname, Sweden, Switzerland, Thailand, Togo, Turkey, United Kingdom, and Yugoslavia.

E-2 visas are for foreign nationals who wish to enter the United States to manage business ventures in which they have invested considerable funds. The following are E-2 treaty countries: Albania, Argentina, Armenia, Australia, Austria, Azerbaijan, Bahrain, Bangladesh, Belgium, Bolivia, Bosnia and Herzegovina, Brunei, Bulgaria, Cameroon, Canada, Chile, China (Taiwan), Colombia, Congo (Brazzaville), Congo (Kinshasa), Costa Rica, Croatia, Czech Republic, Denmark, Ecuador, Egypt, Estonia, Ethiopia, Finland, France, Georgia, Germany, Grenada, Honduras, Iran, Ireland, Italy, Jamaica, Japan, Jordan, Kazakhstan, Korea (South), Kosovo, Kyrgyzstan, Latvia, Liberia, Lithuania, Luxembourg, Macedonia (FYROM), Mexico, Moldova, Mongolia, Montenegro, Morocco, Netherlands, Norway, Oman, Pakistan, Panama, Paraguay, Philippines, Poland, Romania, Serbia, Senegal, Singapore, Slovak Republic, Slovenia, Spain, Sri Lanka, Suriname, Sweden, Switzerland, Thailand, Togo, Trinidad & Tobago, Tunisia, Turkey, Ukraine, United Kingdom, and Yugoslavia.

Applying for a temporary worker visa

The application forms and documents for these visas vary, but each generally follows the same process. Any U.S. employer seeking to hire foreign nationals as temporary workers must file Form I-129 to USCIS for approval. A foreign national seeking temporary worker status must file Form DS-160 through the U.S. consulate or embassy in his or her home nation, and upon approval, will be interviewed before being granted a temporary worker visa.

Many of these visas require certification from the U.S. Department of Labor demonstrating the applicant will receive a prevailing wage (compensation equivalent to what a U.S. worker would receive for the same work). On one hand, the prevailing wage requirement helps ensure that temporary workers are paid fairly, and on the other, that foreign workers don't displace U.S. workers.

The length of stay granted by these temporary worker visas generally ranges from one to three years, but O and E type visas can be renewed an unlimited number of times as long as the applicant remains qualified.

The Diversity Visa Program

Summary

- Each year, approximately 50,000 permanent resident cards (also known as green cards) are granted to eligible applicants through this program.
- Applicants must come from countries deemed eligible by the U.S. Department of State. Certain countries with low immigration rates into the United States qualify.
- No fee is required to submit the Electronic Diversity Visa Entry Form (E-DV entry form).
- The E-DV form must be submitted online, and processing usually takes from six to eight months.

What Is the Green Card Lottery?

The Diversity Immigrant Visa Program (Green Card Lottery) is administered by the U.S Department of State and was established by Congress through the Immigration Act of 1990. The purpose of the act is to encourage the immigration of people into the United States from a variety of ethnic and cultural backgrounds. Each year, approximately 50,000 green cards are made available to immigrants through this program. These applicants are randomly chosen by a computer program from qualified entries. Entrants must be citizens of qualifying countries that have had low immigration rates into the United States. Eligibility is also based upon certain educational and employment requirements.

Submitting an application for the Green Card Lottery carries no fee, but all applications must be submitted online within a certain timeframe.

Eligibility Requirements

Applicants must come from qualified countries that have had fewer than 50,000 immigrants enter the United States during the previous five-year period.

Applicants must have the equivalent of a high school education or have at least two years' experience working in a job that has those educational requirements.

If the immigration quota has already been met for a particular country, an applicant from that country may still qualify if his or her spouse is a native of that country. Alternatively, an applicant may qualify if his or her parents were born in an eligible country.

The following countries are not eligible: Bangladesh, Brazil, Canada, China (mainland), Colombia, Dominican Republic, Ecuador, El Salvador, Haiti, India, Jamaica, Mexico, Nigeria, Pakistan, Peru, Philippines, South Korea, United Kingdom (except Northern Ireland) and its dependent territories, and Vietnam.

Application Instructions

Applicants must submit Form DS-5501 (E-DV entry form) through the Department of State's website. This form includes the applicants biographical information, such as name, sex, birthdate and birthplace, current country of citizenship, marital status, and contact information. Applicants must also submit a digital photograph of themselves.

The Department of State's website will reveal the winners of the lottery at the designated time. Applicants must check the website for lottery results. Winners of the lottery will receive permanent resident cards (green cards), which allow them to live and work in the United States. Their spouses and children may also apply for green cards and immigrate to the United States.

H-1B Work Visa

Summary

- A basic processing fee of $325 must be paid—processing can take from three to six months.
- An optional premium processing fee of $1,225 may be paid—processing takes only two weeks.
- Employers with 25 workers or fewer pay a $750 fee; employers with more than 25 workers must pay an ACWIA fee of $1,500; all employers must pay a $500 fraud fee.

H-1B Work Visa Basics

U.S. businesses may sponsor foreign workers in specialty jobs through H-1B visas. Specialized jobs may include positions in the engineering, science, computer programming, and law fields. The H-1B visa allows foreign nationals to work in the United States for a predetermined period—a maximum of six years in three-year increments. These nonimmigrants may be allowed time extensions in certain situations.

Unlike EB-5 visas, H-1B visas do not lead directly to permanent U.S. residence. However, foreign workers may enter the United States on an H-1B visa while applying through another visa category for permanent residence. For example, applicants sometimes first obtain temporary U.S. residence through an H-1B visa before applying for permanent residence through an EB-5 visa.

Currently, the United States government allows only 65,000 H-1B visas yearly. This visa category also allows 20,000 visas for applicants who have a U.S. master's degree or higher. Due to free trade agreements with Singapore and Chile, about 6,800 visas are reserved for workers from those countries.

Applications must be submitted to USCIS prior to the fulfillment of the yearly quota of H-1B visas. Applications will not be considered after the quota has been met, and all remaining applicants must wait until the next year to apply for an H-1B visa—or they can apply for entrance into the United States through another visa type.

Historical H-1B Quota Data

For fiscal year 2012, the visa limit of 65,000 was reached on November 22, 2011. That year's cap of 20,000 visas for applicants with U.S. master's degrees or higher was met on October 19, 2011.

For fiscal year 2013, the quota of 65,000 was reached on June 11, 2012. The quota of 20,000 for those applicants with U.S. master's degrees or higher was reached on June 7, 2012.

For fiscal year 2014, the cap of 65,000 was met on April 5, 2013. For those applicants with a U.S. master's degree or higher, the visa limit of 20,000 was reached on April 5, 2013.

H-1B Work Visa Requirements

Eligible applicants must have at least a bachelor's degree and show proof of qualifications for the jobs at which they will work in the United States. They must also have any license required in their fields of work. An applicant's spouse and unmarried children under 21 may be eligible as H-4 dependents. These dependents may attend school but cannot work in the United States.

U.S.-based employers sponsor H-1B visas. They must ensure that all requirements are met by the applicant. They must not displace U.S. workers, and U.S. workers must be sought before recruiting H-1B visa holders.

Further, H-1B visa holders cannot be placed with another company. In order for a foreign worker to transfer to a new U.S. company, a new H-1B visa must be applied for by the other company. H-1B workers may begin working at the new job when the H-1B application is filed and don't need to wait for full approval from USCIS.

H-1B Work Visa Application Process

First, the employer must file a Labor Condition Application (LCA), Form ETA-9035, with the Department of Labor. In this LCA, the employer must certify that the employee will receive a wage comparable to wages paid a U.S. worker in that position. Completing this form may require the assistance of an immigration lawyer.

After LCA certification, employers must file Form I-129, Petition for a Nonimmigrant Worker. This form is submitted to the USCIS Service Center in the jurisdiction of the state in which the applicant will be working. Upon approval, Form I-797 is sent to the employer, and the American consulate where the applicant will be processed is notified. If the applicant is in the U.S. and has filed a change of status, he or she may remain in the U.S. as a nonimmigrant. The applicant may begin working on October 1 or on the date he or she requested in the application.

If not already in the United States, the H-1B applicant may be processed at the consulate in his or her home country. In such cases, the DS-160 electronic form must be filed through the Department of State's website.

Processing the H-1B visa can take from three to six months at a fee of $325. Premium processing takes place within two weeks, but the fee is $1,225. Employers must pay a fraud fee of $500 and an American Competitiveness and Workforce Improvement Act (ACWIA) fee of $750 (25 or fewer workers) or $1,500 (more than 25 workers).

J-1 (Student) Visa

Summary

- Exchange program applicants may obtain a J-1 visa.
- A DS-2019 and DS-160 must be filed by the applicant.
- An interview at a U.S. consulate or embassy is required.
- The processing fee is $100.
- Approval takes up to six weeks.
- An applicant's spouse and children under 21 may apply for a J-2 visa.

What Is the J-1 Visa?

The J-1 visa grants applicants entrance into the United States to participate in training or exchange programs. The purpose of this program is to promote goodwill internationally through cultural exchange. More than 170,000 foreign nationals visit the United States each month on this type of visa.

In the United States, J-1 visa holders can become involved in certain privately owned companies and in government or academic programs.

Varieties of J-1 Visa Programs

J-1 visa holders may participate in a variety of programs, serving as camp counselors, child or elder caregivers, government-agency visitors, and international visitors with the Department of State. J-1 visa holders may participate in the medical field as interns, physicians, or medical specialists. The education field offers positions for J-1 holders as short-term scholars in secondary schools, colleges, and universities and as teachers, trainees, research scholars, or professors.

The particular program that exchange visitors participate in determines their length of stay. Extensions are sometimes permitted. To qualify for an extension, some J-1 visa holders may be required to return to their native country for two years. Programs with this requirement include the following:

Programs in which funding for the visa holder applicant was obtained from the U.S. government, an international organization, or the applicant's home government.

Programs in which the applicant worked in a position that was listed on the Department of State's Exchange Visitor List or was in demand in their home country.

Programs in which the applicant worked in the Educational Commission for Foreign Medical Graduates program.

Visa Requirements

In order for a foreign national to participate in the J-1 exchange program, a designated sponsor is required. Sponsors may be certain governmental offices, private companies, and universities. Each sponsored program has certain criteria for admission, but all require that J-1 applicants have English skills suitable for their program and sufficient medical insurance. Applicants must also provide the program fees, which may include the U.S. Department of Homeland Security fee, the sponsor program fee, visa insurance, and processing fees. Fees may vary for each particular program.

Application Process

Applicants must obtain Form DS-2019 from their program sponsors. The form will include the timeframe and purpose of the program, the fees, and an explanation of whether the applicant is subject to the two-year home residence requirement. The applicant can then apply for entry into the United States through a U.S. consulate or embassy.

Processing usually takes up to six weeks depending on the applicant's country of origin. J-1 visas are granted for a certain period of time; however, J-1 visa holders may later apply for an additional visa that could allow them to gain permanent resident status.

Until an exchange visitor obtains a green card, he or she will not be allowed to travel; permission to do so must be granted along with the J-1 visa application. The visitor's spouse and any children under 21 could receive J-2 dependent status, which would allow them to join their family member in the United States and apply for authorization to work.

EB-5 and E-2 Investment Visas

Two Primary U.S. Investment Visas: EB-5 and E-2

For foreign nationals who desire to live or work in the United States through investment, two types of visa are available: the EB-5 Immigrant Investor Visa and the E-2 Treaty Investor Visa. The amount of capital required and the residence status afforded by these two investment visa types differ, and so anyone seeking to gain resident status in the United States through an investment should take the time to understand these differences in order to select the path that fits their situation best.

EB-5 Visa

Created by Congress in 1990 through the Immigration and Nationality Act, the employment-based fifth preference visa, or EB-5 visa, is unlike other types of U.S. visas in that it is the only employment-based visa that also requires the applicant to invest in a U.S. commercial enterprise.

The EB-5 Immigrant Investor Pilot Program is administered by USCIS, and through this program, foreign investors can obtain permanent resident status—and eventually citizenship—for themselves and their dependent family members.

The EB-5 Program requires applicants to invest a minimum of $1,000,000 into a new commercial enterprise in the United States. This investment threshold is only $500,000 for investments located within targeted employment areas—which are rural areas or areas of higher-than-average unemployment.

In addition to the required capital, a number of criteria must be met in order for the investor to qualify for a green card. For example, the new commercial enterprise must create 10 full-time jobs per EB-5 investor, and the investor must be sufficiently engaged in the ongoing management of the enterprise. If all of the criteria for the EB-5 Program are met, the investor and his or her family will be able to apply for permanent resident status and ultimately for U.S. citizenship.

E-2 Visa

The E-2 visa is a nonimmigrant classification that enables foreign nationals from treaty countries to enter the United States on the basis of a business investment. This investment may establish a new enterprise or purchase an existing business.

In addition to the investor, his or her employees (or the employees of a qualifying organization) may be eligible for the E-2 classification. The dependent family members of treaty investors and eligible employees may also be able to apply for E-2 nonimmigrant status.

The E-2 visa allows an initial stay of no more than two years, though extensions of up to two years can be granted. And E-2 nonimmigrants may be granted an unlimited number of extensions.

Key Differences between EB-5 Visa and E-2 Visa

One of the key differences between the EB-5 visa and the E-2 visa, however, is that EB-5 investors are seeking permanent residence in the United States while E-2 treaty investors must maintain an intention to leave the United States upon the expiration or termination of their status.

The EB-5 Program

EB-5 Visa Program Basics

The United States Immigrant Investor Program—also known as the employment-based fifth preference visa program, or just the EB-5 Program—was created by Congress through the Immigration Act of 1990 and codified in Title 8 of the U.S. Code, § 1153(b)(5). The program is administered by USCIS. Foreign investors who satisfy the requirements under the EB-5 Program are able to obtain a green card and a path to U.S. citizenship in exchange for their job-creating investment.

This program was created to stimulate the U.S. economy through the infusion of foreign capital tied specifically to job creation. For foreign nationals, the EB-5 Program offers the opportunity to gain permanent resident status through investment. And for developers, this program offers access to inexpensive financing.

In order to gain permanent resident status through the EB-5 Program, a foreign national must invest in a new commercial enterprise—a broad classification that encompasses a variety of organizational structures as long as they are for-profit and were created or restructured after November 29, 1990. The minimum investment is currently $1,000,000—although certain rural areas or areas of higher-than-average unemployment, known as targeted employment areas (TEAs) may be eligible for a lower minimum investment of $500,000. TEAs are designated by state agencies and are subject to change. The capital investment in the new commercial enterprise must create 10 qualified full-time jobs. This investment can either be a direct investment by the foreign national into the new commercial enterprise or an indirect investment made through a regional center.

EB-5 Regional Centers: Why Most EB-5 Projects Use a Regional Center

Regional centers are economic units created in 1992 by the Immigrant Investor Pilot Program, which has been extended by Congress with no changes since its inception. By affiliating with a regional center, an EB-5 investor enjoys less restrictive job creation requirements because in addition to direct jobs, indirect and induced jobs may be counted toward the program's job creation requirement. Any public or private organization can seek regional center designation through USCIS.

USCIS has set aside EB-5 visas specifically for designed regional centers based on proposals for promoting economic growth, improved regional productivity, job creation and increased domestic capital investment. Almost all EB-5 applications are currently conducted through regional centers. The regional center streamlines the process for potential EB-5 applicants by making it easier to demonstrate job creation. Specifically, only regional centers may use the "indirect" method of calculating jobs through an approved economic methodology. This means that the investor/applicant need merely to demonstrate their funds were spent according to the business plan versus showing actual job positions created and held for the two year period. Another implicit benefit of this difference in job creation calculation is an overall increase in the total amount of EB-5 capital that can be raised for the investment project.

EB5AN maintains multiple USCIS-approved regional centers with broad geographic coverage, enabling EB5AN to immediately sponsor strong EB-5 projects across the United States.

Primary EB-5 Visa Investment Requirements

1. Minimum investment of $1,000,000, which is typically reduced to $500,000 for investments made in a rural or high unemployment area (a "Targeted Employment Area" or "TEA"). Almost all of EB5AN's projects are located in TEAs to reduce the investor's at-risk capital.

2. Creating or preserving at least 10 full-time jobs for qualifying U.S. workers that last a minimum of two years.

3. The investment must be in a new commercial enterprise or a troubled business.

4. The investment must be at-risk and the investment funds must be lawfully sourced.

The EB-5 Program has enjoyed strong support from Congress and as a result has grown dramatically since its inception, creating thousands of jobs for American citizens across the country. EB5 Affiliate Network is proud to continue to provide first-class service to EB-5 clients, developers and investors in furtherance of this goal.

Benefits of EB-5 for Foreign Investors

An EB-5 visa provides the same green card as other qualifying processes, allowing the investor and his or her immediate family to live, study, work, and retire anywhere in the United States. The EB-5 Program helps foreigners obtain a coveted piece of American life while stimulating the US economy through job creation.

For foreign nationals with the necessary capital, the EB-5 Program can be an excellent way to obtain permanent resident status in the United States. Unlike other immigrant visa options, the EB-5 visa requires no U.S. employer to act as a sponsor, nor does it require any specialized knowledge, skills, or experience. Further, the EB-5 Program is not limited to foreign nationals from specific treaty nations.

Upon making a qualifying investment and receiving approval from USCIS, an EB-5 investor, his or her spouse, and any unmarried children under age 21 will be granted conditional permanent residence. Two years later, if the investment has proven to meet the program's requirements, the investor and his or her family will have the conditions removed from their resident status.

185

Five years after first receiving conditional permanent resident status, they can become naturalized citizens.

EB-5 visa benefits for foreign investors include the following:

- One of the fastest methods to gain permanent residence in the United States for the investor, his or her spouse, and unmarried children under 21 years of age
- Freedom to live and work anywhere in the United States without restriction, including in states such as Florida or Texas with no state income tax
- Education benefits such as access to public elementary, middle, and high-school schools and lower cost in-state tuition at public colleges and universities
- No visa sponsor requirements
- No H-1B work visa needed for employment
- Investment must be "at risk" but can be secured by collateral in a real estate project to minimize downside risk. EB5AN focuses on projects with structural downside protection
- In the event of a political change or significant event in the investor's home country, he/she and family can immediately gain entry to the United States without delay
- Potential for U.S. citizenship after minimum five years of established permanent residence in the United States.

Application Challenges for EB-5 Investors

Applicants to the EB-5 Program face certain challenges associated with the application process and the program itself. This section outlines the challenges investors may face at each step of the application process as well as some more general obstacles investors may wish to consider when doing their due diligence to determine whether the EB-5 Program suits their immigration and investment goals.

Step 1: Form I-526

The first step in applying for the EB-5 Program is to file an I-526 petition, the two main components of which are the project documents and the proof of a lawful source of funds. USCIS adjudicators will scrutinize these documents to ensure they comply with the requirements of the EB-5 Program and U.S. law in general and will determine the investor's eligibility for approval based on a preponderance of evidence.

Project documents must be thorough in laying out how investment funds will be used and how the project will meet the program requirements as a new commercial enterprise capable of creating 10 full-time jobs per investor. These documents will generally include a business plan and economic impact report outlining the objectives of the enterprise, its marketing plan, and its financial projections. These should be reviewed thoroughly by both the investors themselves and the project developers as well as immigration attorneys, securities attorneys, and other counsel to ensure the project is legally sound.

The investor also must be able to prove that the investment funds have been sourced legally. For investors from countries such as China, where tracing the path of funds can be problematic because of banks' reluctance to issue statements, proving the source of investment funds is a significant hurdle. Some countries, such as India, also impose strict limits on how much currency can be transferred abroad, which means investors may need to work through banks in other countries to transfer the EB-5 investment. Regardless, investors must be able to fully account for the sources of the investment funds to pass a USCIS review.

Government agencies may also conduct due diligence investigations during this stage of the application. For example, USCIS may visit the site of the commercial enterprise to evaluate its financial and job creation prospects, and the Securities and Exchange Commission (SEC) will investigate suspected cases of fraud in the program if tipped off by USCIS or by concerned investors themselves. It is therefore crucial that both investors and project developers work with experienced counsel and research the program requirements to ensure full compliance.

Step 2: Consular Processing or Adjustment of Status

Investors successful in their I-526 petitions proceed to the next step, which is either consular processing for investors residing abroad or adjustment of status for investors holding nonimmigrant status in the United States. As part of these applications, investors must submit any required legal or medical documents to prove their eligibility to immigrate to the United States.

Investors undergoing consular processing will face a thorough review of their supporting documents by the National Visa Center (NVC) as well as an interview with the U.S. consulate in their country of origin. Investors applying for an adjustment of status will undergo a further USCIS review. In either case, inconsistencies in previously submitted documents may delay processing of the application.

Step 3: Form I-829

The final stage of application to the EB-5 Program is for the investor to submit an I-829 petition to remove the conditions of permanent residence. This requires the investor to prove that the EB-5 investment has created the required 10 full-time jobs in the two years following approval of the I-526 petition, which should be supported by the initial financial report and proved using payroll records and other proofs of employment.

Additionally, because the EB-5 Program requires that the investment funds be at risk throughout the application process, the investor must prove that none of the original EB-5 investment has been repaid to him or her. The financial records provided should be consistent with those filed along with the I-526 in that they account for the investment funds entirely and show how those same funds were required to create the requisite 10 jobs. USCIS may conduct additional site visits while adjudicating the I-829 petition to verify these claims.

Challenges of the EB-5 Program

Aside from the challenges inherent to each step of the application process, the nature of the EB-5 Program itself can create obstacles for investors. The most significant of these are outlined below to assist investors in making informed decisions.

Changes in policy

The EB-5 Program is a permanent law, but changes in legislation can affect different aspects of the program, such as the minimum investment amount and fund sourcing requirements. An example of recent changes in this area is the regional center program, which was recently set to expire on April 15, 2019, but was renewed by Congress until September 30, 2019. Investors whose current petitions are contingent upon aspects of the regional center program could be affected by any changes in this regard and should be aware of this possibility.

Denials and requests for evidence

If USCIS believes not enough evidence exists to justify approval of a petition, it may issue a request for evidence (RFE) to collect further information. There is also the chance that USCIS may issue a notice of intent to deny (NOID), which signifies that the adjudicator believes the petition should be denied but wishes to present the investor the opportunity to clear up any areas of concern. Both of these notices may delay an investor's petition and involve additional costs to revise the petition materials, for example, to consult with counsel.

An investor has the option of requesting an administrative review if his or her petition is denied, but this involves a significant waiting period. Luckily, the approximate approval rates for I-526 and I-829 petitions are 85% and 90%, respectively.

Fraud

Despite the efforts of USCIS, the SEC, and other government agencies to enforce the legal aspects of the EB-5 Program, cases like the recent *SEC v. A Chicago Convention Center* illustrate the risk of fraud when developers and other agents misrepresent elements of the program or individual projects to investors. However, such cases are relatively rare.

Investors applying to the EB-5 Program face unique challenges and opportunities. By providing thorough application materials and exercising due diligence, as with any other investment, investors can increase the likelihood of a smooth petition process.

Defining EB-5 Targeted Employment Areas

The benchmarks used to delineate TEAs within the context of the EB-5 Program have recently been under contention, as regional centers have successfully developed projects in wealthy cities by taking advantage of the opportunity for multiple investors to contribute to such projects with lower investment amounts under the TEA exception. This exception, as outlined in the Immigration Act of 1990, states that while EB-5 investors in general must commit a $1,000,000 investment, investors in a project developed within a TEA may commit only half that amount, meaning $500,000.

When establishing the criteria used to determine a TEA, Congress chose to use unemployment as the target metric over other measurements of poverty, such as average household income. As such, a TEA must experience unemployment of at least 150% the national average. This allows for situations in which areas with low average incomes but high employment would not qualify as TEAs, whereas areas with high average incomes but low employment would qualify. While this seems counterintuitive, one of the goals of the EB-5 Program is to create employment, and targeting areas with low employment through TEA incentives is consistent with this goal.

As the majority of regional center investments are made in the reduced $500,000 amount, it is clear that TEAs play a significant role in the success of the EB-5 Program. This section explores how targeted employment areas are defined and what the consequences of these definitions are for EB-5 investors.

How Are TEAs Defined?

While requirements for targeted employment areas are outlined in the Immigration Act of 1990, each state has the authority to designate TEAs based on available data. For example, while one state may designate a wide swath of rural land as a TEA, another might designate a small neighborhood within a large and otherwise prosperous city. This is meant to allow states to tailor the program to suit the needs of their populations in a way that would not be possible with overarching federal designations. However, while USCIS, which administers the EB-5 Program, generally defers to state designations of TEAs, adjudicators will verify the calculations and data used when approving or denying EB-5 petitions.

Under the current definition, it is possible for a TEA to span a region encompassing multiple income and employment levels if the average employment level for the entire region is low enough. For example, if a TEA comprises six neighborhoods in a major city, one of which has an employment level much higher than the rest, a project located in the wealthier neighborhood would still be within the TEA. This allows for the development within the TEA of impactful projects such as luxury hotels, which benefit from being located in wealthier neighborhoods because of increased tourism to those areas, for example. In the scenario of the six neighborhoods given above, such a development would create economic growth throughout the TEA based on the logic that those without employment, meaning those from the neighboring disadvantaged areas, would benefit from the jobs created by the project.

Criticisms of the current designation criteria center on the argument that the sole metric of high unemployment is not adequate to allow for an accurate delineation of economically depressed areas. More effective criteria might be a combination of several factors, such as employment, income, education and crime levels, and others, for example. As such, critics argue that EB-5 investment funds are not currently being applied where they would be of most benefit. However, if the sole goal of the TEA designation is to encourage EB-5 projects to create jobs where a need for jobs exists, the current criteria is inarguably useful in that regard.

Considerations for Investors

The benefits of investing in a TEA project are significant, as investors are able to take advantage of a lower investment amount than would be possible with a regular project. A regional center may obtain a TEA designation when its I-924 is approved, meaning when USCIS has designated the organization as an official regional center under the EB-5 Program. However, changing unemployment figures may affect the delineation of a TEA after that time, and because USCIS will confirm the TEA status of a project only when an investor files his or her I-526 petition, investors should request a current letter from the regional center proving that a project is located within a TEA before committing any funds.

State strategies for delineating targeted employment areas may also change over time, so investors benefit from consulting with an attorney experienced in these procedures to confirm the possibility of investing in a TEA project.

Investment Options: Direct versus Regional Center

The fundamental difference between direct and regional center investment models is that while regional centers are able to count indirect job creation toward the required number of full-time jobs created per investor, direct investment results in only direct job creation. Aside from this, the two models are alike in that they require the same amount of investment capital, with both being able to take advantage of a lower amount in targeted employment areas, and in that investors for both experience the same average wait times for adjudication of their I-526 petitions, according to USCIS estimates.

The difference between indirect and direct job creation requirements does create some practical considerations for investors that may affect their decision whether to invest directly or through a regional center. First, below are some other points investors might take into account when making this decision:

- Regional centers must file an I-924 form to request formal designation from USCIS, so investors must receive confirmation of this status before working with a center. This is aside from filing the I-526 petition for conditional permanent residence and later the I-829 for removal of conditions, which investors in both models must do. A little under one third of the visas issued annually under the EB-5 Program are specifically reserved for regional center investors, though in practice these investors claim the majority of visas.
- Regional centers offer an established infrastructure through which to secure funding for large projects, distribute funds to the appropriate entities during project development, and properly administer and report on fund use. However, these services may result in significant administrative fees that investors could avoid through direct investment.
- USCIS and Congress may propose changes to minimum investment amounts and targeted area designations for the EB-5 Program, which would affect all investors. However, regional center investors are also affected by legislation specific to the regional center program. For example, the program has only been authorized through September 30, 2019, meaning it will face potential renewal or nonrenewal on that date. Direct investors are not affected by this possibility.

Considerations for Investors

The direct investment method is often preferred by foreign investors seeking to open and operate their own commercial enterprise in the United States. These investors are seeking to have full control over their investment and are looking to build a successful business. A common goal among direct investors is to expand their existing business operations into the United States and increase their profits. Typically, this means that the investor is looking to make an investment in a more urban, business-friendly area that may or may not qualify as a TEA due to the local unemployment rate. Most foreign investors are not seeking to open new commercial enterprises in rural areas, even though rural areas automatically qualify as TEAs. If the investor chooses to locate his or her business in an area that does not qualify as a TEA, then the investment must be $1,000,000 instead of $500,000. Generally, direct EB-5 investments are more suitable for investors that desire to have greater control over their investments and operate independently.

The regional center investment method is the most popular EB-5 investment method by far because it allows each investor to become part of a new commercial enterprise as a passive investor with minimal to no daily management responsibilities. In a regional center investment, multiple EB-5 investors are typically pooled together to make an investment in a new commercial enterprise. Since EB-5 capital in a regional center project tends to be a small portion of the total project capital, this pooled approach typically results in a large job cushion, providing more than the required 10 jobs per investor. Such a cushion reduces the stress placed on an EB-5 investor. For those who choose direct investment, the EB-5 investor is personally responsible to meet the 10 jobs per investor requirement.

Below are three example scenarios which demonstrate the differences between these investment models and their job creation potential:

- Small businesses such as restaurants are better suited to direct investment because they require few investors and create few jobs, only enough to satisfy the requirements for those investors. The direct investment model allows those few investors to avoid the various administrative fees associated with a regional center investment.
- Real estate developments are among the most common regional center projects, as they require significant capital from multiple investors but are able to support this through high job creation via construction jobs, tenant jobs, and the economic impact of sourcing materials. Direct investors would be unable to count these indirect jobs in a real estate project and would thus be unlikely to meet the required total.
- Hotels and resorts are well suited to both investment models depending on the goals of investors. The regional center model allows investors to avoid a management role in the hotel itself, as the new commercial enterprise serves merely to raise capital for the hotel as the job-creating entity, and any jobs created are indirect. These jobs would include construction and operations as well as the supply of materials, and thus a hotel developed through a regional center could support a number of investors. Direct investment in a hotel would allow the investor to take on a management role, but only jobs created by the operation of the

hotel itself, as verified by payroll documents, would count toward the total.

Filing Procedures

EB-5 investors seeking to make a direct investment can submit their applications by themselves with the help of a qualified immigration attorney. Direct EB-5 investors are therefore typically responsible for assembling all supporting documentation for their specific new commercial enterprise investment, whereas EB-5 investors seeking to make a regional center investment must work with the regional center to obtain and correctly prepare the necessary project documentation for the selected investment. Regional center EB-5 investors do not need to prepare any project-specific documentation since all of the required project documentation has already been completed and assembled by the regional center.

Investors must carefully consider several factors when deciding between the direct and regional center investment models, mainly concerning the role the investor wishes to take in the new commercial enterprise. While regional centers are able to count indirect jobs toward the investment total and thus are able to facilitate larger projects, investors generally play a passive role in managing the new commercial enterprise, the only role of which is to serve as a lender for the job-creating entity. Direct investment projects do not benefit from the same level of funding and administrative support as regional center projects, but investors are able to take on an active management role. Each model has its own benefits and drawbacks, and investors must thoroughly explore their options before committing to one or the other.

Due Diligence and Fraud Prevention

The Importance of Due Diligence for EB-5 Investors

Although EB-5 investors come from a wide range of backgrounds and are generally experienced with conducting due diligence in their respective fields, many are unsure how to proceed with due diligence in the unique EB-5 context. In the regional center model, investors must conduct two levels of due diligence, the first on the EB-5 project and its developers and the second on the regional center itself. Aside from allowing investors to inform themselves and better protect their investments, due diligence can provide an idea of the chances of successful immigration under the EB-5 Program based on the track record of the regional center.

This section discusses the importance of due diligence in the EB-5 context and outlines five questions investors should ask when conducting due diligence for their potential investments.

Investment/Project Concerns for EB-5 Investors

EB-5 investors have two central concerns. The first is whether investing in an EB-5 project will allow them to become permanent residents of the United States. The second is whether a project will provide a return on the investment.

The EB-5 Program requires that investors submit two visa petitions. The first is the I-526 petition for conditional permanent residence, which the investor files after he or she has made the initial investment. This proves the source of the investment funds and demonstrates to USCIS that the project will be capable of creating the required 10 full-time jobs in the United States per investor. At the end of the residence period of two years, the investor files the I-829 petition for removal of the conditions of permanent residence and must provide documentation that the EB-5 project has fulfilled the program requirements as outlined in the I-526 petition. This process takes approximately six years, but investors from China may experience longer waits as a result of recent visa retrogression concerns.

Aside from evaluating whether a project will be financially capable of sustaining itself throughout this visa application period, investors must determine whether the new commercial enterprise established under the program will be able to repay the investment amount afterward. This is generally a significant sum of $1,000,000 or $500,000 if the enterprise is located in a targeted employment area, so investors are understandably wary of entering into a loan agreement without proper assurance that they stand to be repaid at the appropriate juncture.

Due diligence in confirming the viability of a project is thus crucial within the EB-5 context.

Due Diligence Questions for Investors

An investor must take several factors into consideration when conducting due diligence. First and foremost, he or she must evaluate the regional center, its track record of success with USCIS, and its ability to manage a project that will provide a return on the investment amount. The following are key questions investors should examine when investigating a regional center in this regard.

1. Has the regional center previously facilitated successful visa petitions?

A regional center should be able to provide investors information on how many previous investors have filed visa petitions successfully. If any previous investors have been denied permanent residence, the center should likewise be able to provide the legitimate reasons for those denials and show that it has taken steps to prevent such issues with future petitions. Investors should keep in mind, however, that petitions are sometimes denied for reasons not owing to the regional center, as in cases where the denial is based on an issue with the source of investment funds, for example.

2. How long has the regional center been operational?

Investors should look into when the regional center was designated as such by USCIS and whether it has previously managed any projects. A regional center experienced with the unique concerns surrounding projects and funds in the EB-5 context will be able to more adequately account for the areas of focus of USCIS visa petition adjudicators and additionally will have the knowledge and competence to deal with any issues as they arise. As USCIS has recently begun reviewing regional centers which have not met the goals of the EB-5 Program, a proven track record will increase the chances that the regional center itself will remain operational throughout an investor's conditional residence.

3. Has the project been approved by USCIS?

The first visa petition associated with an EB-5 project includes an additional level of USCIS review regarding the business plan and economic impact report for the project. This increases the adjudication time for that petition, and thus investors may benefit from entering a project after it has already passed this initial USCIS review. The regional center should be able to confirm the status of the project for potential investors. Aside from this, a project may require various licenses or permits, and investors should confirm that these have been granted to avoid additional delays after having committed funds.

4. Can the project support the required number of jobs?

To be granted a visa under the EB-5 Program, each investor must be able to prove that his or her investment has resulted in the creation of 10 full-time jobs within the employment area. As such, regional center projects drawing on multiple investors must time job creation carefully to ensure each investor is credited with the correct number of jobs. Investors must carefully review the project documentation to ensure developers have included an adequate buffer in terms of the number of jobs created. A project should not aim to create only 10 jobs per investor, as investors may be left short under those circumstances if contingencies affect the number of jobs created.

5. Does the regional center have a redeployment plan for the investment funds?

Because the investment amount must remain at risk throughout the conditional residence period, regional centers must carefully account for the possibility that a loan may be repaid early. One option is to not allow borrowers to repay the loan before the I-829 petition is adjudicated. Another option is for the regional center to immediately reinvest any repaid investment funds into another project to ensure they remain at risk for the necessary amount of time. Investors should consult with a financial advisor to determine which strategy best suits their needs.

Consulting with EB-5 Practitioners

In conducting their due diligence, investors benefit from working with professionals experienced in the requirements of the EB-5 Program. A financial advisor can help an investor guard against the possibility of fraud or misrepresentation in a project and can provide valuable financial advice to help the investor negotiate favorable loan and repayment agreements. Similarly, an immigration attorney will work with a regional center on behalf of the investor to gather documentation for the I-526 and I-829 petitions. This includes the project offering, financial statements, and source of funds documents as well as payroll records and other proof of job creation.

In conducting due diligence on regional centers and projects, investors gain the ability to make informed investment decisions and increase their chances of a successful visa petition. As the stakes are so high in terms of both the investment amount and the permanent residence of the investor and his or her family in the United States, due diligence plays a key role in assisting investors during the planning stages and in allowing them to invest in EB-5 projects with confidence.

Due Diligence: Financial Risk

For a foreign investor considering an investment in an EB-5 regional center sponsored project, two main types of risk must be evaluated:
- Immigration risk to get the permanent green card
- Financial risk to get their $500,000 or $1,000,000 investment back at the end of the investment term, or to get the initial capital contribution back along with any administrative fees as soon as possible in the case of an I-526 denial

This section will focus on evaluating the financial risk of EB-5 regional center investments.

1. What Is the Track Record and Reputation of the Project Developer (EB-5 Capital Borrower) and Any Other Lenders/Banks Involved?

When evaluating the financial risk of an EB-5 project, the track record and reputation of those involved is the most important factor. The EB-5 investor's capital will be managed by the project developer, and so it is critical to have confidence in the development team and their experience, reputation, and alignment of incentives.

The following are key project developer questions to ask:
- How many projects like this one has the developer completed successfully?
- How much total development experience does the developer have?
- How much developer equity capital is at risk in the project?
- Has the developer previously done business with the lender/bank involved in the project?
- Has the developer ever defaulted on a loan?
- Is the developer currently involved in any serious litigation?

2. How Will EB-5 Capital Be Released to the Project (Escrow Structure)?

Many EB-5 investors would prefer that their capital remain in escrow until their respective individual I-526 petitions are approved. Given the long and unpredictable processing times for I-526 approvals from USCIS, however, most project developers utilize a hybrid escrow release structure. The most common hybrid structure is one in which a portion of the EB-5 investor's capital is released upon the investor's I-526 petition submission, and the remaining capital of each EB-5 investor is released from escrow when the respective investor's I-526 petition is approved.

3. If an Investor's I-526 Petition Is Denied, When and How Will the Investment Be Returned? Will the Administrative Fee Be Returned?

Best practice is for EB-5 projects to specify exactly what happens in the case of an investor receiving an I-526 denial.

In the worst projects, the EB-5 investor may have to remain an investor in the project through completion without any immigration benefit whatsoever. In other projects, the EB-5 investor's capital contribution will be returned within 1–2 years of the I-526 denial. The most attractive projects are those that provide an I-526 denial guarantee whereby the EB-5 investor will receive a full refund of his or her capital commitment within 60–90 days of the final I-526 denial. Furthermore, investors should understand what entity is making this denial refund guarantee and be sure that the corporate entity has the necessary capital and the liquidity to stand behind this guarantee. A guarantee from an entity without any assets is essentially worthless.

In addition to their capital contribution, EB-5 investors usually are required to pay an administrative fee (typically about $50,000). Different repayment terms are often applied to the $500,000 or $1,000,000 capital contribution and the administrative fee. Here, the worst projects are those that make a "best effort" to return the full administrative fee—this is highly unlikely to occur and is usually at the sole discretion of the EB-5 project. The best projects are those that provide a full I-526 denial refund guarantee of both the capital contribution and the administrative fee from a well-capitalized and liquid corporate entity.

4. What Percentage of the Total Capital Stack of the Project Is EB-5 Capital?

This question ties into job creation and cushion as well as the availability of other sources of financing for the project. The worst projects are ones that cannot get traditional bank lending at a reasonable LTV rate (above 50%) because they are too risky, and so these projects will tend to have a higher percentage of EB-5 capital. A good rule of thumb is that projects with EB-5 capital above 40%–50% should usually be avoided, and projects with less than 25% EB-5 capital should be investigated further.

The other key factor here is job creation and cushion. Projects with a smaller percentage of EB-5 capital tend to have a larger job cushion, which is safer for EB-5 investors. Therefore, a smaller percentage of EB-5 capital in the project is usually a very good sign for EB-5 investors because it means that EB-5 capital is less critical to the successful completion of the project and that the project has a larger job cushion.

5. What Percentage of the Total Capital Stack of the Project is Developer Equity?

EB-5 investors should avoid projects with minimal developer equity (below 10%) once EB-5 capital has been factored in. Traditional banks in the United States often require a minimum of 15%–20% of developer equity in a deal at all times, and so EB-5 investors should not consider projects in which the developer equity is much less than that range.

6. Does the Project Have a Credible Exit Strategy (Repayment of EB-5 Investors)?

EB-5 investors should understand what the anticipated project exit strategy is and whether or not it is credible. Additionally, EB-5 investors should realize that since the EB-5 capital must be kept at risk under USCIS rules, there can never be a guaranteed return of the original capital contribution or a return on the committed capital. EB-5 projects that include such a repayment guarantee will not be approved by USCIS as this does not meet the "at risk" requirement of the program. Therefore, the best an investor can do is understand what the proposed exit strategy is and verify the assumptions made by the project sponsor and the developer concerning the likelihood and credibility of the proposed exit strategy coming to fruition.

A great indicator of whether a project has a credible exit strategy is whether a major third-party senior lender has underwritten the project and has loaned it millions of dollars in capital. The logic here is that if a major U.S. bank felt comfortable with the developer's exit strategy/plan to repay the bank, the exit strategy is likely credible.

7. What Is the Project's Return on the EB-5 Investment (ROI)?

Most EB-5 investments today offer between 0% and 1% annual interest return to EB-5 investors. Since the difference between interest rates is negligible, the interest rate to EB-5 investors is usually one of the least important factors in determining the safety of an EB-5 project.

Due Diligence: Immigration Risk

For a foreign investor considering an investment in an EB-5 regional center sponsored project, two main types of risk must be evaluated:

- Immigration risk to get the permanent green card
- Financial risk to get their $500,000 or $1,000,000 investment back at the end of the investment term, or to get the initial capital contribution back along with any administrative fees as soon as possible in the case of an I-526 denial

This section will focus on evaluating the immigration risk of EB-5 regional center investments.

1. Is There a Contingency Plan in the Event That Not All Desired EB-5 Capital Is Successfully Sourced?

This is the single most important question when evaluating immigration risk. From an immigration perspective, the safest projects are those that will still be completed in the event of an EB-5 shortfall. This can be in the form of an initial bridge loan or through having additional equity/other debt sources as a fall back option. This sounds counterintuitive, but the reality is that the single most important project question for an EB-5 investor (and the best way to minimize immigration risk) is to know whether or not the project can be completed without the full amount of EB-5 capital. The safest projects from an immigration perspective are those that can be successfully constructed and operated even in the event of an EB-5 shortfall.

At the end of the day, only two immigration questions matter when evaluating a potential EB-5 project:

- Will the project be completed? The following factors actually matter to answer yes:
  - Developer cash irrevocably committed
  - Senior loan executed with a major bank
  - Construction completion guarantee executed from parent entity
  - Project well under construction
- Will the required number of jobs be created when the project is completed? The following factors matter:
  - How many jobs are created from construction alone
  - How much of a job cushion there is from construction alone
  - How much of the total construction cost has been spent to date when EB-5 investor capital enters the project

If the answer to the two questions above is a clear yes, then the investor's immigration risk in the EB-5 project has effectively been minimized.

How does an investor find a project that answers yes to those two questions? Let's break down each of the questions and determine what has to be true for each to be considered a clear yes.

Will the project actually be completed?

At the root of this question is whether the project actually gets built as described and projected in the EB-5 compliant business plan. This means that the projected amount of capital for construction is spent, that no major time delays occur during construction, and that the project experiences no cost shortfalls or overruns.

If a project has identified options for the full capitalization and has alternatives (even if vastly more expensive) to EB-5 funding then the immigration risk of the project not being completed has been minimized.

For example, consider a $100,000,000 hotel project in which the developer has committed to invest $30,000,000 of cash equity and has taken a senior bank loan for the remaining $70,000,000. For this scenario, assume that the senior loan can only be executed once $30,000,000 of total developer equity + EB-5 has been committed to the project. If the developer was seeking to raise $15,000,000 of EB-5 and have $15,000,000 of equity in the project then the sponsor could execute the senior loan when $30,000,000 of cash is available. The developer could either (i) wait for the EB-5, (ii) utilize a bridge loan for $15,000,000, or (iii) utilize bridge equity that is anticipated to be recapped out once EB-5 funding is identified.

If the developer has plans to move forward in all three of the above scenarios, regardless of how many EB-5 investors enter the project (one investor or the maximum 30 investors needed to reach $10,000,000) the project has sufficient capital for completion, and so success is not determined by how much EB-5 capital (or how many EB-5 investors) is found for the project. If the project moved forward without the full amount of EB-5 it could significantly hamper the developer from completing their next project if they have to over-commit on the anticipated equity, but from an immigration perspective at least the project will still be completed.

This issue is vitally important since the EB-5 market today is quite competitive and very few projects achieve full subscription quickly (i.e., find the target number of EB-5 investors within the expected fundraise time frame).

Will the required number of jobs be created when the project is completed?

The key to this question is job creation. Many projects today determine job creation as a combination of both construction expenditures and operational revenues. The safest projects are those in which the job creation from construction expenditures alone creates several times the required number of jobs per investor. To reduce the immigration risk even further, investors should seek projects that are already well under construction with very high job cushions.

Consider again the $100,000,000 hotel project example above. Let's say that this project creates a total of 1,200 EB-5 compliant jobs, and of these jobs,

1,000 are attributable to construction expenditures and 200 to operating revenues (once the hotel is open). Now, if the hotel costs $100,000,000, that means that once $50,000,000 is spent on construction, roughly 50% of the jobs have been created; in this case, 500 jobs. Since the project has no more than 20 EB-5 investors, and it must create 10 jobs per EB-5 investor, the project needs to create only 200 jobs. The project creates 1,000 jobs from construction alone, which means the project has a 500% job cushion. This level of job cushion is very attractive for EB-5 investors since it means the project has a much lower immigration risk.

If an EB-5 investor invested in this project halfway through the construction period, essentially all of the EB-5 investor's immigration risk is eliminated. Why is this the case? Once the project is 50% complete, approximately $50,000,000 has been spent on construction expenditures, and therefore roughly 500 of the 1,000 jobs have already been created. Since only 200 jobs are required for 20 EB-5 investors to get their permanent green cards, this means that the project still has a 250% job cushion even if it stopped construction and was never completed after the EB-5 investors entered the project at the halfway point.

Let's say, for example, that all 20 EB-5 investors did invest the combined $10,000,000 in EB-5 capital into the hotel project when the project was halfway through the construction period. Then, the following week, an earthquake hit the local area and the entire hotel site was swallowed up by a sink-hole, and the land became unusable as a result. In this case, all 20 EB-5 investors would still get their I-526 and I-829 petitions approved since the project did create the 10 required jobs per investors, despite the fact that the project was not successfully completed. As long as the job requirement is met, the project does not have to be successfully completed in order for EB-5 investors to get their I-526 and I-829 petitions approved.

The safest possible EB-5 project from an immigration perspective is one where the required EB-5 job creation for all EB-5 investors in the project has already occurred when the first EB-5 investor enters the project.

This type of project is not uncommon in the market today, and EB-5 investors should ask all of the questions above to determine whether a project truly meets these criteria.

The bad news: EB-5 investors beware

Almost every EB-5 project agent will tell potential EB-5 investors that the project (being sold) will happen regardless of how many EB-5 investors come into the project and that any amount of job cushion makes a project safe. The reality, however, is that the devil is in the details; most of these projects are misleading investors with exceptions built into their project documents that either allow other types of financing to come in senior to EB-5 capital if there is a shortfall or allow the EB-5 loan to be cancelled if a certain capital threshold is not met. Other common terms include escrow release provisions that require a certain amount of capital prior to release of funds. In such cases, if the target capital raise is never reached, then the EB-5 investors who did invest face multiple years of delays and potential capital loss. The reality is that many of these "shortfall commitments" are not actually enforceable from third-party lenders, and many project developers do not want to commit to take in EB-5 capital unless it is for a certain amount within a certain timeframe.

Investors should always conduct detailed due diligence on the EB-5 projects presented to them and utilize this framework as a starting point to screen out and avoid higher risk EB-5 projects.

2. Does the Project Include Any Job Cushion (Construction Jobs Only)?

For every single EB-5 investor, at least 10 jobs (indirect, direct, and induced) must be created by the project. The higher the job cushion, the safer the project. Projects are especially safe when the required 10 jobs can be met from construction expenditures alone and do not require any operational jobs. Many projects on the market today have a job cushion of at least 20%, but investors looking to minimize immigration risk should target a job cushion of 100% or more.

3. When Will the EB-5 Job Creation Occur?

USCIS regulations require that the job creation of a project occur after the EB-5 investment has been made into the project and within two-and-a-half years following approval of the investor's I-526 petition. If the project does not create the required number of jobs within the allotted time period, EB-5 investors will be at risk of losing their conditional permanent resident status at the I-829 stage of the EB-5 process.

USCIS has issued a policy memorandum that states that bridge financing (equity or debt) in the project prior to the entrance of EB-5 capital can be applied toward the total job creation calculation of the project. This means that even though a project started construction before EB-5 capital was invested, all of the construction expenditures and resulting jobs from the beginning of construction can be counted toward the EB-5 requirement of 10 jobs per investor.

4. Has the project been pre-approved by USCIS (I-924 project "exemplar")?

Investors filing I-526 petitions should ask whether the project has been pre-approved by USCIS as a project "exemplar." However, since the processing time for a project "exemplar" can be 12–16 months, this application is often still pending with USCIS when investors file their I-526 petitions. Since filing a project "exemplar" is not required (even though it is a best practice), investors should confirm with the project sponsor that a project "exemplar" application has been submitted to USCIS and that a receipt notice can be provided as evidence. If a project is a USCIS-approved "exemplar" or an individual I-526 has been approved by USCIS, the project has successfully met the USCIS standards for the EB-5 Program and any future investors and I-526 petitions should be approved (usually at an expedited rate).

5. Is the project located in an officially designated TEA? When was the TEA letter issued and how long is the TEA letter valid?

Answering these questions is critical for determining whether the EB-5 investment will qualify as a $500,000 investment instead requiring the standard $1,000,000. The TEA letter must be issued by the appropriately designated state agency and must be valid at the time of the I-526 or I-924 project "exemplar" submission(s) to USCIS.

6. Does the project have an EB-5/*Matter of Ho* compliant business plan?

One of the most basic EB-5 requirements is that the business plan must be *Matter of Ho* compliant. The primary consideration here is whether or not the business plan meets the requirements of the EB-5 Immigrant Investor Program in terms of job creation, the amount of EB-5 capital, and the key assumptions made for the successful development and operation of the business in question.

Detecting and Preventing Fraud in EB-5 Projects

Recent actions by the SEC have brought increased attention to the issue of fraud within the EB-5 Program, with notable cases having involved the misappropriation of funds. Regional centers, investors, and other EB-5 agents have taken notice of this issue, and many will conduct significant due diligence before committing to a project for this reason. This section outlines four strategies investors can use to detect and prevent misappropriation.

1. Conduct Due Diligence on Fund Managers and the Project

Before entering into any agreement, investors should be satisfied with the integrity of the parties involved in the project, particularly in the management and disbursement of funds. Background checks can be used to verify the industry experience and legal standing of those who will have access to the investment funds, as can a call to relevant professional associations to confirm that a member is in good standing.

Investors should take note of arrangements in which the new commercial enterprise (NCE) is closely related to the job-creating entity (JCE). In a typical arrangement, the NCE collects funds and disburses them to the JCE, and each will review the flow of funds independently. In cases where the principals of the NCE and JCE are the same or where there is overlap, only one review would be conducted by those individuals. This is a common setup and not a red flag in and of itself, but investors should again take care to verify the integrity of the principals of both entities.

Investors can also take the step of investigating a project in person via a site visit. Legitimate projects will facilitate this sort of due diligence and will be eager to reassure investors by providing a live visual tour of the site via webcam to avoid the need for travel costs. Investors can also search online periodically for information about the project and any parties involved to remain apprised of local news.

Regional centers typically take care to work with experienced fund managers with good industry standing. Such managers will structure the project so as to deter fraud, and this foresight can prove invaluable. Nonetheless, investors are encouraged to confirm the backgrounds of all those with access to the investment funds.

2. Carefully Account for Fund Disbursement

The disbursement agreement for the project should outline in detail how funds will be used at each stage of planning, construction, and operations. In a project involving multiple parties, each will be required to verify and authorize any expenditures according to this agreement. Investors especially must review the project documents to ensure that their investment funds are being used specifically to fund job creation as required by the EB-5 Program, as proving this will be necessary when investors file their I-829 petitions.

An investor must file his or her I-829 petition to remove the conditions of permanent residence within 90 days prior to the expiry of the two-year conditional residence period. The I-829 documentation requires the investor to show that the use of the funds has complied with EB-5 regulations and has been consistent with the documents submitted with the I-526 petition. The petitioner must trace the path of funds from escrow through to job creation using financial proof such as bank statements, payroll records, and other receipts.

If USCIS denies an investor's I-829 petition on the grounds that the full investment fund amount was not used for job creation, this is a sign that misappropriation may have occurred, and the investor must look into the matter further.

3. Work with an Institutional Lender

Regional centers typically work with institutional lenders to hold the investment funds in escrow until they are released to the JCE. Institutional lenders are an ally to investors in that they aim to protect the interests of all parties by overseeing the disbursement of funds from the moment the investor sends them to the NCE. The lender will generally also work with a title company to ensure that ownership of the project site is secure in that no liens or other claims are in place. The title company will therefore carefully document all expenditures. For example, each contractor will sign a lien waiver confirming receipt of payment for services and forfeiting the right to place a lien on the property. This introduces an increased level of oversight and deters misappropriation.

Institutional lenders may also wish to have an architect review monthly construction expenditures to detect any signs of fraud during that stage. Finally, most lenders will require that the developer sign a contract stating that the project will be completed regardless of cost. This is known as a completion guarantee and assures investors that the JCE will be operational in order to create the 10 full-time jobs required under the EB-5 Program.

4. Seek Third-Party Reviews and Assistance

Investors should work with experienced advisors to safeguard their investments from fraud. While regional centers will generally work with an accountant to audit the performance of the fund manager, investors should ensure that this accountant is from an independent firm not associated with the project principals. If the project has received any national, state, or local funds, as with tax credits or grants, those governments will likely conduct their own audits of expenditures as well to ensure all funds have been spent as disclosed.

Investors should also work with their own attorneys to conduct due diligence and prepare any documentation necessary for the project and the EB-5 Program. An attorney experienced in the nuances of the program can offer valuable guidance when filing the I-526 and I-829 petitions and can assist the investor in detecting any signs of fraud by other parties.

Investors take on a considerable risk when participating in the EB-5 Program regardless of the possibility of fraud. As such, investors must use the strategies outlined above to confirm the integrity of any parties to the project and prevent their investments from falling victim to misappropriation.

Immigration and Financial Planning

Steps to Obtain an EB-5 Green Card

The EB-5 Immigrant Investor Pilot Program, which is overseen by U.S. Citizenship and Immigration Services (USCIS), allows foreign investors and their families to gain permanent resident status through qualifying investments. The process is relatively complex, but broadly speaking, investors must complete five basic steps in order to obtain lawful permanent resident status.

Step 1: Finding the Right EB-5 Project

The first step in obtaining U.S. residence through the EB-5 Program is to find the right project to invest in. Investors can either invest directly into a new commercial enterprise project or through a USCIS-approved regional center. Whether investing directly or through a regional center, EB-5 investors should conduct ample due diligence to ensure a prospective investment is a good match for them and that the regional center (if applicable) has a track record of success.

Direct investments require the direct creation of 10 full-time jobs, and so many investors opt to invest in projects sponsored through regional centers, which can also count indirect and induced jobs toward the job creation requirement. Additionally, regional centers enable EB-5 investors to easily pool their funds with other investors, which allows for larger projects and favorable job creation margins. Migration agents are often involved in matching potential EB-5 investors with compatible projects. In order to invest in EB-5 projects, foreign nationals must be considered accredited investors.

The EB-5 Program requires investments to be made in new commercial enterprises (NCEs), which are defined as for-profit businesses established after November 29, 1990, engaged in lawful commercial activity. Businesses formed before this date may be eligible for EB-5 investment if they have been restructured or expanded such that a 40% increase in net worth or number of employees has occurred.

EB-5 investors can also choose to invest in troubled businesses, which are defined as businesses that have experienced 20% or higher net loss in the past 12 or 24 months. For troubled business investments, EB-5 investors are not required to create 10 new full-time jobs—instead, the NCE must maintain employment at the pre-investment level.

Step 2: Investing the Necessary Capital and Filing an I-526 Petition

Once the investor has selected a project, he or she must invest the amount of capital required by the EB-5 visa program. A minimum investment of $1,000,000 is required unless the project is located within a TEA, in which case the minimum investment is $500,000. USCIS requires EB-5 investors either to make their investment in full and upfront or to demonstrate that their capital is irrevocably committed to the investment. Typically, the invested capital is placed in escrow until the investor's I-526 petition is approved.

The I-526 petition is filed with USCIS and must demonstrate that the proper amount of capital was invested in a project that is expected to generate the required 10 jobs per EB-5 investor. For the purposes of the EB-5 visa program, sufficient engagement entails either direct, day-to-day management in the NCE or a role in its policy formulation. NCEs are often structured as limited partnerships, in which case EB-5 investors are considered sufficiently engaged by virtue of their role as limited partners. USCIS also expects thorough documentation that proves the investor's funds were lawfully obtained.

Step 3: Obtaining Conditional Permanent Resident Status

After an applicant's I-526 petition is approved, he or she can apply for two-year, conditional permanent resident status. Investors who do not yet have an immigrant visa must submit Form DS-230 to the National Visa Center and be processed through their home country's U.S. consulate or embassy. Investors who are already lawfully residing in the United States must file Form I-485, which will change their status to conditional permanent resident. Typically, either process requires the assistance of an immigration attorney.

Conditional permanent resident status is effective for two years, during which time the investor must physically reside in the United States. The investor may travel abroad without jeopardizing his or her status, but certain limitations apply. In order for the conditions to ultimately be removed at the end of the two-year conditional period, the investor must also be able to demonstrate that the NCE he or she invested in and the investment itself were maintained throughout this time.

Step 4: Filing an I-829 Petition and Removing Conditions from Resident Status

Conditional permanent resident status expires after two years and cannot be renewed—in order to maintain permanent resident status, the investor must file an I-829 petition. This petition must be filed within the last 90 days of the conditional residence period and must demonstrate that the investor has fulfilled the requirements of the EB-5 green card program. Therefore, the petition and its accompanying documentation must clearly show that the required amount of capital was invested in an NCE that actually created or sustained the necessary number of jobs to meet the employment requirement

Step 5: Permanent Residence

Once the conditions are removed via approval of the investor's I-829 petition, the investor's status will convert to lawful permanent resident status granting the investor indefinite permanent resident status and work permission in the United States. Five years after they received their initial conditional permanent resident status, the investor and his or her family have the option to become U.S. citizens.

EB-5 Immigration Planning for Chinese Parents

The EB-5 Program provides a significant opportunity for investors seeking to immigrate to the United States to create a better future for their children. The growth of the middle class combined with the stressors of increasing competition in education, pollution and other environmental issues, and the limits imposed by an authoritarian government have created a booming market for U.S. visas among wealthy Chinese families. As such, investors often base their immigration and investment strategies on the needs of their children.

The EB-5 Program is a promising option for these investors. Under the regional center model in particular, an investor must invest $1,000,000 in a new commercial enterprise, but this required amount drops to $500,000 if the enterprise is located in a targeted employment area, meaning an area with a low population or a high unemployment rate. USCIS maintains a list of designated regional centers, which are monitored to ensure they fulfill the goals of the EB-5 Program and comply with U.S. laws. The investment must result in the creation of 10 full-time jobs in the area, and the investor is not required to manage the enterprise directly but must play a role in policy formulation as a voting partner.

This model offers several advantages to Chinese investors who wish to immigrate to the United States for the sake of their children, as it requires little direct involvement from the investor and costs less than other investment programs such as the EB-1C visa. Although USCIS does not release its approval rates for the adjudication of EB-5 visa petitions, investors who work with experienced regional centers, counsel, and other partners to adhere to the program requirements can achieve permanent residence in the United States as well as a return on their investments.

This section outlines the factors affecting Chinese investors' decisions to emigrate and provides a case study to illustrate the type of situation in which the EB-5 Program could be a viable option to achieve a family's goals.

Why Investors Choose to Immigrate to the United States

Prior to choosing an immigration strategy, potential investors should consult with an attorney experienced in the requirements and benefits of U.S. visa programs to determine which might suit their unique goals and circumstances. The following points should be addressed as part of this exploration process:

- Why do the investors hope to immigrate?
- How much money can the investors access for this process?
- Do the investors have children?
- If so, how many, and how old are they?
- Do the investors wish their children to attend school in the United States?
- Do the investors wish to conduct business in the United States?

- If so, do they wish to play an active or passive role in managing the business?
- Are the investors familiar with U.S. cultural practices, and do they speak English?

The EB-5 regional center model, described above, is well suited to investors who wish for their children to be able to immigrate but who may not themselves wish to immigrate or directly manage a U.S. business. The case study below illustrates the circumstances under which this may be the best option.

Example: The Case of Mei Chan

Mei is the CEO of a successful computer manufacturing company in Beijing that has multiple employees. She and her husband have an established social circle and lifestyle in China and do not wish to emigrate, and Mei additionally feels she would be unable to branch out successfully to the United States given her inability to speak English and her unfamiliarity with the business culture overseas. However, Mei and her husband have one son, Ling, who attends university in Los Angeles and wishes to remain in the United States after completing his studies. His parents want to help him achieve this goal.

Ling has majored in business, meaning he will face fierce competition for jobs after graduation as well as the additional hurdle of finding an employer who will sponsor his H-1B nonimmigrant visa and thereby allow him to remain in the United States. Also of concern are his chances of being selected as part of the annual H-1B lottery process USCIS uses to determine which visas will be adjudicated when demand outstrips supply, as it has done recently. Because of this, Ling would rather prefer to remain in the United States as a permanent resident and explore his own options for starting a business, so Mei has considered expanding overseas to allow Ling to apply for an L-1 visa and then permanent residence through the EB-1 Program.

However, this strategy is not ideal given that Mei would prefer to avoid doing business in the United States because of her unfamiliarity with that market. Ling and Mei would additionally have to build up the U.S. branch of the company for at least one year to allow Ling to qualify for a green card under the EB-1 Program, and doing so might not be possible given the challenges Mei would face in the initial expansion process. As Ling would have fairly little experience as a recent graduate at that point, Mei would likely have to make multiple trips to the United States to oversee the hiring of new employees, establish an office, and generally manage the launch of the U.S. branch. The cost of this expansion would be monumental, much more than the $500,000 or even $1,000,000 required for the EB-5 Program. However, direct investment through the EB-5 Program would pose similar issues, given that one of the requirements of that model is a willingness to directly manage the new commercial enterprise.

Given these circumstances, the EB-5 regional center model is the best option for Mei and Ling. To fulfill the requirements of the program, Mei can gift her son $500,000 to invest in a new commercial enterprise in a targeted employment area through a designated regional center, and Ling would therefore be able to file for an I-526 petition for conditional permanent residence. Taking on a more passive role in the management of the enterprise through the regional center would additionally allow Ling to gain valuable business experience and would avoid the issue of Mei having to take on a managerial role in the United States. If Mei and her husband later decide, perhaps in their retirement, that they wish to join their son in the United States, Ling could sponsor their green cards through an immediate relative petition.

Mei is representative of thousands of Chinese parents who wish to help their children achieve a better life in the United States. As a wealthy potential investor, Mei would have several options in terms of pursuing immigration, and she would most definitely consult with a qualified U.S. immigration lawyer to discuss which programs would benefit her and her son and allow them to meet their respective goals. Because the sole purpose of Mei establishing a business in the United States in this case would be to allow Ling to pursue a green card, the EB-1 and EB-5 direct investment options are not well suited to her needs, as she has no desire to immigrate herself or to manage a business abroad. A knowledgeable attorney would therefore recommend the EB-5 regional center model, which meets all Mei and Ling's investment and immigration criteria.

The regional center model is therefore ideal for the significant proportion of Chinese EB-5 investors who share these goals. Such investors can benefit from speaking with an attorney to learn more and further explore their options.

Minor Children as Primary EB-5 Applicants

Recent delays in the processing of Chinese EB-5 applications caused by retrogression quotas have caused many parents to seek to have their minor children named as primary investors in an I-526 petition. Whereas these children would otherwise have aged out of the system at 21 and therefore have been ineligible to immigrate as derivative beneficiaries with their parents under the EB-5 Program, being named as a primary applicant allows a child to later obtain a green card.

However, the issue of minor applicants poses certain legal risks to EB-5 projects and investors. This section discusses how this procedure is viewed under U.S. and Chinese law and how investors might approach the need to name a minor as a primary applicant for an EB-5 petition.

Minor Investors under U.S. Law

While USCIS regulations do not require that an EB-5 investor be of legal age to sign a contract, U.S. law makes such contracts risky for all parties involved with the EB-5 project. State laws specify that minors under a certain age, which varies from state to state but usually falls between 18 and 21, are not considered legally competent to sign contracts. Because of this, a minor investor who signs a subscription agreement would have the right to later void that agreement and reclaim the investment, meaning both investment funds and escrow banks will generally not accept funds from minor investors.

Despite this, USCIS considers 13 to be the maximum age at which a child can pay a reduced fee when filing an I-485 petition for permanent resident status, while children over 14 must pay the full adult fee. While not stated explicitly, this implies that minors over age 14 would be considered adults for the purposes of filing the original I-526 petition, as well. Additionally, USCIS has accepted minors as principal applicants for other employment visas, such as the EB-1A visa for "extraordinary ability aliens."

These issues remain untested as of this year, however, as no petitions have yet been filed by a derivative child as a principal applicant.

Minor Investors under Chinese Law

Chinese law allows parents or guardians to represent a child in legal matters including the signing of EB-5 subscription agreements. As such, EB-5 projects may wish to specify Chinese law as the governing law to execute such an agreement and other documents required for the EB-5 application to allow the parents to co-sign on behalf of the minor child, who would be considered the primary applicant. The parent would also be required in such a case to attest that he or she is the legal guardian of the minor child, that both are Chinese citizens, that the parent has reviewed all documents signed by the minor child, and that the parent has provided the EB-5 investment funds.

U.S. courts will generally accept the choice of law specified by the parties of a contract, in this case Chinese law as selected by the representatives of the EB-5 project and the investors. As the purpose of a subscription agreement is to allow the minor child to qualify for an EB-5 visa and as the parent has approved of and provided the funds for the investment, a U.S. court would be able to justify the use of Chinese law for the subscription agreement in the face of a legal challenge.

However, investors and EB-5 project representatives should be careful to review any state policies which might preclude the selection of Chinese law for these cases.

U.S. Legal Strategies for Investors

If an EB-5 project is unable or unwilling to select Chinese law for the subscription agreement, investors may be able to rely on other options under U.S. law. Below are two such strategies, these being gifting the funds to a minor or transferring the investment to the investment project outside of escrow.

Gifts or Transfers to Minors

Firstly, the parent or guardian of the child has the option of gifting funds to the minor applicant under the laws of the state where the EB-5 investment fund is based. Under the Uniform Gifts or Transfers to Minors Act, a version of which has been adopted in every U.S. state, parents and other persons are allowed to make a gift to a minor without a formal trust agreement with the provision that the person gifting the funds will control them until the minor reaches the age of majority as defined in that state. Additionally, the instrument conferring the funds must be structured as specified in the laws of the given state.

Because this arrangement means that both the custodian and the minor will be named on the subscription agreement, EB-5 projects adopting this strategy may run the risk of a greater chance for denial of the I-526 petition. While no such cases have yet been tested, the retrogression quotas have made aging out of the derivative immigration option a real possibility, and USCIS may see such cases in the near future, at which point investors will be able to refer to those rulings as a guideline.

Accepting Funds out of Escrow

As mentioned above, escrow banks in the United States are generally unwilling to accept funds from minor investors. If an escrow bank is unable to accept the subscription agreement, it may be willing to facilitate the transfer of the investment to the EB-5 investment fund outside of escrow with certain provisions. In this arrangement, an investor, in this case the minor child, will not receive any repayment from the escrow holdback if his or her I-526 petition is denied. As such, the EB-5 investment fund will need to prepare a separate agreement with the parent and the minor investor to specify that the investors waive both the deposit of their funds in an escrow account and any benefits they would have received if their funds were held in an escrow account.

The two strategies outlined above have not been tested in the context of EB-5 cases, so investors must ensure they work with experienced professionals to protect their assets with the proper legal agreements in the United States.

Future Considerations

Because the Chinese retrogression quotas emerged only in 2015, all procedures surrounding the I-526 applications of minor children as primary investors are part of unexplored legal territory. Demand from Chinese applicants, who represent a large majority of EB-5 investors, continues to grow, so regional centers and other project developers can expect to contend with the minor investor question in the coming years. It remains unclear whether USCIS will accept the strategies outlined above as part of an investor's EB-5 application, but they have stated that upcoming regulations may address this question.

Of additional concern is the stance of U.S. courts in the case of a dispute. In the meantime, EB-5 investors run risks in adopting these strategies to assign the role of primary applicant to a minor child. Given these limitations, EB-5 investment funds might choose to enter into contracts only with investors who meet the legal age for civil conduct in the target state, though this also carries the risk that any minor children might age out of the opportunity to immigrate to the United States as a derivative under the auspices of the EB-5 Program.

Changes to U.S. law might also resolve this issue. In its current state, the Child Status Protection Act, 8 U.S.C. § 1153(h), allows a child to deduct the amount of time a visa petition has been pending from his or her age. The alternative, to freeze a child's age as of the date of filing of a parent's I-526 petition, would allow parents to apply for the EB-5 Program themselves as intended without running out the clock on the potential for their children to immigrate. Congress may very well consider such a change in the coming months as the EB-5 Program is reevaluated.

The most plausible scenario is that aside from setting a clear age cut-off for principal EB-5 applicants, USCIS will adjudicate each case based on its unique circumstances. Investors and EB-5 project representatives therefore have the freedom to create agreements according to U.S. and Chinese laws as necessary to meet the needs of all parties to an arrangement, including a minor child as the primary investor if necessary. Key strategies as outlined above are to work under Chinese law, to gift the investment funds to a minor child, or to transfer the investment funds to the project out of escrow, but each of these has its drawbacks and uncertainties.

Luckily, with average waiting times of between five and six years, it is currently unlikely that an investor would need to set up an application with a minor child under 13, as such a child would still qualify as a derivative by the time his or her parent's I-526 petition were adjudicated. The status of children over 14 remains unclear, with USCIS treating that age as the cut-off for payment of the full adult filing fee for an I-485 petition. Without further clarification, Chinese investors and their U.S. investment fund counterparts must work within the current guidelines and legal limits.

Proving the Lawful Source of EB-5 Funds

Foreign investors are required under the EB-5 Program to document the lawful source of any funds invested in an NCE in the United States. USCIS therefore requests that investors provide supporting documents to evidence that all such funds have been obtained lawfully. This is required both by the EB-5 Program and by U.S. laws.

Investors are required to make an investment of $1,000,000 or $500,000 if the NCE is in a targeted employment area, this being an area with a low population or high unemployment. However, investors may also face administrative costs relating to the investment, and the funds used to cover that amount must also be sourced lawfully and documented in the materials provided to USCIS for the I-526 petition for conditional permanent residence.

The following subsections discuss methods to prove the most common lawful sources of EB-5 funds.

Salary

An investor using his or her salary to fund an investment must include the following documents with the I-526 petition:

- The investor must submit a capital source statement explaining in detail that the investment funds are derived from his or her salary. This must include the name of the company with which the investor has been employed as well as records of the investor's salary payments and the total amount accumulated over time. The investor must likewise provide bank statements proving receipt of those salary payments.
- If the investor has relied on a spouse to cover living expenses so as to save his or her salary for the EB-5 investment amount, the spouse must also provide a capital source statement explaining in detail his or her employment history and income over the time period during which the investment amount was accumulated.
- The investor must submit his or her employment contract as well as an income certificate from the employer supporting the salary payments over time as claimed in the capital source statement.
- Additionally, the investor must provide his or her personal income tax returns for the previous five years if available. If not, as may be the case for investors from countries where income tax is not collected, the investor may submit a declaration from a tax professional from his or her country of origin detailing the required information and explaining why records cannot be furnished.

If an investor uses salary payments to make up only part of the investment amount, the lawful source of the remaining amount must also be accounted for. This may require the investor to submit further documentation, such as a gift letter or property sale record, in addition to the materials listed above.

Stock Proceeds

When submitting the supporting documents for an I-526 petition, an investor using stock proceeds to fund his or her EB-5 investment will need to provide the following evidence:

- The investor must provide USCIS with a capital source statement detailing how the investor came to acquire the stock and that the proceeds from the sale of the stock are being used to fund the EB-5 investment. The investor must also provide USCIS with bank statements proving receipt of the proceeds from the sale of the stock.
- If the investor purchased the stock, USCIS additionally requires that he or she prove the legal source of the purchasing funds, as well. This may require the investor to submit employment and payment records, property sale records, bank statements, or other supporting documents on the source of the purchasing funds.
- The investor must additionally submit with the above supporting materials the written purchase contract and sale contract for the stock in question along with any share transfer agreements tracing the path of the stock from the initial owner to the investor and then to the subsequent purchaser.
- Additionally, the investor must submit individual income tax returns or other similar documents filed in the previous five years. An investor unable to provide income tax returns for legitimate reasons, as in the case of investors from countries where income tax is not collected, may instead be able to submit a declaration from a tax professional in his or her country of origin.

Gifted Funds

An investor using gifted funds to make up the investment amount will be required to submit the following evidence with the I-526 petition:

- The investor must provide a capital source statement detailing that the investment funds were gifted to him or her. The person who gifted the funds and the method by which those funds were acquired by that person must also be identified in detail. In this same vein, the investor must also provide bank statements proving receipt of the gifted funds.
- The person who has gifted the funds must likewise provide the investor with a capital source statement to be submitted with the petition materials. This statement must detail how the gifted amount was obtained and should agree with the investor's capital source statement in this regard.
- The person who has gifted the funds should also provide the investor with a gift letter stating the gifted amount and clarifying

223

that the EB-5 investor is not obligated to reimburse that amount. The investor must include this letter with the petition materials.

- The investor must submit his or her own personal income tax returns and other similar documents filed in the previous five years as well as those same documents filed by the person who gifted the investment funds for the same time frame. An investor unable to submit income tax returns may be able to instead submit a declaration from a tax professional in his or her country of origin detailing the required information and explaining why official records are unavailable.

An investor may need to provide additional documents depending on how the gifted funds were obtained. For example, funds obtained through the sale of stock or real estate would require the provision of property sale records or purchase and sale records in addition to the documents detailed above.

Real Estate Proceeds

Investors using real estate sale proceeds must provide the following documents:

- The investor must submit a capital source statement explaining that the investment funds are derived from the sale of real estate. Additionally, the investor must detail how he or she obtained the real estate, for example, how the funds used to purchase the real estate were acquired. The investor must also include a bank statement proving receipt of the sale proceeds.
- The investor must provide the purchase contract and sales contract for the
- To establish ownership of the property, the investor must submit an ownership certificate as well as any tax certificates to evidence the payment of taxes related to the property.
- The investor must also include with the application his or her personal income tax returns for the previous five years. An investor legitimately unable to provide these records, as in countries where government records are destroyed after a certain length of time, may instead furnish a declaration from a tax professional from his or her country of origin detailing the necessary information and stating why official records are no longer

An investor using real estate sale proceeds to fund an EB-5 investment will likely need to provide additional documentation to more fully trace the path of the investment funds prior to the purchase of the real estate. For example, an investor who has been gifted the real estate property will need to submit a gift letter and capital source statement from the person who has bestowed the property, whereas a person who has purchased real estate using his or her salary will need to support that claim with employment records and additional bank statements.

Investors and regional centers should seek the services of financial advisors and attorneys experienced with the unique requirements of the EB-5 Program to ensure that any documents submitted with the I-526 petition support the lawful source of the investment funds. As lawful fund sourcing is required not only by the EB-5 Program but also by U.S. law, investors and regional centers can avoid legal consequences and improve the likelihood of a successful application by ensuring that all financial documentation is thorough and accurate.

Consequences of Material Changes for EB-5 Projects

When adjudicating visa petitions filed under the EB-5 Program, USCIS allows for a degree of flexibility between project documents and actual outcomes. Though ideal circumstances would have the project proceed exactly as planned in the documents submitted with investors' original I-526 petitions, commercial projects face the possibility of unforeseen events and contingencies that create discrepancies between any original documents and those submitted when filing the I-829 to remove the conditions of residence.

Such discrepancies become an issue when they materially affect a project and thus put at risk investors' visa eligibility under the EB-5 Program. Material changes are those concerning significant aspects of a project, which therefore have the potential to affect adjudication decisions. These include changes made in an effort to remedy deficiencies in a petition between filing and adjudication and other changes affecting major aspects of a project, such as fund sourcing or elements of the business plan.

When do material changes create an issue?

Material changes are not in and of themselves a problem within EB-5 projects. For example, USCIS will not deny an I-829 petition simply because a project has strayed from the plan outlined in the I-526 documents if the investor can demonstrate that the original business plan and other project documents were submitted in good faith and that all efforts were made to comply with those conditions. Additionally, the investor must demonstrate that the material changes made during the conditional residence period have not affected his or her eligibility under the EB-5 Program, as would be the case if investment funds ceased to be at risk during that time, for example.

Material changes are also not an issue if made between approval of an exemplar I-526 petition and the actual filing of a petition by an investor afterward. However, in this scenario investors would not benefit from potentially shortened wait times resulting from the preapproval of the project, as USCIS would review the project documents a second time to verify continued eligibility.

A problem arises when changes affect information USCIS may use to adjudicate a visa petition, such as changes made between filing and adjudication. For example, if an investor files his or her I-526 petition based on the establishment of a new restaurant but later decides to instead establish a bed and breakfast using the investment amount before the petition is adjudicated, USCIS would likely deny the I-526 petition based on that significant change to the business plan.

Material versus Nonmaterial Changes

USCIS has followed fairly consistent patterns in deciding which changes are considered material versus nonmaterial for the purposes of visa petition adjudication:

- Changes in the scope of the investment project, such as an investor switching projects entirely, are considered material. For example, if an investor files his or her petition for a project associated with one regional center but later decides to invest with a different center or with a different job-creating entity within the same regional center, the I-526 petition would be denied.
- Changes to aspects of the investment project that do not affect its overall eligibility are not considered material. For example, if an investor files an I-526 petition with the intention to establish an Italian restaurant but then chooses to focus on Mediterranean cuisine in general, such a change would not affect the eligibility of the project or the adjudication of the I-526
- Changes to the structure of an investment or affecting the actual investment of funds are considered material. For example, consider a case in which an investor has stipulated certain clauses in the investment agreement that guarantee the return of funds upon a certain date. USCIS determines that this arrangement means the funds are not at risk and issues a request for evidence with regard to the I-526 petition. If the investor nullifies those clauses of the agreement, this would be considered a material change.
- Changes that simply clarify inconsistencies in loan agreements or otherwise do not depart substantially from the original documents are not considered material. For example, if an investor submits documents with the I-526 in which the loan agreement contains an unintentional inconsistency and later amends the agreement to rectify that error, the change would not be considered material.

In addition to the above, USCIS tends to be lenient in cases where investors anticipate potential changes when filing their I-526 petitions. For example, in a regional center project in which funds might be repaid early and then redeployed to another job-creating entity so as to ensure the investment amount remains at risk, the I-526 petition should account for this possibility so that when the time comes to file the I-829, USCIS will be aware of the reason for the change in fund deployment.

Strategies for Investors

Investors must take into consideration the potential consequences of material changes for the adjudication of their EB-5 visa petitions. To avoid hurdles brought about by such changes, investors should consider adopting the following three key strategies:

- Vet projects carefully to verify that they will proceed according to the plans provided with the offering documents. A business's activities during the conditional residence period are most relevant in this regard.
- Work with regional centers that have demonstrated the ability to successfully complete EB-5 projects. These centers are at a lower risk of losing their designation, an event which would force associated investors to materially change their investment strategies.
- Ensure that the I-526 petition is comprehensive in demonstrating how the investor has fulfilled or will fulfill the requirements of the program. If USCIS issues a request for evidence regarding a significant aspect of the petition, rectifying that oversight might require a material change. Any changes following a request for evidence should stress continuity between the new documents and the originals.

Material changes following approval of the I-526 petition and the granting of conditional permanent residence are of less concern. However, investors should notify USISC of any significant developments in preparation for filing the I-829, which must demonstrate how the project has attempted to adhere to the original project documents. If investors continually consider how USCIS might view any changes to a project, the various issues outlined above can be proactively avoided.

Redeployment: A Viable Strategy for EB-5 Investors

With demand for EB-5 visas having recently outstripped supply, USCIS began 2019 with a backlog of almost 22,000 EB-5 visa petitions awaiting adjudication. The resulting wait times, especially for Chinese applicants, among whom the EB-5 Program has become increasingly popular over the past several years, have prompted investors to explore new strategies to ensure they continue to meet the conditions of the program.

A main area of concern has centered on the requirement that EB-5 investment funds be maintained at risk throughout an investor's conditional residence period, beginning from the time he or she enters the United States following approval of the I-526 petition and ending when the I-829 petition is adjudicated and unconditional permanent residence is granted. With retrogression causing wait times of six to 10 years for some investors, fulfilling this requirement has become increasingly challenging.

This section examines the redeployment of investment funds within a new commercial enterprise, one adaptation strategy investors have used in response to this obstacle.

What is the at-risk requirement?

The purpose of the EB-5 Program is to create jobs within the United States. As such, those filing for visas under the program are required to make an initial investment of $500,000 or $1,000,000 in a new commercial enterprise depending on whether the project is located in a TEA, which is a region experiencing unemployment levels significantly higher than the national average. This investment amount must be made available in its entirety to the new commercial enterprise for the explicit purpose of job creation.

That the investment must be maintained at risk means the investor cannot be repaid this initial amount until his or her conditional residence period has ended. While the investor is permitted to see a return on that investment, such as a distribution of profits from the operation of the new commercial enterprise, the original loan to the enterprise cannot itself be repaid. Guidelines from USCIS have additionally clarified that the amount cannot simply be held in escrow by the new commercial enterprise during this time but must be continuously deployed in a project.

This requirement creates a problem for investors dealing with increased wait times as a result of retrogression: if the wait time for adjudication extends beyond the term of the loan and the loan is repaid during or even prior to the conditional residence period, the funds are no longer at risk. In this scenario, the investor would fail to meet the EB-5 Program requirements and would risk losing his or her visa. For investors who have relocated their families and created new lives in the United States in an effort to obtain permanent residence under the program, this possibility poses a significant risk.

Redeployment of Investment Funds

The majority of EB-5 investors apply through the regional center model, in which the regional center as the new commercial enterprise loans the investment funds to a second enterprise responsible for job creation. In the case of a real estate development, for example, the regional center loans the funds to a development firm, which uses those funds to create construction jobs. At the end of the loan term, the firm repays the loan, and the regional center returns the funds to the investor.

Traditionally, loan terms of five years satisfied the at-risk requirement well, providing enough time for the investor to file and receive approval for an I-526 petition, live in the United States for a conditional residence period of two years, and then file and receive approval for an I-829 petition. However, increased wait times mean these loan terms are no longer sufficient and indeed create an additional risk for the investor: aside from the possibility of the new commercial enterprise failing during the wait, the investor also risks losing his or her visa by failing to meet the at-risk requirement.

While resolving the issue of early repayment, longer loan terms are not desirable in all cases. As such, redeployment creates a potential solution for this issue by allowing the new commercial enterprise, the regional center, to ensure the investment funds are maintained at risk by continually deploying repaid funds into new job-creating projects. While the initial deployment of the investment must fill the job creation quota, redeployment simply allows investors to meet EB-5 Program requirements in cases where the loan is repaid prior to the end of conditional residence.

Investors should keep the following key points in mind when considering redeployment as a potential fund management strategy:

- The potential for redeployment must be outlined in the private placement memorandum for the initial offering. Although it is not necessarily possible to plan for redeployments years in advance, as the business climate may change in the intervening years, the plan should be as detailed as possible so as to allow investors to make informed decisions and minimize risk.
- The EB-5 Program does not allow for material changes to projects, meaning substantive changes not outlined in the business plan approved with the I-526 petition. As such, as mentioned above, job creation must occur during the first deployment of funds, which is the focus of the original business plan.

USCIS has not yet published definitive guidelines as to what constitutes an acceptable redeployment of funds, though redeployment to a project similar to the one outlined in the original I-526 business plan should theoretically meet the criteria. As wait times continue to pose an issue for EB-5 investors over the coming years, adjudication decisions will likely provide clarification on this matter and allow investors and project developers alike to adapt with appropriate redeployment strategies.

The Potential of Private Equity Real Estate (PERE) Funds for EB-5 Investors

Private equity real estate funds have recently emerged as a promising avenue for investors already in the process of achieving permanent residence in the United States under the EB-5 Program. The potential for changes in the program have encouraged EB-5 practitioners to diversify their business models, and investors may also seek multiple investment avenues in an effort to provide maximum financial security for themselves and their families.

Although Congress has renewed the EB-5 Program until September 2019 and will likely continue to do so, lawmakers face pressure to review targeted employment area designations in light of the fact that investors are generally more attracted to large cities such as New York and Los Angeles, leaving rural areas lacking. As job creation is one of the pillars of the EB-5 Program and such areas typically suffer from higher unemployment, Congress may consider redrawing the map concerning targeted investment areas.

Such a change would present not only a shift in the program but also an opportunity for foreign investors seeking additional investment opportunities in the United States. Real estate is a relatively stable asset which can offer consistent growth, and regional center managers have thus begun to investigate facilitating investments in private equity real estate (PERE) funds as well as EB-5 projects. The United States offers one of the most promising commercial real estate investment environments for foreign investors, and PERE funds are considered worldwide to be among the safest investment methods because they are not affected by volatility in public markets.

This section discusses how PERE funds are a reliable recommendation for EB-5 investors seeking to explore avenues of investment aside from their initial EB-5 commitment. Regional centers and other EB-5 practitioners can therefore harness the opportunities offered by PERE funds to create sustainable investment models for their clients.

The Benefits of PERE Funds

PERE funds make up a significant amount of assets under management worldwide, with real estate investment reaching $1.8 trillion in the 12 months leading up to October 2018. Each fund is overseen by an experienced manager with knowledge of the unique nuances of the regional market, and most funds are diversified to further lessen the risk to investors, as underperformance in one market is balanced by over-performance in another. PERE funds have an additional advantage in that they allow investors to avoid trade and business income tax by investing through a blocker corporation rather than directly in the private equity fund. In this model, the investor is not considered a partner in the fund, allowing for a reduction in his or her taxable income basis.

For Chinese investors, who comprise nearly 80% of EB-5 visa applicants, U.S. PERE funds can provide additional security. The government devaluation of the renminbi in 2015 has encouraged Chinese investors to adopt more caution when building their portfolios. Nonetheless, the growth of the middle class in China has led to an abundance of capital and a strong desire to safeguard funds against further volatility in the domestic market. It is for this reason that PERE funds using foreign currencies have consistently raised more capital among Chinese investors than those using the renminbi. In 2013, according to a report by Chinese commercial bank Ping An Bank, foreign currency PERE funds making up only 3% of the total number of funds in China accounted for nearly a quarter of the entire amount of funds invested.

These figures highlight the desire among Chinese investors to safely commit their capital in foreign markets. As such, for regional center managers and other EB-5 practitioners in the United States who are frequently approached by those seeking additional opportunities to invest, PERE funds are an excellent recommendation, providing significantly less risk than other investment options as well as proven returns. Practitioners seeking to expand their client bases and diversify their business models can additionally benefit from working with PERE funds, which can facilitate relationships with networks of investors both nationally and internationally.

Partnering with PERE Funds

EB-5 practitioners seeking to branch out into the PERE fund market face the challenge of finding suitable partners in this endeavor. While most practitioners have established a network of experienced consultants over the years with the necessary credentials and knowledge for their particular areas of expertise, professionals such as residential real estate brokers and property managers may lack experience in managing complex portfolios for foreign investors. As such, these consultants may outsource the work of building and maintaining the investment assets to colleagues specializing in those areas.

This model introduces increased risks for investors, as the original EB-5 practitioner will not have the ability to vet each party, whose ability and commitment to managing the investment may vary. The involvement of multiple parties also increases the risk of misappropriation or fraud, which practitioners should be careful to guard against. As such, while existing connections may continue to offer support in other areas, they are likely not the best candidates to facilitate the acquisition and management of a diverse portfolio of real estate holdings for foreign investors.

Partnering with a local PERE fund provides practitioners with the assurance that the asset will be managed by a devoted professional experienced in the unique requirements of PERE investors. Unlike consultants who focus narrowly on their own roles, fund managers are able to view the portfolio of real estate assets as a whole and thereby assure investors of balanced performance over time. PERE fund managers generally have a proven ability to navigate the U.S. real estate market and create profitable assets, and because they have a vested interest in the success of the investment, they are better able to work in investors' best interests.

Additionally, because PERE fund managers are experienced in the acquisition of real estate assets, they are typically able to leverage existing business relationships and negotiate proprietary deals, thereby eliminating the need for a real estate broker, allowing for more efficient acquisition of new properties, and ensuring those properties are purchased at the best price. The fund manager will typically also consolidate the acquisition and maintenance process, including asset sourcing, payment via escrow, and property management, among other services, to minimize risks for investors.

Foreign investors coming from the EB-5 context, in which fraud and misappropriation of funds have become increasing concerns in recent years, will be assured by the fact that PERE funds are overseen by the Securities and Exchange Commission as well as the Financial Industry Regulatory Authority, a private corporation which regulates brokers in the United States. PERE funds are subject to strict reporting and auditing requirements, resulting in a transparent environment for investors. An additional level of assurance exists in that fund managers are only compensated once investors have received their shares of the profit plus interest.

Foreign investors, especially those facing an increasingly volatile market in China, can benefit from diversifying their investments in the United States in addition to their primary investments in EB-5 projects. Regional center managers and other EB-5 practitioners can play a key role in facilitating stateside relationships for such investors. In expanding their client bases and business models to take advantage of the promise of PERE funds, practitioners can allow investors to achieve higher returns and additional security in their lives post EB-5.

The Visa Process

I-526 Petition Requirements

Once an EB-5 investor has selected a project and made the necessary investment, he or she must complete Form I-526, Immigration Petition by Alien Entrepreneur, and submit it, along with all supporting documents, to U.S. Citizenship and Immigration Services (USCIS). USCIS will then evaluate Form I-526 and determine whether the applicant is eligible for an EB-5 visa.

Usually, immigration attorneys compile and submit I-526 petitions on behalf of their clients. The USCIS fee for filing Form I-526 is $1,500. If any information is missing or inadequate, USCIS will send an RFE, which will delay the approval of the petition. The average processing time for Form I-526 is around 14 months.

USCIS evaluates an investor's I-526 petition based on the following five (5) criteria:

1. Investment Amount Meets EB-5 Requirements

An EB-5 investor's I-526 petition must demonstrate that the minimum required capital was invested in an NCE. For projects located within a TEA, the minimum investment amount is $500,000. Projects not located in a TEA, however, require a minimum investment of $1,000,000.

In order to meet USCIS requirements, the invested capital must also be considered "at risk" and irrevocably committed to the NCE.

2. Investment Capital Was Lawfully Obtained

The EB-5 investor must also be able to clearly demonstrate on his or her I-526 petition that the invested capital was obtained lawfully. The investor must trace the capital from its source—a salary, investment distribution, sale of property, etc.—to the NCE. Funds given to the investor must also be traced back to their source.

If the investor earned money in the United States without the proper employment status, those funds cannot be invested since they are not considered lawfully obtained.

3. Capital Was Invested in a New Commercial Enterprise

An EB-5 investor's I-526 petition must demonstrate that the necessary amount of lawfully obtained capital was invested in an NCE.

A new commercial enterprise is defined as a for-profit entity engaged in ongoing, lawful commercial business activity. The enterprise must have been established after November 29, 1990. Furthermore, the NCE can be structured in a number of ways (e.g., sole proprietorship, partnership, joint venture, corporation, etc.), and it may be public or private.

4. New Commercial Enterprise Creates Required Number of Jobs

Investing in an NCE is not, by itself, sufficient for EB-5 visa approval. USCIS requires that the NCE create at least 10 full-time jobs for each EB-5 investor involved.

For those who make direct investments, these 10 positions must be created by the NCE itself, and they must be permanent, full time (at least 35 hours per week), and filled by W-2 employees. Positions filled by nonimmigrant aliens or the investor and his or her family cannot be counted toward the minimum job creation requirement. The investor's I-526 petition must demonstrate that at least 10 jobs have been or will be created. To demonstrate future job creation, the I-526 must include a clear description of the NCE's hiring plan, including which positions will be created and when they will be filled.

When sponsored by a regional center, an NCE must still create a minimum of 10 positions per EB-5 investor, and these must also be full-time, but they can be created either directly or indirectly. Indirect jobs are those created through the revenues of the NCE. Any indirect jobs counted toward an investor's minimum job creation requirement must be demonstrated in the investor's I-526 petition through an economic report.

5. Investor Is Actively Involved in the New Commercial Enterprise

In addition to demonstrating that a sufficient amount of lawfully obtained capital was invested in an NCE—and that the investment was responsible for the creation of 10 job positions—an I-526 petition must demonstrate that the EB-5 investor is actively engaged in managing the NCE.

Those who make direct investments in an NCE may manage the enterprise, act as a member of the entity's Board of Directors, maintain voting control, or otherwise demonstrate day-to-day involvement with the business.

Typically, NCEs sponsored by a regional center are structured as limited partnerships. In such cases, an EB-5 investor is a limited partner, and within the framework of the Uniform Limited Partnership Act, he or she is considered sufficiently engaged in managing the NCE to satisfy the requirements of USCIS. The same applies for limited liability companies.

Conclusion

USCIS approves I-526 petitions that clearly meet the criteria listed above. Once approved, investors and their families can apply for their EB-5 visas. EB-5 visas grant foreign nationals conditional lawful permanent resident status for two years, at which time the investor must file Form I-829, Petition by Entrepreneur to Remove Conditions. This petition must clearly demonstrate that the applicant's investment in the NCE was sustained for the two-year conditional period and that the necessary jobs were created.

Visa Interview Preparation for EB-5 Investors

Once an EB-5 investor's I-526 petition has been approved by USCIS, the investor and any dependent family members living outside the United States can apply for immigrant visas. This application, Form DS-260, is submitted through the U.S. embassy or consulate in the investor's home country.

After the application is reviewed by the U.S. National Visa Center, the investor and his or her family will be notified of when they will be interviewed and what documentation they will need to bring. This immigrant visa interview will be conducted at the U.S. embassy or consulate in the investor's home country and is intended to determine the applicant's admissibility into the United States.

The interviewer will review the documentation provided by the applicant and will ask related questions. Therefore, before this interview, the investor should review all the required documentation and ensure it is accurate. Additionally, interviewees must know the content of the documents under consideration and should be prepared to answer any related questions.

Documents Needed for the EB-5 Visa Interview

Each person being interviewed will need the following documentation, as applicable:
- Birth certificate
- Marriage certificates
- Divorce decrees
- Police certificates
- Color passport photograph
- Passport (valid until at least six months after the intended date of U.S. entry)
- Sealed results of a medical examination
- A copy of his or her Form DS-260 submission

In addition to these personal documents, the investor must provide evidence that the appropriate amount of capital has been released from escrow for use in the EB-5 project. Typically, a letter from the financial institution that manages the project's escrow account is sufficient evidence.

Any documents not written in either English or the official language of the interviewee's home country must be accompanied by a translation.

EB-5 Visa Interview Questions

An applicant may be denied an immigrant visa for various reasons, which include a misrepresentation of the material facts in Form DS-260, prior illegal entry into the United States, criminal history, and more.

An applicant should adequately prepare to answer questions regarding his or her past, especially items that might be considered red flags. The interview might also include questions about any prior visits to the United States.

Additionally, the investor should be prepared to answer questions about his or her I-526 petition, the new commercial enterprise he or she has invested in, and the source of the capital used for the EB-5 investment.

Adequate Preparation

The success of the visa application process is not solely determined by having all the right documentation—an immigrant visa applicant must be prepared for his or her interview. At this point in the EB-5 visa interview process, an investor should strongly consider seeking the counsel of a qualified EB-5 professional who can help the investor and his or her family work through their immigrant visa applications and interviews.

On the day of the interview, each applicant should arrive early with all of the necessary documentation. Typically, immigrant visa interviews take 30 to 45 minutes.

Forms I-485 (Change Status) and DS-260

These applications make it possible to achieve conditional permanent resident status and are typically filed with the assistance of an immigration attorney.

Form I-485

EB-5 immigrant investors who are already in the United States can file an I-526 petition to have their status changed. Approval of Form I-526 allows the applicant and each dependent to file an I-485 application to become conditional permanent residents in the United States. It typically requires a fee of $985 and a biometrics fee of $85.

Biographical information must be recorded on Form I-485 so USCIS can determine the eligibility of the applicant. Approval of the application allows applicants to adjust their visa status or apply for permanent residence. The assistance of an immigration attorney is often required.

I-485 Requirements

To have Form I-485 accepted by USCIS, the following requirements must be met:

1. Proof of eligibility: The applicant received Form I-797C when their I-526 petition was approved. A copy of this form should be submitted with Form I-485.

2. Personal records: The applicant must include copies of his or her birth certificate and any marriage and divorce certificates.

3. Photos: The applicant must submit two identical photographs taken within the previous 30 days.

4. Passport and nonimmigration visas: Copies of all immigration-related documents and complete passport must be included.

5. Criminal history records: The applicant must include written evidence of criminal history, if any.

6. Medical records: Copies of medical exam results and vaccination records must be included.

7. Biographic information: A completed Form G-325A must be submitted for applicants between age 14 and 79.

8. Biometrics: After submission of Form I-485, USCIS will notify applicants where to go for their biometrics services, which will include fingerprinting.

I-485 Application Process

Form I-485 is submitted by mail to the USCIS lockbox facility in Arizona or Texas.

Currently, when the applicant's I-526 petition is accepted, the I-485 application can be filed immediately by the applicant's immigration attorney. A filing fee of $985 and a biometric fee of $85 must accompany the application. Applicants age 79 or older are not required to pay the $85 biometrics fee.

The processing time for the I-485 application is usually six to 12 months. USCIS notifies applicants by email or physical mail when their applications have been processed.

EB-5 applicants can file Form I-765, Application for Employment, which allows them to work while their I-485 application is being processed. They can also travel during the processing time by submitting Form I-131, Application for Travel Document. EB-5 applicants are granted two-year conditional permanent residence upon approval of their I-485 application.

Following the two years of conditional permanent residence, the applicant may file an I-829 petition to remove conditions. Upon approval of the I-829 by USCIS, the EB-5 investor obtains full permanent residence. The investor, spouse, and unmarried children under age 21 may then live and work in the United States permanently.

Form DS-260

Upon the approval of his or her I-526 petition, an EB-5 investor and any eligible family members not yet living in the United States must file Form DS-260. This is filed by EB-5 investors and eligible family members at the U.S. consulate or embassy in their home nations; an interview is required. An immigration attorney may file this form for the applicant. Once approved, the DS-260 grants the applicant an immigrant visa that allows conditional permanent residence in the United States.

DS-260 Application Basics

Upon the approval of his or her I-526 petition, an EB-5 investor and any eligible family members not yet living in the United States must file Form DS-260, Application for Immigrant Visa and Alien Registration. For EB-5 investors already in the United States, Form I-485 must be filed instead.

The DS-260 application is filed with the U.S. consulate or embassy in the investor's home nation. The investor and each family member seeking to live in the United States must file a separate Form DS-260, and once approved, the applicant is granted conditional permanent resident status in the United States.

DS-260 Application Process

In Part I of Form DS-260, the applicant provides biographical information; this part of the form is completed and submitted by the applicant and may involve the assistance of an immigration attorney. In addition to basic biographical information, Part I of Form DS-260 requires information about previous places of residence, the applicant's job history going back 10 years, and any record of military service.260260

A consular worker helps the applicant complete Part II of Form DS-260 during the interview conducted at the U.S. consulate or embassy in the applicant's home country. For this interview, the applicant will be required to provide certain documentation, which may include his or her birth certificate, passport, and any marriage or divorce certificates.

Once the interview is finished, the DS-260 application is signed and the process is complete.

EB-5 Conditional Permanent Resident Status (CLPR)

Under the Immigration Reform and Control Act of 1986 (IRCA) and the Illegal Immigration Reform and Immigrant Responsibility Act of 1996 (IIRAIRA), eligible immigrants can apply for permanent resident status through the EB-5 visa program based upon a qualified EB-5 investment. Once their application is approved, EB-5 investors are awarded conditional permanent resident status.

CLPR Expiration

Once a foreign national's permanent resident status is approved, the two-year CLPR period begins. Upon approving an immigrant's EB-5 conditional permanent resident status, U.S. Citizenship and Immigration Services (USCIS) will issue a permanent resident card, commonly referred to as a green card. The green card shows the approval date and expiration date of an immigrant's conditional resident status.

Two years after approval, EB-5 conditional permanent resident status expires automatically. A foreign national whose CLPR status has expired may face deportation.

I-829 Petition to Remove Conditions on Immigration Status

In order to remove the conditions on permanent resident status, an EB-5 investor must file an I-829 petition with USCIS within 90 days of the expiration of his or her CLPR status. An I-829 must demonstrate to USCIS that the foreign national made an investment in a U.S. commercial enterprise in accordance with the EB-5 visa program. The contents of an I-829 petition will need to include proof that the EB-5 investment generated the necessary employment (e.g., I-9s, W-2s, and payroll records) as well as the investment's business license, its property lease, its financial records, etc.

Once USCIS approves the I-829 petition, the applicant's resident status is no longer conditional. (Note that the two-years of residence during the CLPR period are included when determining length of residence for naturalization.) If, however, an EB-5 investor fails to submit an I-829 petition within 90 days of the expiration of his or her CLPR status, permanent resident status will be terminated and the U.S. Department of Homeland Security will issue a Notice to Appear (NTA) in removal proceedings.

The United States will deport a foreign national and his or her dependents unless he or she is able to demonstrate that extenuating circumstances prevented the timely submission of the I-829 petition.

Primary Challenge to Removing Conditions on Immigration Status

Properly preparing and submitting the I-829 petition represents the primary challenge to removing conditions from an EB-5 investor's permanent resident status.

In order to remove the conditions on his or her immigration status, an EB-5 investor must prove to USCIS that the original requirements of the approved I-526 petition have been met. Particularly, this involves clearly demonstrating that the required investment was made—either $1,000,000 or $500,000 if the investment was in a TEA—and that this investment created 10 full-time jobs. As a result, having a properly prepared I-829 petition is essential.

Every year, a few investors choose to file their I-526 petition on their own—without the aid of an immigration attorney or firm that specializes in EB-5 investments. For such investors, it is vital that they fully understood all the requirements of the EB-5 visa program and the conditions that apply to their immigration status.

If USCIS determines that an investment does not fulfill all the requirements set forth in the investor's approved I-526 petition, the I-829 petition to remove the conditions on the investor's permanent resident status will be denied—and the investor and his or her family may face deportation.

Each EB-5 Investor's Situation Is Unique

Each EB-5 investor's situation is unique, and so each I-526 petition is unique. As a result, the requirements that must be fulfilled and demonstrated in an I-829 petition are specific to each investor.

For instance, whether or not the commercial enterprise is located within a TEA determines how much capital must be invested by an EB-5 investor. Also, the means by which the investment was made—either a direct investment or an investment facilitated by an approved regional center—determines the kinds of jobs that can be counted toward the job creation requirement.

Because most foreign nationals who consider an EB-5 investment do so specifically to obtain permanent resident status, ensuring that the process is handled correctly from start to finish is essential. As a result, we recommend that anyone considering an EB-5 investment consult with a professional company to ensure all the requirements of the EB-5 visa program are met.

Processing Times for EB-5 Program Investors

The EB-5 Program currently has the longest processing time of any employment-based immigrant visa category. As any investments under this program must remain at risk throughout the visa application process and until the investor's I-829 petition is adjudicated, investors face considerable risk due to processing times. This section outlines each stage of the EB-5 process so investors can learn whether the program is well suited to their immigration goals and time frames.

Step 1: Form I-526

The first stage of applying to the EB-5 Program is to submit Form I-526, Immigration Petition by Alien Entrepreneur, with USCIS. This form declares the investor's intent to immigrate to the United States under the EB-5 Program and provides detailed evidence that the investor has made or is making an investment in a qualifying new commercial enterprise that will create 10 full-time jobs within the two years of the conditional residence period. Supporting evidence such as bank statements and a business plan are necessary to corroborate the information submitted.

USCIS has stated that the I-526 petition has a current average processing time of over 14 months. However, many petitions take over two years to adjudicate, and this delay puts a strain on investors, who are forced to accept additional risk and to perfectly time their job creation so as to adhere to the program requirements. While investors have the option of filing a writ of mandamus with the U.S. courts to compel USCIS to adjudicate their petitions, this process takes time and costs money.

Step 2: Consular Processing or Adjustment of Status

Approval of the I-526 petition prompts the next stage of the process, wherein investors apply for conditional two-year permanent residence in the United States. For investors residing overseas, the second step is consular processing, whereas for investors holding nonimmigrant status in the United States, the second step is adjustment of status. Each of these is outlined below.

Consular Processing

Investors and their derivative family members must file either the DS-230 or the DS-260 application with the National Visa Center (NVC) to gain admission to the United States. After the NVC reviews an application, it is forwarded to the U.S. consulate in the investor's country of origin for processing and so the applicant can be interviewed. Chinese investors will be interviewed at the U.S. consulate in Guangzhou, for example. Wait times between the NVC and the consulate are also lengthy, sometimes over one year.

Chinese EB-5 investors should keep in mind that the current retrogression quotas have introduced further delays in the application process. Investors with approved I-526 petitions must review the USCIS issues each month to determine when they are eligible to file their DS-230 or DS-260 applications with the NVC. Most Chinese investors have a final action date two years after their I-526 filing date, meaning even those whose I-526 petitions are approved earlier than that may need to wait two years before being able to enter the United States as a conditional permanent resident.

Adjustment of Status

Investors and their derivative family members in the United States with nonimmigrant status must submit Form I-485 to adjust their status to that of a conditional permanent resident. While adjustment of status is generally faster than consular processing, investors must again review the USCS filing charts each month to determine by what date they will be eligible to submit their I-485 applications.

For Chinese investors, retrogression will affect the filing date for adjustment of status regardless, as well, meaning a wait following approval of the I-526 petition. While it is possible for an investor and his or her family to maintain nonimmigrant status in the United States throughout the waiting period, consular processing through the NVC is sometimes the only option for those who cannot.

Step 3: Form I-829

After an investor has entered the United States as a conditional permanent resident, he or she will have two years to prove that the EB-5 investment has created 10 full-time jobs. Within 90 days of this deadline, the investor must file an I-829 petition for removal of conditions of permanent residence. USCIS has given the current wait times for adjudication as 15 months, but it may take much longer than that. The fact that the investment is at risk throughout this process creates an additional hurdle for investors.

At the end of this process, investors are not guaranteed a green card, as the I-829 petition approval is based on whether the investment funds have created the requisite number of jobs. The EB-5 Program requires that the investment be at risk throughout this time period, meaning each investor faces some level of uncertainty. While investors are permitted to insure the investment with a third party, that insurance itself is also placed at risk if the third party goes out of business. Therefore, if a new enterprise fails before the investor has filed his or her I-829 petition, USCIS may deny the petition because the jobs no longer exist, meaning the investor may lose the investment and will additionally be ineligible for a green card.

The above factors mean that the EB-5 Program is not suited for every investor. Chinese investors especially face potential wait times of over six years between filing of the I-526 petition and adjudication of the I-829, meaning the investment is at risk during that time, and job creation must be timed within the appropriate two-year window. Investors have the option of instead applying for another employment-based visa, such as any one of the EB-1, EB-2, EB-3, or EB-4 Programs, to gain entry to the United States and earn a green card.

The EB-5 Program has specific requirements and poses significant risks for certain investors. As such, those wishing to apply for the program must consider the wait times and associated risks to their investments as outlined above and conduct their due diligence to determine whether the EB-5 Program is right for them.

EB-5 Program Processing Statistics

USCIS EB-5 petition processing times from January 2014 to October 2015 reveal that I-924 processing times have dropped by several months, while I-829 and I-526 times remain stable. This is illustrated in Figure 22.

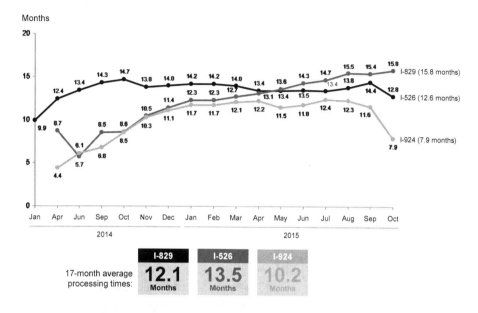

Figure 22. Petition processing times, 2014–2015.

I-526 USCIS Form for Immigrant Petition by Alien Entrepreneur

While the Investor Program Office (IPO) struggled to keep up with the number of I-526 petitions submitted from 2010 to 2017, it has finally reversed course. In 2018, the IPO processed more than twice the number of I-526 petitions it received, cutting down on its large backlog and reducing 2019 wait times to less than one year. This is a marked decrease from the 13-month average processing time from 2015. It is possible that the current shorter processing times might increase slightly given the recent influx of new I-526 petitions caused by the September 30, 2019, extension deadline.

I-829 USCIS Form for Petition by Alien Entrepreneur to Remove Temporary Conditions

Based on the most recently released USCIS data, processing times for I-829 applications increased in 2015. According to the data, the average processing time for I-829 applications between January 2014 and October 2015 was 12.1 months. This increase was likely the result of a chain reaction or bullwhip effect caused by an increase in I-526 applications approved 2–3 years earlier that are now due for I-829 filings.

I-924 USCIS Form for Application for New Regional Center Approval or Project "Exemplar" Status under the Immigrant Investor Pilot Program

Based on the most recently released USCIS data, I-924 processing times increased significantly in 2014 but have begun to stabilize in 2015, and they actually saw a significant decrease in processing time in October 2015. According to the data, the average processing time for I-924 applications between January 2014 and October 2015 was 10.2 months, which is almost three months above the most recently released monthly processing average of 7.9 months in October 2015. It is important to note here that USCIS does not segment out I-924 applications for new regional center designation from those I-924 applications that are for pre-approval of actual projects, or "exemplar" projects that are seeking approval by USCIS. These I-924 "exemplar" applications are submitted to USCIS without an individual investor attached to them, and so they are very similar to an actual I-526 investor petition—just without the information for an actual individual investor. Overall, it remains to be seen if this improved processing time is an anomaly or a trend that will continue into the future. If this is a trend of reduced processing times for I-924 applications, particularly I-924 "exemplar" project applications, this would be very positive news for the EB-5 community as many project-related milestones and key EB-5 lending provisions often include a project's I-924 "exemplar" approval as one of the trigger points for the release of EB-5 funds out of escrow and into the project's operational account—thus making EB-5 funding available sooner for project developers.

New I-526 Application Denial Rate Drops by ~50%

Figure 23 presents the filing statistics for Form I-526, Immigrant Petition by Alien Entrepreneur, as of November 18, 2015.

Fiscal Year	FY2013					FY2014					FY2015				
Quarter	Q1	Q2	Q3	Q4	Total	Q1	Q2	Q3	Q4	Total	Q1	Q2	Q3	Q4	Total
Receipts	1,935	1,350	1,437	1,624	6,346	2,143	2,540	3,005	3,240	10,928	2,959	2,337	2,502	6,575	14,373
Growth Rate (Quarterly)	3%	-30%	6%	13%	-	32%	19%	18%	8%	-	-9%	-21%	7%	163%	-
Growth Rate (Over Year)	50%	-9%	4%	-14%	5%	10%	47%	52%	50%	42%	38%	-8%	-17%	103%	31.5%
Approvals	693	833	1,001	1,172	3,699	1,453	1,429	1,133	1,100	5,115	1,652	1,978	2,941	2,185	8,756
Approval Rate	72%	79%	88%	79%	80%	64%	85%	90%	94%	80%	93%	88%	92%	85%	89%
Growth Rate (Quarterly)	3%	20%	20%	17%	-	24%	-2%	-21%	-3%	-	50%	20%	49%	-26%	-
Growth Rate (Over Year)	-36%	-19%	11%	74%	1%	110%	72%	13%	-6%	38%	14%	38%	160%	99%	71%
Denials	263	220	142	318	943	811	257	125	73	1,266	133	273	268	377	1,051
Denial Rate	28%	21%	12%	21%	20%	36%	15%	10%	6%	20%	7%	12%	8%	15%	11%
Growth Rate (Quarterly)	45%	-16%	-35%	124%	-	155%	-68%	-51%	-42%	-	82%	105%	-2%	41%	-
Growth Rate (Over Year)	18%	36%	-64%	75%	-1%	208%	17%	-12%	-77%	34%	-84%	6%	114%	416%	-17%
Pendings	6,095	6,074	6,506	7,131	7,131	7,363	8,302	10,375	12,453	12,453	13,526	13,731	13,129	17,367	17,367
Growth Rate (Quarterly)	-	0%	7%	10%	-	3%	13%	25%	20%	-	9%	2%	-4%	32%	-
Growth Rate (Over Year)	-	-	-	-	42%	21%	37%	59%	75%	75%	46%	65%	27%	39%	39%

Figure 23. USCIS filing statistics for I-526 petitions.

USCIS I-526 EB-5 petitions: From the most recent USCIS data, it appears as though USCIS has begun to approve more new I-526 applications than it has previously. The I-526 denial rate has decreased from a rate of 20% in 2014 to almost half that figure at 11% in 2015. This decreased rate of denials is a signal that increasing I-526 application processing times may be starting to result in an increased rate of I-526 approvals by USCIS as the number of pending I-526 applications continues to grow despite increased numbers of USCIS adjudicators. The year 2015 saw a 31.5% increase in I-526 petitions submitted (14,373 total) to USCIS and an impressive 71% increase in the number of I-526 applications approved by USCIS. This large increase in I-526 submissions was clearly driven by both (i) an increase in popularity of the EB-5 Program overseas, and (ii) a response to the anticipated legislation in Q4 2015 that was first expected on September 30, 2015, and again on December 11, 2015. Congress ended up passing a ten-month extension of the EB-5 regional center program with no programmatic changes (e.g., minimum investment amounts, definitions for TEAs) to the existing program for the duration of this extension. Going forward, all new I-924, I-526, and I-829 petitions will continue to be accepted and adjudicated as normal until a new EB-5 bill is passed, until another extension is given, or until the expiration of the EB-5 Program on or before September 30, 2019.

More I-526 Applications Are Pending Now Than Ever

Figure 24 illustrates trends in the number of I-526 petitions pending by quarter (FY2013–FY2015, Q4).

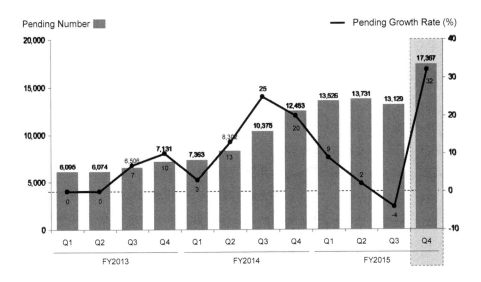

Figure 24. Pending I-526 petitions, 2013–2015.

Pending I-526 applications: The number of pending I-526 applications started to decrease in Q3 of 2015 as USCIS worked through their backlog of pending applications. In the final quarter of 2015, however, this number spiked as foreign investors rushed to submit their applications prior to the anticipated September 30, 2015, and subsequent December 11, 2015, EB-5 Program renewal deadlines.

Visa retrogression: With additional/expedited USCIS processing capacity still an open question, it is unclear how this large spike in new pending I-526 petitions will impact investors from China, who are already facing increased processing times due to visa retrogression. Demand from the Chinese market continues to outstrip the number of EB-5 visas allocated to mainland China, which has resulted in a significant pending I-526 backlog at USCIS. This visa retrogression issue, however, does not affect petitioners from countries outside of mainland China, and therefore processing times for non-Chinese applications should be significantly lower than the reported USCIS average. In any case, EB-5 immigrants from all countries, including mainland China, can continue to file and obtain approval of I-526 immigrant petitions. In fact, filing an I-526 petition as early as possible is more important now than ever since it is the I-526 USCIS receipt date that is ultimately used for quota purposes and to calculate visa retrogression for Chinese applicants.

USCIS Form I-829 Approvals Drop by 94%

Figure 25 displays I-829 petition quarterly statistics (FY2013–FY2015, Q4).

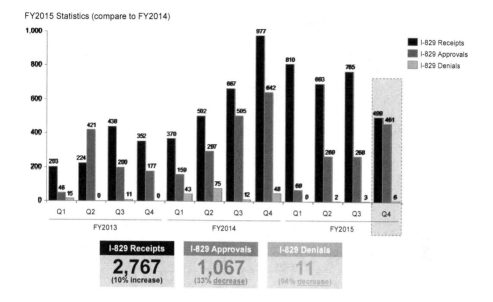

FY2015 Statistics (compare to FY2014)

Figure 25. I-829 statistics, 2013–2015.

The year 2015 saw a 10% increase over 2014 in the number of I-829 petitions submitted to USCIS (2,767 total). USCIS's increased processing times, however, resulted in 33% fewer I-829 petitions being approved in 2015 (only 1,067 approvals). Significantly, USCIS denied only 11 individual I-829 petitions out of the 1,078 I-829 petitions that were processed—this is a remarkable 94% decrease in the number of denied applications from 2014, during which 183 individual I-829 petitions were denied.

EB-5 Program Investment ($) Jumps 71% in 2015

Figure 26 shows EB-5 foreign direct investment (FDI) in millions ($) by fiscal year (FY1992–FY2015).

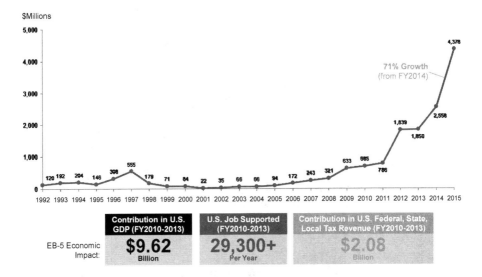

Figure 26. Economic impact of the EB-5 Program.

The rapid growth of the EB-5 Program in the past five years has contributed significantly to growth in the overall U.S. economy by significantly impacting new job creation, new business development, and increases in government tax revenue. Global interest in the EB-5 Program began to grow after the 2008 recession, when traditional funding sources became scarce. The program has exploded in the past two years as it has become more popular with foreign investors and U.S. EB-5 project developers. In the past year alone, foreign direct investment made possible through the EB-5 Program has increased a remarkable 71% from ~$2.6 billion to ~$4.4 billion.

According to recently released data, the EB-5 Program has made the following economic impacts over FY2010–FY2013:

1. Contribution to U.S. gross domestic product (GDP): $9.62 billion
2. Jobs supported: more than 29,300 jobs per year
3. Contribution to U.S. federal, state, and local tax revenue: $2.08 billion
Source: IIUSA.

EB-5 Visa Statistics for 2018

Every year, the U.S. Department of State (DOS) releases statistics related to visa issuance and use. These statistics are presented in a number of tables organized by visa preference, foreign state of chargeability, issuance office, and more. The 2018 statistics are now available.

Statistics related to the employment-based fifth preference visa (EB-5) are found in Table V, Part 3 of the Report of the Visa Office 2018. Figure 27 provides a summary of this table and lists the 10 foreign states with the highest quantity of EB-5 investors who were issued visas in 2018.

Foreign State	Direct Investors	Regional Center Investors	EB-5 Category Total	% Total
China (mainland)	188	4,454	4,642	48.3%
Vietnam	15	678	693	7.2%
India	67	518	585	6.1%
South Korea	21	510	531	5.5%
China (Taiwan)	27	425	452	4.7%
Brazil	31	357	388	4.0%
Venezuela	34	203	237	2.5%
Hong Kong	19	181	200	2.1%
Mexico	19	155	174	1.8%
Russia	8	126	134	1.4%
Top 10 Total	429	7,607	8,036	83.7%
Grand Total	581	9,021	9,602	100.0%

Figure 27. Recipients of EB-5 visas in 2018 by country.

Discrepancies in percentages are due to rounding.

Total Number of EB-5 Visas Declines

In 2018, the DOS issued a total of 9,602 EB-5 visas, 488 fewer than in 2017, which represents a decrease of ~5%. The difference between the number of visas issued in 2017 versus 2018 was likely due to continued visa retrogression for mainland-born Chinese nationals.

EB-5 Regional Center Investments Remain Dominant

When comparing the number of visas issued by investor type, direct investors were vastly outnumbered by those who invested through regional centers. Of the 9,602 EB-5 visas issued, only 581 (6.1%) were for direct investors. These DOS numbers reflect the overall preference of EB-5 investors to invest in projects sponsored by regional centers. In practice, this preference is primarily attributed to the desire of EB-5 investors to limit their involvement in the daily management of their EB-5 projects by becoming limited partners in the new commercial enterprise.

Chinese Nationals Receive the Majority of EB-5 Visas but Face Rising Competition

In the summary table above, the number of visas issued to EB-5 investors from the top 10 foreign states represents 83.7% of the total number of visas issued to EB-5 investors in 2018. More specifically, 48.3% of all EB-5 visas were issued to mainland-born Chinese nationals. Historically, China has held the top spot for EB-5 visa issuance, and this is unlikely to change in 2019. However, China's dominance has somewhat dropped since 2015, when an entire 83.5% of EB-5 visas went to mainland-born Chinese nationals. Countries such as India, Brazil, and Vietnam are quickly becoming larger players in the EB-5 market.

The EB-5 Program continues to gain popularity throughout Asia. The number of South Koreans receiving EB-5 visas skyrocketed from 195 in 2017 to 531 in 2018. Visas issued to Indian nationals rose even more drastically, from 174 in 2017 to 585 in 2018. The number of visas issued to Vietnamese investors increased as well, from 471 in 2017 to 693 in 2018. Of the top 10 foreign states listed in the summary table above, six are located in Asia.

Data Increasingly Important as Future of EB-5 Program Uncertain

These U.S. DOS metrics are important since they offer insight into the trends that currently characterize and have continuing effects on the EB-5 industry. The ongoing uncertainty concerning the reauthorization of the EB-5 Immigrant Investor Pilot Program—and the possibility that the investment threshold may be increased—make these data particularly valuable.

Implications of Retrogression for Chinese EB-5 Investors

A recent surge in EB-5 visa petitions from Chinese investors has resulted in a significant backlog, and USCIS has offered little clarification on the length of waiting periods investors should expect. This has created issues for EB-5 investors and projects alike, as the current structure of the program requires that the initial investment amount remain at risk for the duration of an investor's conditional residence period.

This section explores the current retrogression situation and some of the obstacles it has posed for investors under the EB-5 Program.

What is retrogression?

The United States grants a limited number of visas per fiscal year, just under 10,000 of which are allocated to investors and their families within the EB-5 Program. Additionally, since demand for EB-5 visas has outstripped supply in recent years, the number of visas available for investors from any one country has been further limited to 7% the total amount.

This has largely affected investors from China, who make up the majority of EB-5 applicants. Rising EB-5 markets in India, Vietnam, South Korea, and Brazil could face retrogression in the future as well. While unallocated visas from the worldwide total can be reassigned to Chinese investors, the number of visas available still falls far short of the number of applicants, and USCIS thus began 2016 with a backlog of nearly 22,000 petitions awaiting adjudication.

The process of applying for an EB-5 visa begins with the investor filing an I-526 petition, which proves that the investor has already invested (or is in the process of investing) the required amount of capital in a new enterprise in the United States. This amount is significant, either $1,000,000 or $500,000 depending on the nature and location of the project, and it must remain at risk until the investor's conditional residence period comes to an end.

A problem arises in that the waiting period between filing and adjudication of the I-526 petition, at which point the conditional residence period begins, can stretch anywhere from several months to over five years. With additional waiting periods following the filing of the I-829 petition, the adjudication of which determines whether unconditional permanent residence is granted, Chinese EB-5 applicants can expect their investments to remain at risk for anywhere from six to 10 years.

Several aspects of the EB-5 Program are affected by increased wait times. These include loan terms, maintenance of the at-risk requirement for investment funds, and the types of jobs qualifying for EB-5 job creation. Below, we outline some points investors should keep in mind.

257

Points of Consideration for EB-5 Investors

Facing a potential wait time of up to 10 years following the initial investment and filing of the I-526 petition, Chinese investors must plan carefully to ensure they meet all requirements of the EB-5 Program. The granting of unconditional permanent residence is contingent on the following factors, all of which must be met by the time an investor files his or her I-829 petition:

1. The investor must invest either $500,000 or $1,000,000 as applicable in a new commercial enterprise in the United States. This investor must typically meet or be in the process of meeting this requirement by the time he or she files the I-526 petition.

2. The investment must be maintained at risk throughout the conditional residence period, which begins when the investor enters the United States on an EB-5 visa following approval of the I-526 petition. This means the full investment amount must be made available to a new commercial enterprise for job creation purposes, and the investor must not be repaid until the conditional residence period ends following adjudication of the I-829 petition.

3. The full investment amount must be allocated for job creation and must result in the creation of 10 full-time jobs in the United States. Although USCIS has not clarified whether the jobs must exist at the time of filing or approval of the I-829 petition, the current assumption is that this must be the case if those jobs are to count toward the job creation requirement.

As a result of the retrogression wait times and the specific requirements of the EB-5 Program outlined above, Chinese EB-5 investors thus face two potential obstacles:

- **Loan repayment.** If an investor enters into an agreement with a new commercial enterprise based on a loan term of five years, the loan will be repaid by the end of that term and potentially within the conditional residence period. Early repayment means those funds are no longer at risk and thus no longer satisfy the requirements of the EB-5 Program. As such, investors must carefully negotiate loan terms to ensure either that the initial loan will not be repaid prior to the end of the conditional residence period or that the investment funds will be redeployed into a new job-creating entity and thereby maintained at risk.

- **Job creation.** The calculations used to determine job creation numbers depend on the nature of an EB-5 project. While most regional center projects benefit from the opportunity to include construction jobs in the job creation total, some projects rely on the creation of operations jobs, meaning the business must be operational at the time of filing of the I-829 petition for those jobs to be counted. With waiting periods of up to 10 years, the risk of a business failing before its investor is able to file his or her I-829 petition is not insignificant. Investors must therefore carefully consider both the viability of the new commercial enterprise and the methods used to determine job creation, as both factors affect the fulfillment of EB-5 requirements.

Retrogression has created major uncertainties for Chinese investors, who face the possibility of losing their permanent residence if the conditions of the EB-5 Program are not met within specific timeframes. With ultimate visa approval potentially resting on the long-term success of new commercial enterprises, the coming years may see an increased focus on largescale urban construction projects, meaning investors will likely be less able to take advantage of the lower investment amount required for projects in underemployed areas.

An additional possibility is that Congress will address the backlog by increasing visa quotas over the coming years and that USCIS will publish new guidelines to clarify the aforementioned EB-5 Program requirements affected by retrogression. As always, investors should consult with experienced EB-5 advisors to keep apprised of any developments in the program.

Form I-829 Basics

Two years after a foreign national's Form I-526 has been approved by USCIS, he or she must submit Form I-829, Petition by Entrepreneur to Remove Conditions. Specifically, this form must be filed within the last 90 days of the investor's two-year conditional residence period. Failure to submit this form within this timeframe may jeopardize a foreign investor's ability to gain lawful permanent resident status.

An I-829 petition must prove to USCIS that the investor has met all the requirements of the EB-5 Program. Once the I-829 petition is approved by USCIS, an investor and his or her qualified family members will be awarded lawful permanent resident status.

Accompanying Documentation

Since Form I-829 is a petition to remove the conditions from the investor's permanent resident status, the investor must demonstrate he or she possesses conditional permanent resident status. This can be accomplished by providing a photocopy of the investor's green card.

Also, because removing the conditions from the investor's resident status is contingent upon successfully completing all the requirements of the EB-5 Program, the investor must provide accompanying documentation that demonstrates he or she has met all the criteria of the EB-5 Program.

To demonstrate that a new commercial enterprise was established, the investor will need to provide federal tax returns that document the enterprise's existence.

In addition to proof that the enterprise was created, the I-829 and accompanying documentation must show that the enterprise existed through the duration of the investor's two-year conditional residence. Acceptable evidence may include state and federal tax returns, quarterly tax statements, bank statements, contracts, licenses and certifications, receipts, and invoices.

The investor will also need to provide proof that the requisite capital was invested. Such proof may include bank statements, audited financial statements, or some other form of evidence that demonstrates the investor's capital was received by the new commercial enterprise.

Additionally, the EB-5 Program requires that the investor's capital investment result in the creation of 10 full-time jobs. Certain tax documents and payroll records can be used to demonstrate this requirement was met.

For an applicant with a criminal history, certain legal documents must also be provided, such as related court records, law enforcement statements, or any records of arrest, sentencing, probation, or parole.

Filing Form I-829

Typically, Form I-829 is prepared and filed by immigration attorneys on behalf of their EB-5 investor clients. The USCIS fee for filing Form I-829 is $3,750; if required, the biometrics services fee is $85.

This petition is sent to the USCIS California Service Center. Generally, it takes six months or more for USCIS to process Form I-829, and once processed, USCIS may request more information or schedule an in-office interview.

When an investor's I-829 is approved by USCIS, his or her conditional status is replaced by lawful permanent resident status, and he or she will be issued a new green card to reflect this status change. If desired, the investor may apply for citizenship five years after initially being granted conditional permanent resident status.

EB-5 Permanent Resident Status

For foreign nationals participating in the EB-5 Immigrant Investor Program, the goal is to gain permanent resident status in the United States. Conditional permanent resident status is granted to an EB-5 investor upon the approval of his or her I-526 petition by USCIS. This conditional status is valid for two years and allows the investor to be sufficiently engaged in the daily management of his or her investment.

Within the last 90 days of this conditional period, the EB-5 investor will file Form I-829, Petition by Entrepreneur to Remove Conditions. Upon approval of the I-829 petition, the investor and his or her spouse and dependent children will be granted permanent resident status. Five years after first receiving conditional permanent resident status, the investor and his or her family will be able to apply for U.S. citizenship.

Upon earning permanent resident status, an immigrant will receive a permanent resident card, also referred to as a green card. Permanent resident status entails certain rights and responsibilities, which are outlined below.

Rights of Permanent Residents

U.S. permanent resident status grants immigrants many rights and privileges. Green card holders may live and work anywhere in the United States, and they are fully protected under federal, state, and local law. Permanent residents are also free to travel abroad using a valid passport issued by their home country; however, in order to remain permanent residents, they must fulfill the physical presence requirement, which is discussed in the next section.

In addition to these rights, permanent residents enjoy numerous other benefits, including access to world-class higher education and excellent health care. They also have the option to obtain U.S. citizenship.

Responsibilities of Permanent Residents

Along with the rights and privileges mentioned above, permanent residents are expected to fulfill certain responsibilities:

- Permanent residents are required to pay all applicable state and federal income taxes. They must file income tax returns with the Internal Revenue Service (IRS), paying taxes on their gross worldwide income. Immigrants from countries with whom the United States has tax treaties may be able to obtain credit for the payment of their foreign taxes.
- Like all male U.S. citizens from age 18 to 25, male green card holders must register with Selective Service. Registration for Selective Service does not, in itself, entail service in the U.S. military, but it does mean that any male permanent residents from

age 18 to 25 will be subject to the draft should the U.S. government choose to conscript men into military service.

- In addition to paying taxes and registering with Selective Service, permanent residents are expected to be of good moral character.

In order to maintain permanent resident status, an immigrant must fulfill the physical presence requirement, which generally entails physically residing within the United States for six months or more in any given year. If a permanent resident spends more than one year outside of the United States, he or she must obtain a reentry permit or face losing permanent resident status.

If outside of the United States for two or more years after being issued a reentry permit, a Returning Resident (SB-1) immigrant visa is necessary. While outside the United States, permanent residents are still required to file U.S. income tax returns, and failure to do so may jeopardize their status. Permanent resident status will be considered abandoned if a green card holder moves to another country and no longer intends to reside in the United States.

Permanent Resident Status versus Citizenship

Permanent resident status is not the same as U.S. citizenship. While permanent residents are able to live and work in the United States, they remain citizens of their home nation. As such, permanent residents cannot obtain U.S. passports, cannot vote in U.S. elections, and are not allowed to run for U.S. elected office.

U.S. citizens may be able to more easily bring into the United States family members who are foreign nationals. Citizens also have more access to federal jobs as well as federal assistance and benefits—including Social Security and Medicare.

To become a citizen of the United States, a permanent resident must file for citizenship through USCIS. EB-5 investors may apply for citizenship after maintaining their permanent resident status for five years. This five year period starts when an EB-5 investor is granted conditional permanent resident status.

Figure 28 offers a comparison of rights for permanent residents versus U.S. citizens.

RIGHT	PERMANENT RESIDENT	U.S. CITIZEN
May live and work anywhere in the U.S.	Yes	Yes
Enjoys protection under U.S. law	Yes	Yes
Gains access to U.S. higher education	Yes	Yes
Gains access to U.S. health care	Yes	Yes
May travel outside of the U.S.	Yes	Yes
Eligible for U.S. passport	No	Yes
May vote and run for most elected offices	No	Yes
Gains access to federal assistance and benefits	No	Yes
Must abide by residency requirements	Yes	Yes

Figure 28. Permanent residence versus citizenship.

Traveling Abroad as a Green Card Holder

The primary goal of an EB-5 investment is permanent resident status for the investor and his or her family. When a foreign national obtains a green card and becomes a permanent resident of the United States, certain considerations must be made when traveling abroad.

If the government believes a lawful permanent resident (LPR) does not intend to permanently reside in the United States, USCIS might determine that the LPR has abandoned his or her permanent resident status.

Maintaining Permanent Resident Status

In order for LPRs to maintain permanent resident status, their primary place of residence must be the United States. As such, when they travel abroad, they must do so with an intent to return. When LPRs spend prolonged periods away from the United States, USCIS might determine that they have abandoned their permanent resident status.

In general, LPRs may spend fewer than six months abroad within the span of a year. If away for longer than six months but less than one year, USCIS may ask for proof of intent to return to the United States.

USCIS will suspect an LPR does not intend to permanently reside in the United States when time spent abroad exceeds one year. In such cases, intermittent visits to the United States will not likely be perceived as an intent to maintain permanent resident status.

Determining Intent to Return

When determining whether an LPR has abandoned his or her permanent resident status in the United States, USCIS is largely concerned with the LPR's intent. Any LPR who leaves the United States must have an intent to return and must be able to clearly demonstrate this intent.

USCIS may consider several factors to determine whether an LPR intends to return to the United States and continue living here permanently. These factors include but are not limited to the following:
- Historic travel patterns
- Family ties
- Business ties
- Property ownership
- Financial accounts and activity
- S. driver's license status

Abandoning Permanent Resident Status

USCIS may determine that an LPR has abandoned his or her permanent resident status under a number of circumstances:

- The LPR has moved and clearly intends to permanently reside within another country.
- The LPR fails to file income tax returns while abroad or files as a nonimmigrant.
- The LPR spends more than one year abroad and fails to obtain a reentry permit.
- The LPR remains abroad more than two years after being issued a reentry permit and fails to obtain a Returning Resident (SB-1) immigrant visa.

Note that USCIS may determine an LPR to have abandoned his or her permanent resident status for absences of any length, not only for absences greater than one year.

Frequently Asked Questions

Project Developers

General Questions

Does the EB-5 Program differ from state to state?

No, the EB-5 Program is a U.S. federal program, and therefore it is not different from one state to another. The only part of the program for which states are responsible is determining what qualifies as an employment-based TEA.

What experience, education, qualifications, or skills are required of an EB-5 investor in order to fulfill the program's requirement to actively participate in managing the NCE?

While the EB-5 Program requires investors to be involved in managing the NCE through either day-to-day management or policy formation, no specific background experience, education, etc., are required. For direct investments in which the investor will likely take a more active role in management, certain business or financial experience may be helpful—but the primary requirement is that the NCE creates the necessary number of jobs.

What source of funds documentation is required if an EB-5 investment is greater than the minimum investment threshold?

For investments greater than the minimum $1,000,000 ($500,000 for projects in TEAs), only the funds necessary to satisfy the requirement of the EB-5 Program must be accompanied by lawful source of funds documentation.

Can a new commercial enterprise be a charitable organization?

Because a new commercial enterprise is strictly defined as a for-profit entity, it cannot be a non-profit. A non-profit may, however, be able to participate in the EB-5 Program in other ways—for example, as a regional center or in cooperation with a for-profit entity.

What services do immigration attorneys provide to EB-5 project developers?

Immigration attorneys help developers create EB-5 compliant projects. Typically, this involves the formation of a multidisciplinary team of professionals who will put together all the necessary documentation, including securities offering documents, an economic analysis, and the project's business plan. Immigration attorneys can also help projects apply for regional center designation and gain exemplar status. Essentially, a good immigration attorney will be able to advise a project developer on all aspects of the EB-5 Program from start to finish.

How much of an EB-5 investment can originate from loan proceeds?

A loan may be used as the source of part or all of an EB-5 investment as long as the loan is secured by the investor's personal assets and the funds used to purchase those assets can be traced to a lawful source.

What requirements does the EB-5 Program have for project developers?

For a project to be eligible for the EB-5 Program, it must fit the program's definition of a new commercial enterprise. Furthermore, it must involve a sufficient need for capital so that at least one EB-5 investor can make a qualified investment of $1,000,000 ($500,000 for projects in TEAs). Finally, it must produce at least 10 jobs per EB-5 investor.

What regulations must potential EB-5 investors follow when looking for an investment?

Investors are not restricted from seeking an investment opportunity—they can contact whomever they feel necessary (e.g., developer, regional center, etc.) to find and vet an opportunity. Issuers, however, must follow certain SEC regulations regarding marketing to potential investors.

What parts of the EB-5 process tend to be the most challenging for immigration attorneys and other professionals?

Many aspects of the EB-5 Program are complicated and challenging, and each professional involved will certainly have some particular aspect that he or she considers most difficult. Some of the most challenging parts of the process tend to include documenting lawful source of funds, ensuring the business plan is compliant, and conducting regional center due diligence.

What are the basic requirements for a business to obtain EB-5 funding?

Generally speaking, any for-profit business is eligible for EB-5 funding. To satisfy the program's requirements, a business must meet the definition of an NCE, have a compliant business plan, and ultimately create 10 jobs per EB-5 investor.

What legal responsibility does a U.S. citizen bear toward an EB-5 partner?

A U.S. citizen who has partnered with an EB-5 investor bears only the responsibility assigned in the partnership agreement or business arrangement. With respect to illegal conduct, the U.S. citizen bears no responsibility and is otherwise not liable for the actions of the EB-5 investor.

How might someone earn money referring clients to EB-5 projects?

For U.S. citizens and permanent residents, the Securities and Exchange Commission (SEC) governs who may receive finder's fees. As a general matter, only licensed and registered brokers may accept finder's fees, unless an exemption applies. If an individual is a licensed and registered broker or is working outside the United States where no such license is required, he or she would need to contact individual regional centers about investor referrals.

How might small businesses and startups find direct EB-5 investors?

Finding investors generally requires some form of marketing. One option is to contact a migration agency that can promote the business to foreign investors. Before a small business or startup markets a project to potential EB-5 investors, however, the business should retain an immigration attorney with relevant EB-5 experience to ensure the business is EB-5 compliant and marketable. Securities counsel should also be consulted to ensure compliance with all SEC regulations throughout the process.

How might a businessperson add EB-5 funds to a project's capital stack?

In order for someone to add EB-5 funds to a project's capital stack, the project must comply fully with all EB-5 and SEC regulations. As a result, the first step in securing EB-5 funding is to retain an immigration attorney with EB-5 experience, who will not only provide counsel regarding EB-5 compliance, but will also be able to help set up the necessary team of professionals to create a marketable EB-5 project. Once a project is EB-5 compliant and marketable, it can be marketed to potential investors, which is often accomplished using foreign migration agents.

Will changing EB-5 business locations after I-526 filing be considered a material change upon I-829 filing?

A change to the business's location will not likely constitute a material change as long as the other facts of the case remain the same. For instance, if the project is sponsored by a regional center, the new location would need to be within the regional center's geographic scope. Also, if the project was in a TEA, the new location would likewise need to be in a TEA. Job creation based on regional economic analysis would also need to remain unchanged. An immigration attorney and economist may need to be consulted to determine whether a change of location will result in any material changes to the EB-5 case.

What are the responsibilities of a business owner who partners with EB-5 investors?

The primary responsibility of a business owner seeking EB-5 investment is to ensure compliance with the Securities and Exchange Commission (SEC), which will likely require the business owner to retain securities counsel. Other than that, a business that markets itself to EB-5 investors should ensure it is compliant with the EB-5 requirements so that investors will be able to successfully obtain their visas based upon their investments in that business.

Project Job Creation

How does employee turnover affect an EB-5 business?

The EB-5 employment creation requirement is to create 10 full-time, permanent job positions, not to hire 10 individual employees. If an employee quits, then a new employee must be hired as soon as is practical in order to maintain the job position. When an investor files Form I-829, he or she must demonstrate that 10 full-time, permanent positions are on payroll.

Can part-time jobs from an existing business be made into full-time jobs to meet the EB-5 job creation requirement?

Because the EB-5 Program requires the creation of new jobs, simply adding hours to existing jobs will not likely satisfy the program's employment creation requirement. It would be prudent to seek clarification from USCIS before proceeding.

What are the greatest risks of direct EB-5 investments?

Because direct investments can only count the jobs created directly by the EB-5 project, the greatest risk of such investments is the failure to create enough jobs to satisfy the requirements of the EB-5 Program. Almost all EB-5 projects are sponsored through regional centers since such projects are able to count direct, indirect, and induced job creation.

How long must the jobs created through an EB-5 investment be maintained?

This depends on how the jobs are being counted. For indirect and induced jobs, employment creation is calculated based on expenditures, and so once the money is spent, the jobs are considered created. For direct jobs, it is best to have them created before an investor's I-829 petition is filed and maintained until after the petition is approved. Because job creation is key for obtaining permanent resident status, it is vital to retain experienced immigration counsel to review the project's business plan and economic analysis.

How does an EB-5 project select the employees that will meet the employment creation requirement?

For jobs created directly by the project, employees are hired in the same way that any business hires employees—the only requirement is that the positions be full time and filled by U.S. workers (i.e., citizens or permanent residents). Indirect and induced job creation, on the other hand, is based on money spent and does not involve any hiring on the part of the project.

Can EB-5 funds be used for any part of a project, including the purchase of land?

EB-5 funds can be applied to any part of a project. By itself, however, the purchase of land is not generally accepted as an EB-5 expenditure. Therefore, in terms of job creation, land purchases do not provide any direct benefit to EB-5 investors. That said, the key requirement for an EB-5 project is that its spending—excluding the cost of land and any other ineligible expenses—will create the necessary number of jobs.

How does having multiple investors affect the job creation calculation of a project?

The EB-5 Program requires that each EB-5 investment create 10 or more jobs, and so the total number of jobs created by a project is divided by the total number of EB-5 investors. All eligible jobs are counted, even ifEB-5 funds represent only a small percentage of a project's total capital stack. In other words, job creation is attributed only to EB-5 investors—thus the smaller the percentage of EB-5 funds used by a project, the more favorable the job creation figures will tend to be for EB-5 investors.

How might jobs in two separate locations be counted toward EB-5 job creation?

Jobs created in two separate locations may be acceptable, but EB-5 compliance may be complicated. First, if working with a regional center, the regional center's jurisdiction must cover the whole project. Second, if investments are made at the lower TEA threshold of $500,000, all jobs will need to be located in the TEA. Third, if the separate locations reflect a split company structure, one of the companies must be the wholly-owned subsidiary of the other. Due to the complexity of such a scenario, an experienced EB-5 immigration attorney should be consulted before proceeding.

How are jobs created via EB-5 capital verified by USCIS?

For projects counting direct, indirect, and induced job creation, USCIS will require documentation of the expenditures from which job creation has been calculated. For projects counting direct jobs only, W-2s and payroll records will need to be submitted.

What are the EB-5 Program's basic requirements for job creation?

An EB-5 investor is required to make a minimum investment of $1,000,000—or $500,000 if the project is located in a TEA—and that investment must be responsible for the creation of at least 10 full-time, permanent jobs for U.S. workers. For EB-5 purposes, "full time" is defined as 35 or more hours per week and "permanent" means that the job cannot be seasonal or temporary in nature. For projects sponsored by regional centers, jobs may be calculated using economic models and can include indirect and induced job creation, but the basic requirement remains: each EB-5 investor must create 10 or more jobs.

What is a "permanent" job for EB-5 purposes?

Within the context of the EB-5 Program, a permanent job is one that is not temporary or seasonal in nature. The EB-5 definition of "permanent" does not reflect a requirement that a job position must exist for a certain length of time. However, the necessary number of jobs must exist when the investor files Form I-829.

Can a direct EB-5 investor count contract employees toward job creation?

Direct EB-5 investments can count only those jobs created directly by the NCE itself toward the EB-5 Program's job creation requirement. For projects sponsored by regional centers, indirect jobs such as contract labor can be factored into the job creation calculation.

How is the job creation requirement and job allocation determined for mixed-capital projects?

The EB-5 employment creation requirement is calculated based on the number of EB-5 investors who invest in a project—not on the project's total capital. A project must create 10 full-time, permanent jobs per EB-5 investor. All full-time, permanent jobs created by a project are counted toward the EB-5 job creation requirement. If, for example, a project created 500 full-time, permanent jobs, it could support up to 50 EB-5 investors with 10 jobs being allocated to each investor. If that same project had only 20 EB-5 investors, however, the 500 jobs would be divided among them, and each investor would be allocated 25 jobs—far more than the 10 jobs required.

What factors disqualify a job from being counted toward EB-5 employment creation?

Generally speaking, any job position in any industry can be counted toward job creation as long as the position is not part-time (less than 35 hours per week), temporary, or seasonal. Construction jobs may be counted as long as construction lasts for two or more years. In order to be counted, each job must be filled by a U.S. citizen, permanent resident, refugee, or asylee—it cannot be filled by a nonimmigrant with work authorization or an undocumented worker. For direct investments, only jobs created directly by the new commercial enterprise may be counted—indirect and induced jobs do not qualify. Investments through regional centers, however, are able to count indirect and induced job creation.

Project Structure

How many EB-5 investors can invest in an NCE?

Any number of foreign nationals from any number of countries may invest in an NCE. The primary issue is job creation—in other words, will the project create 10 permanent, full-time jobs for each EB-5 investor?

Can a foreign national start a business using seed funding to create jobs and qualify for an EB-5 visa?

The EB-5 Program requires the investment of personal funds, which may be derived from a gift or loan (as long as the loan is backed by the investor's personal assets). Simply creating 10 jobs does not qualify a person for an EB-5 visa.

What steps must a business entity take in order to start receiving EB-5 funding?

For businesses that want to count direct, indirect, and induced jobs toward employment creation, the first step is to find a regional center to sponsor the project. For businesses planning to meet the EB-5 Program's employment creation requirements through direct jobs only, a business needs a compliant business plan, a TEA designation letter (if applicable), securities documents (e.g., private placement memorandum, corporate governance documents, etc.), and finally the necessary number of investors. Securities documents should be prepared by qualified securities counsel, and finding investors may require the assistance of an agent or consultant. Any business seeking EB-5 capital should retain an immigration attorney with EB-5 experience to help navigate the complicated requirements of the program.

How can an existing business experiencing losses qualify for the EB-5 Program?

Under specific conditions, existing businesses experiencing losses—referred to as a troubled business—may qualify for the EB-5 Program. Essentially, the business must have sustained at least a 20% net loss to net worth in the past 12 to 24 months. In such cases, the program's employment requirement is met when at least 10 jobs are preserved or created.

Can a direct EB-5 investor partner with non-EB-5 investors?

Yes, a direct EB-5 investor can make an investment in a new commercial enterprise that has additional EB-5 or other investors as long as at least 10 jobs are created by the enterprise for each EB-5 investor. An EB-5 investor need not be a majority partner as long as he or she maintains active participation in the company.

Can an EB-5 investor invest in a regional center project that has already started?

Yes, as long as a project remains open to EB-5 investment, an EB-5 investor may invest in that project. While most good regional center projects close out quickly, it is possible for an opening to be created due to certain circumstances—such as an investor backing out or not meeting the investment requirements. When investing in such projects, it is particularly important to conduct due diligence and retain experienced counsel.

Can an online business qualify as an NCE in the EB-5 Program?

An online business can qualify as an NCE under the EB-5 Program, but eligibility will depend on the nature of the business. Essentially, the necessary number of jobs must be created in a particular U.S. geographical area. It would be prudent to retain an immigration attorney with EB-5 experience to help ensure such a project is compliant with the program.

Is an approved I-526 petition the same as an exemplar petition?

No, an I-526 petition submitted by another investor and approved by USCIS does not count as an exemplar petition, which is submitted by the regional center as part of its I-924 petition to gain regional center status. If, however, USCIS has approved another investor's I-526 petition, this means that the project's business documents have been examined and approved by USCIS, and so the project's other EB-5 investors can expect I-526 approval as long as their source of funds documents are accepted.

How can an investment in a current, successful business qualify for the EB-5 Program?

An EB-5 investment may be made in a current and successful business under certain circumstances: (i) the existing business is restructured such that a new commercial enterprise results or (ii) the investment results in either a 40% increase in the net worth of the business or a 40% increase in the number of persons employed by the business. Potential EB-5 investors considering an investment in an existing business should consult an experienced immigration attorney to ensure the investment will meet all EB-5 Program requirements.

Can an EB-5 investment be used to start a company and acquire other businesses that will create new jobs?

Yes, new jobs created by business acquisitions can satisfy the EB-5 Program's employment creation requirements, but only in certain circumstances. The jobs must be actual new positions, and the acquired businesses must be wholly-owned subsidiaries of the new commercial enterprise. Due to the complex nature of such an investment and business strategy, it would be best for an EB-5 investor to consult with experienced corporate and immigration counsel before proceeding.

What industry sectors qualify for EB-5 investments?

The EB-5 Program is not limited to any particular sector—any business in any industry qualifies as long as it is a lawful, for-profit entity that meets the USCIS definition for new commercial enterprise.

What constitutes a material change in an EB-5 project?

The specific nature of a "material change" within the EB-5 Program is somewhat of a mystery—USCIS determines what constitutes a material change on an individual basis. Generally speaking, however, changes to the investment structure, business activity, location, economic methodology, or uses of funds are likely to be seen as material changes.

What percentage of an NCE must an EB-5 investor own?

The percentage itself does not matter—any level of ownership is acceptable as long as (i) the investor makes the necessary investment of $500,000 or $1,000,000, (ii) the investment results in the creation of 10 or more jobs, and (iii) the investor is actively engaged in the daily operation or policy formation of the NCE.

TEA/Rural Areas

For an EB-5 project to qualify as a TEA, when does the TEA requirement need to be met?

To qualify as being located in a TEA, an EB-5 project must have a valid state issued TEA letter if the project is located in an area with at least 150% of the national unemployment rate or a qualified rural area. The EB-5 investor must establish that the EB-5 project had a valid TEA when his or her EB-5 investment was made or when his or her I-526 petition was submitted to USCIS.

What is a "rural" TEA?

For EB-5 purposes, "rural" means any area not located within a metropolitan statistical area (MSA) and not located within a municipality that has a population of 20,000 or more people. If both requirements are met, the "rural" area grants investors the benefit of a lower minimum investment threshold—currently $500,000. The rural designation does not affect what type of NCE can be created, nor does it affect the minimum employment creation requirement of the program.

What is the difference between the EB-5 Program's minimum investment thresholds of $500,000 and $1,000,000?

The smaller investment threshold of $500,000 is allowed for projects located within TEAs. A TEA is either (i) a rural area outside of a metropolitan statistical area with a population of less than 20,000 or (ii) an area experiencing an unemployment rate 50% greater than the national average unemployment rate. For any project not located within a TEA, the minimum investment is currently $1,000,000.

For a direct EB-5 investment, when must the investor prove that the necessary funds are available to invest?

USCIS generally expects the full investment amount to be at risk when the I-526 petition is being adjudicated—and so the funds should either already be invested or placed in escrow when the petition is filed.

How long are TEA letters valid?

TEA designation letters are valid as long as they are based upon the data currently used by the issuing state. Unemployment data is updated annually, and therefore TEA letters are valid for no more than about one year. For most states, data is updated at the end of April.

Will USCIS consider a project to be in a TEA if employees often perform work outside the TEA?

In order for an EB-5 project to qualify for the lower investment amount of a TEA, the NCE is required to be principally doing business within the geographic boundary of the TEA. One element of the "principally doing business" requirement is the location of employees. If the NCE's principal place of business is in a TEA and the employees are hired and paid from within the TEA, performing work outside the TEA may be acceptable.

Project Timing

What is the correct timing for an EB-5 project with multiple EB-5 investors pooling capital together?

The investments into the EB-5 project can be staggered if structured correctly. The key is the timing of job creation for the EB-5 investors. As long as each individual investor can meet his or her individual job creation requirement (ten jobs per investor) without additional EB-5 investment from the other investors in the anticipated pool of capital, then each investor should proceed to file/invest as soon as they are able. However, if the project requires the successful subscription of multiple EB-5 investors at once, before the project can get underway and jobs can be created, then the EB-5 investors should wait to commit their capital and submit their I-526 petition until all of the required EB-5 investors are committed to the project.

What is the process for developers to begin accepting EB-5 capital?

For a developer that wants to add EB-5 funds to its project's capital stack, the first step is to consult an immigration attorney with EB-5 experience. This attorney should be able to guide the developer through the entire process, which consists of creating a compliant business plan and the necessary securities offering documents—and may also involve requesting TEA designation, forming or affiliating with an EB-5 regional center, conducting an economic analysis, and more. Once all the proper documentation is in place, the project can then seek EB-5 investors.

Equity versus Debt

Can an EB-5 investment take the form of a loan instead of equity?

EB-5 regulations do not require an equity investment, but in order to fund an EB-5 project using a loan model, certain considerations apply. According to 8 CFR § 204.6(e), a loan to an NCE is not a qualifying investment. For project's sponsored by regional centers, however, an NCE can make a loan to a project's JCE since indirect jobs are counted toward job creation. For projects using the direct investment model, the NCE could make a loan to a wholly owned subsidiary. Additionally, the source of the funds for investment can be a loan.

When using a loan to fund an EB-5 investment, what collateral is acceptable?

A foreign national can use loaned funds for an EB-5 investment as long as it is secured by the investor's personal assets. The collateral for the loan cannot be the EB-5 project or any assets owned by the new commercial enterprise.

Can funds be given to a U.S. business and still qualify as an EB-5 investment?

No, the funds from an EB-5 investor must be invested in a qualified U.S. business—the capital must be placed at risk and irrevocably committed to the enterprise. The funds cannot be in the form of a gift from the foreign national to the enterprise.

How long does it take for a project to raise EB-5 funds?

How long it takes to raise EB-5 funds depends on a number of factors, including how much EB-5 funding is being sought and how marketable the project is. One option may be to structure the project's capital stack such thatEB-5 funds are used to replace other financing, which would allow a project to move forward before the full amount of EB-5 capital is raised.

At-Risk Requirement

How can an EB-5 investor know his or her investment is considered at risk?

For an EB-5 investment to be considered at risk, there can be no guarantee of a return of the investment (e.g., a redemption agreement). Due diligence should be conducted to determine whether or not such language is included in the project documentation, and particular attention should be paid to the exit strategy.

Where should the funds of an EB-5 investment be upon filing Form I-526?

When adjudicating the I-526 petition, USCIS expects to see that the funds have been invested in the new commercial enterprise. In practice, this means the funds should already be transferred to the escrow account of the project, where the funds will remain until I-526 approval.

How is an EB-5 investment made?

This depends on whether the investment is being made directly into a new commercial enterprise or into a project sponsored by a regional center—as well as how the project is structured. Most EB-5 investments are in projects sponsored by regional centers, and most regional center investments involve the investor transferring funds into an escrow account that is authorized to release the funds into the investment vehicle. Before making an EB-5 investment, a foreign national should retain experienced immigration and securities counsel.

Must the NCE be profitable in order for an EB-5 investor to gain permanent residence?

Technically speaking, profitability is not a requirement of the EB-5 Program—only job creation based on an eligible investment. If a business plan isn't viable, an investor's I-526 petition may be denied. If the NCE becomes unprofitable after the I-526 petition is already approved, however, profitability should have no bearing on I-829 approval as long as the necessary number of jobs can be sustained and the NCE doesn't go bankrupt.

How long must an EB-5 investor's funds be considered at risk?
An EB-5 investment must remain at risk until after the I-829 petition is adjudicated. If no longer considered at risk when the I-829 is being adjudicated, the petition will be denied.

Can a real estate development project guarantee an EB-5 investor a home in return for investment at the end of the EB-5 process?
No, the guarantee of a home in return for investment is problematic in two major ways: (i) the value of the home would be counted against the at-risk capital of the EB-5 investment, which would likely cause the investment amount to fail to meet the required minimum; (ii) an EB-5 investor cannot be guaranteed any return of his or her investment, in part or in full—any guarantee would indicate the investment is not truly at risk.

Return on Investment

How does return on investment (ROI) work in the EB-5 Program?
The EB-5 Program is about gaining U.S. permanent resident status, and generally, the returns of EB-5 investments are low, ranging from about 0.5% to 1.0%. Returns may be distributed annually, quarterly, or even monthly depending on the project. Note that while a return on investment is permitted, a return of the investment is not—the principal of the investment must remain at risk until unconditional permanent resident status is granted.

What kind of return on investment (ROI) can an EB-5 investor expect?
The rate of return will depend entirely on the specific details of the investment. While ROI cannot be guaranteed, investors in EB-5 projects that employ a loan-based model might earn 1–2%, while equity investors' earnings will vary based upon the profitability of the enterprise. Because the primary purpose of an EB-5 investment is obtaining a green card, not making a profit, the main consideration of any EB-5 investor should be the immigration risk of a project, not its earning potential. A low-earning project that is safe from an immigration perspective is generally better than a project with a higher rate of return but greater immigration risk.

For EB-5 projects using a loan model, what is the standard term for loan repayment?
While there is no set industry standard, loan repayment often takes place in five or more years to account for the requirement that EB-5 funds be at risk until I-829 approval. Note, however, that EB-5 regulations require that invested funds be fully at risk, and so repayment cannot be guaranteed.

Direct versus Regional Center Projects

What does it mean to maintain a direct EB-5 investment?

In order to maintain an EB-5 investment, no part of the invested capital can be used for non-business purposes, nor can it be returned to the investor. An investor can receive profit distributions, but the principal must remain in the new commercial enterprise.

Can an EB-5 direct investment be used to purchase a residence from which the NCE operates?

Purchasing and using a residence as a business location will not likely be accepted by USCIS since the EB-5 investment must be in a new commercial enterprise and must remain at risk. Renovations and add-ons may be acceptable, but it would be best to consult an experienced EB-5 immigration attorney before proceeding.

What are direct, indirect, and induced jobs?

Direct jobs are positions created directly by the NCE, either through construction (if the construction lasts two or more years) or through operation of the business. These jobs can be counted easily because they are actual positions filled by actual people. Indirect jobs are those created as a result of the NCE's spending on goods and services, and induced jobs are created by the spending of the NCE's employees within the region. Indirect and induced jobs are calculated using economic models—and only projects sponsored by regional centers may count indirect and induced jobs toward the EB-5 employment requirement.

What form is used by EB-5 investors for direct investment projects?

No special form is used for a project not sponsored by a regional center—the EB-5 direct investor simply files an I-526 petition. Along with this petition, however, the investor will need to include the necessary project documentation, such as the EB-5 compliant business plan.

Are EB-5 investments protected in any way?

No, in order for an investment to qualify for EB-5, it must be considered "at risk" and have no guarantee of being returned in the end—or that it will generate returns while invested. Certain projects, however, are safer than others. Due diligence is a vital part of the investment process for any potential EB-5 investor.

EB-5 Program Status

When does the EB-5 Program next need reauthorization, and what does that mean for investors?

In February 2019, the EB-5 Regional Center Pilot Program was reauthorized with no changes; it will need to be reauthorized again by

September 30, 2019. If reauthorized, the investment amounts may be increased and other changes could be made. It is unclear what exactly might change and how such changes might affect investors and the industry as a whole.

How might a legislative audit of the EB-5 Program affect future EB-5 investments?

Whether or not Congress conducts a legislative audit of the EB-5 Program, and what such an audit might change, is impossible to determine. The program is up for renewal September 30, 2019, and so it is possible that changes will occur at this time. Any changes will likely have some bearing on future investments, but the specific effects will be unknown until changes are actually put into action.

Will Congress increase the minimum EB-5 investment threshold?

The current minimum investment threshold of $500,000 for projects located in TEAs can be changed—and such changes have been discussed in recent years. Any change to the EB-5 Program will require approval by Congress, but whether this will happen, and when, is unknown.

How will congressional changes to the TEA minimum investment amount affect current EB-5 projects and pending I-526 petitions?

Whether or not Congress changes the EB-5 Program, and how, is still unknown—and so it is impossible to determine how these changes will affect current projects and pending petitions. Many industry professionals assume that any changes would be prospective, not retroactive, and thus would affect future projects and petitions only.

Investors

General Questions

What are the potential consequences of filing an incomplete Form I-526 and submitting the missing documents later?

Submitting an incomplete I-526 petition will result in an RFE or a denial. Since RFEs cause delays, it is better to wait to send a complete application than face potential I-526 denial. If the missing information is sent after the petitioner receives a receipt notice but before an RFE is issued, a delay is still likely, and an RFE might even still be issued.

How often does a green card have to be renewed?

A green card expires every 10 years and must be renewed some time before the expiration date. This does not, however, mean that a permanent resident's status expires. Once a foreign national receives lawful permanent resident status, that status is permanent unless its terms are violated in a way that results in deportation (e.g., certain criminal activity, too much time spent outside the United States).

How much of the EB-5 process can an immigration attorney advise on?

An immigration attorney with EB-5 experience can advise on all relevant immigration issues and the compliance of the project with EB-5 regulations. An immigration attorney can also perform due diligence related to the immigration risk of a project, examining how likely an EB-5 investment will be met with approval by USCIS each step of the way. Except as they relate directly to immigration and EB-5 compliance, an immigration attorney should not be advising on the investment itself or the financial and business considerations of the investment; separate securities counsel and a financial adviser should be retained to assist in these areas.

Can purchasing a house qualify as an EB-5 investment?

No, the purchase of a residence does not qualify as an EB-5 investment. A house may, however, be used as collateral for a loan that could fund, in part or in full, an EB-5 investment.

Can an EB-5 investor make multiple investments in separate projects?

Yes, an EB-5 investor may invest in as many projects as desired, filing a separate Form I-526 for each. If more than one of the I-526 petitions is approved, however, the investor must choose which project will be the basis for his or her conditional permanent resident status—and ultimately the basis for the I-829 petition.

For married couples, which spouse should be the principal EB-5 applicant?

Either spouse may file as the principal applicant—this choice is up to the couple and in most cases has no bearing on the immigration process. Typically, if one spouse generates the funds used in the investments, he or she is the principal applicant, but this is not necessary.

If pursuing a different immigrant visa, when should an EB-5 investor withdraw an I-829 petition?

Because withdrawing an I-829 petition will result in loss of conditional permanent resident status, an investor should consult experienced immigration counsel before making this decision. Generally speaking, the investor should wait for the other immigrant petition to be approved, at which point he or she can withdraw the initial I-829 petition and file an I-485 application to adjust status.

What does the EB-5 priority date refer to, and what is it for?

Also known as the filing date or receipt date, the EB-5 priority date is the date on which the I-526 petition is received and filed by USCIS. The priority date is used to determine an applicant's place in the visa queue. Priority date is particularly important to Mainland-born Chinese nationals due to visa retrogression.

What is an EB-5 regional center management or administration fee, and do direct investments carry such a fee?

A management or administration fee is charged by a regional center to cover their costs, such as those involved in putting the project documentation together and marketing the project. Administration fees are generally around $50,000. A direct investment may or may not have such a fee—and the amount will vary—depending on whether the investment involves the services of legal professionals, consultants, planners, business brokers, management, etc.

What are the requirements for funds transfers from an EB-5 investor to a regional center?

The key requirements for EB-5 investors transferring funds is that the source and path of funds is clearly demonstrable, that the funds were gained and transferred legally, and that the funds belong to the investor.

Why do people apply for visas through the EB-5 Program?

While people apply for visas through the EB-5 Program for various reasons, the primary reason anyone pursues an EB-5 visa is to gain U.S. permanent resident status. People often pursue the EB-5 Program rather than other options because other immigrant visas may involve longer wait times and greater uncertainty.

Can a foreign national travel to the United States with a pending I-526 petition?

Yes, it is possible for a foreign national with a pending I-526 petition to travel to the United States, but the burden to prove nonimmigrant intent is greater. Anyone attempting to travel to the United States with a pending I-526 petition must be able to prove to the border patrol officer sufficient ties to home and obvious intent to return. The officer, however, will ultimately decide whether to allow the investor into the United States.

Can retained income from an investor's business be used as EB-5 investment funds?

Generally speaking, retained earnings cannot be used. The investment must be comprised of personal funds, and so the investor must demonstrate that the income was obtained through a salary, dividends, distributions, etc., and that taxes were paid as necessary.

When is an EB-5 investor able to legally work in the United States?

After an investor's I-526 petition is approved, he or she may apply for employment authorization while applying for adjustment of status. Employment authorization cards are generally issued within two to three months of the application. Apart from obtaining some other employment authorization, such as an H-1B visa, an EB-5 investor is able to legally work only after receiving employment authorization.

What documents will an EB-5 investor with a pending I-485 need at a Customs and Border Protection (CBP) checkpoint?

Any EB-5 investor planning to travel within the United States should consider checking with CBP to ensure he or she will have the proper documentation while travelling. These documents may include the investor's passport, I-485 receipt notice, employment authorization document (EAD), and travel document.

How is an EB-5 investor's country of origin (country of chargeability) determined?

A foreign national's country of chargeability is determined strictly by one's place of birth. Married couples born in different countries may claim either as their country of chargeability.

How many EB-5 investors are in a typical project sponsored by a regional center?

There is no "standard" number of EB-5 investors for regional center projects because each project differs in its financial needs and estimated job creation. Therefore, the number of EB-5 investors will be specifically based on the project, and each project's documentation ought to indicate the number of EB-5 investors it is seeking.

When do EB-5 investors get their invested capital back?

Whether or not EB-5 investors will have their capital returned, and when, depends on the success of the project and the specifics of the offering documents—particularly the exit strategy. In order to comply with the EB-5 Program, an investor's capital must be considered fully "at risk," at least until he or she has received I-829 approval.

Why did the number of denied I-526 petitions rise in 2018?

Generally speaking, if an I-526 petition is fully compliant with EB-5 laws and regulations, USCIS will approve it. An increase in denials in a given year is most likely due to a higher number of noncompliant petitions being adjudicated. Due to the complex nature of the EB-5 Program, petitions may be denied for any number of reasons.

What are the main differences between USCIS and the NVC?

United States Citizenship and Immigration Services (USCIS) is part of the U.S. Department of Homeland Security and is responsible for receiving and adjudicating immigrant petitions. Approved petitions are forwarded to the National Visa Center (NVC), an agency of the Department of State, who then handles the visa application and interview process.

Are there any current proposals to add new immigrant visa options?

While comprehensive immigration reform has recently been discussed by Congress, no such reform has taken place. Congress is not currently considering any additional immigrant visa options.

How might an EB-5 investor obtain clarification concerning EB-5 project documents?

Before entering any agreement, an EB-5 investor should retain competent immigration counsel with relevant EB-5 experience. The investor's attorney should be able to answer all questions concerning the project documentation— or at least be able to guide the investor toward other professionals as needed.

What changes to EB-5 law are likely to occur and when?

The EB-5 Program will continue as it currently exists until September 30, 2019, at which point action will be required by Congress. While Congress is expected to renew the program, it may at that time change EB-5 in a number of ways—the primary expected change is an increase to the minimum investment thresholds. Since 2020 is an election year, some in the industry anticipate another extension without change, but it is impossible to know what will happen with any certainty.

When is the minimum investment threshold for the EB-5 Program expected to change?

The EB-5 Program is up for renewal on September 30, 2019, at which point changes, particularly to the minimum investment threshold, might be made. Whether the EB-5 Program will change—and, if so, by how much—is yet to be determined.

Can an existing U.S. company's retained earnings or undistributed capital be the source of funds for an EB-5 investment?

The retained earnings cannot simply be reinvested by the company since the EB-5 Program requires the invested capital to be the personal funds of the investor. But as long as the capital is distributed or paid out as salary to the investor, who then pays all applicable taxes, this capital could be used by the investor to fund an EB-5 investment.

What is the first step to obtaining an EB-5 visa?

The first step any foreign national considering the EB-5 Program should take is to consult with an immigration attorney with EB-5 experience. Competent counsel will be able to determine if a foreign national is eligible for the program, if EB-5 is the best immigration option, and answer any questions the potential investor may have. If the foreign national decides to pursue an EB-5 visa, the attorney will be able to guide the investor through the entire process.

Why might a foreign national want to pursue the EB-5 Program?

The basic reason for anyone to pursue an EB-5 visa is to obtain permanent resident status in the United States. The reason a foreign national might choose the EB-5 Program over some other means of immigration will depend on the particular circumstances—but in general, for those who are qualified and can afford to make the required investment, the EB-5 Program offers one of the few direct paths to a green card.

What documents will an EB-5 investor need to enter the United States?

After an investor's I-526 petition is approved, he or she must apply for the EB-5 visa through Form DS-260 at the consulate in his or her home country. Once the visa application is approved, the investor will be issued a visa page in his or her passport. This visa is the only document needed to enter the United States.

How negotiable are EB-5 regional center administration fees?

Most EB-5 regional centers charge an administration fee of around $50,000, which is typically not open to negotiation. An interested EB-5 investor may ask, of course, and every regional center has its own policies.

What must an investor do to keep an EB-5 green card?

After receiving I-526 petition approval, an EB-5 investor is able to apply for conditional permanent resident status, which is valid for two years. This status is conditional, meaning it depends on the success of the petitioner's investment; permanent resident status will be maintained only if the investor's I-829 petition is approved. Upon receiving I-829 approval, the conditions on the investor's status are removed, and he or she will be issued a regular green card that must be renewed every 10 years. In order to maintain permanent resident status, the investor must abide by the law and will have to demonstrate that he or she has made the United States his or her place of residence.

Will a legal name change affect an investor's EB-5 application?

A name change in itself will not jeopardize an EB-5 application; the EB-5 investor will simply need to provide USCIS with a copy of the court order to demonstrate that his or her name was, in fact, changed. This court order should be submitted along with future filings, but it may also be submitted independent of any other documents as an interfiling.

What documents are needed to begin the EB-5 process?

Generally speaking, a potential EB-5 investor will need documents proving the lawful source and path of funds used for the investment. Depending on the nature of the source of funds, these documents can vary widely. Documents might, for example, include bank statements, payroll records, tax returns, property ownership documents, sale or loan of property documents, deeds of gift, and personal affidavits. Because the details of every EB-5 case are different, other documents may be needed—a consultation with an immigration attorney is necessary to determine all the specific documents an EB-5 investor will need.

How might multiple EB-5 investors pool their funds?

For regional center investments, pooling multiple investors' funds is the norm and is typically accomplished by forming a limited partnership in which the investors are limited partners. This structure is also viable for direct investments; however, the EB-5 investors involved in a direct investment may structure the business as they so choose. Direct investors interested in pooling funds should consult an experienced EB-5 immigration attorney to ensure their business structure is EB-5 compliant.

How might former membership in the communist party affect an EB-5 application?

Former membership in the communist party will not automatically disqualify someone from pursuing the EB-5 visa—each case is evaluated on an individual basis. Factors that may affect admissibility include whether the former party member joined voluntarily, the level of his or her participation, and how long ago he or she left the party.

Can starting or investing in a residential construction company qualify a foreign national for an EB-5 visa?

Investing in a residential construction company may satisfy the requirements of the EB-5 Program as long as (i) the company meets the definition of an NCE, (ii) the investment meets the minimum threshold of $500,000 (if the NCE is in a TEA) or $1,000,000, and (iii) the investment results in the creation of 10 full-time, permanent jobs for U.S. workers. One potential issue for a construction company in particular is that the new job positions must be permanent, not temporary or contract labor.

What is the typical rate of success for EB-5 investors obtaining green cards?

While statistics are available from USCIS regarding the total number of approved and denied EB-5 petitions, these statistics have little bearing on any individual EB-5 case. For investors looking into a project sponsored by a regional center, a more accurate statistic would be the success rate of the EB-5 regional center in question. For direct investments, however, no such metric is available. In general, the success of an EB-5 petition—whether for direct investments or projects sponsored by regional centers—is totally dependent on the success of the new commercial enterprise to create the necessary jobs using the investor's investment of funds derived from a lawful source.

How can funds be transferred from a country with capital export restrictions, like Sri Lanka, for EB-5 investment?

While it may be difficult to transfer money out of nations that have capital export restrictions, several options may exist depending on the specific country in question. For instance, it may be possible to transfer smaller portions of the investment to friends and family who can then transfer that money into the investor's U.S. account. In some nations, particularly in the Middle East, the Hawala system may need to be used. It is important for anyone in this kind of situation to consult, at minimum, a U.S. immigration attorney with EB-5 experience—though it may be prudent to consult a local professional experienced in this area of law as well.

How are I-526 petitions transmitted to USCIS?

I-526 petitions can be sent in physical form to USCIS via the post office or other mail delivery services. E-filing is available at the USCIS website.

How long are green cards valid?

The conditional green card issued based upon I-526 approval is valid for two years and must be renewed annually after that until I-829 adjudication. The standard green card must be renewed every 10 years.

Must green card holders apply for citizenship?

No, a lawful permanent resident is in no way required to pursue the naturalization process. There are benefits to gaining citizenship, and so those who are eligible should consider applying—but doing so is optional.

What happens if a permanent resident's citizenship application is denied?

If a permanent resident applies for citizenship and is denied, he or she may appeal the decision or refile. Denial of a citizenship application will have no effect on the applicant's permanent resident status unless the reason for the denial is also grounds for removal.

What can be done if an EB-5 investor's visa application is delayed due to administrative processing?

Administrative processing is a security measure triggered by an applicant's name, country of origin, or some other factor through which the Department of State involves other security agencies in the visa application review process. If an applicant is placed in administrative processing, he or she can do little to speed up the process—according to the Department of State, such cases are typically resolved within 60 days, though the length of time varies by country.

Would an inadmissible spouse adversely affect an EB-5 investor's I-526 petition?

No, each applicant's admissibility is determined independently. If the principal applicant's spouse is inadmissible, this determination will have no bearing on the principal applicant's admissibility.

How might a foreign national pursue an EB-5 visa and a degree from a U.S. institution at the same time?

In order for a foreign national to pursue a degree from a school in the United States, he or she must obtain an F-1 visa. If also desiring a green card through the EB-5 Program, the foreign national should secure the F-1 visa first. Once an I-526 petition is filed by an EB-5 investor, obtaining an F-1 visa will be difficult since that visa category requires an intent to return home and a pending EB-5 case indicates an intent to immigrate to the United States.

How much will it cost a foreign national to immigrate through the EB-5 Program?

The EB-5 Program requires an investment of $1,000,000 unless the project receiving the investment is located within a TEA, in which case the minimum investment amount is $500,000. If investing through a regional center, an administrative fee of about $50,000 can be expected. In addition to the investment capital and regional center fee, the I-526 petition carries a $1,500 USCIS filing fee; consular processing costs $345 per applicant while adjusting status through Form I-485 costs $1,070 per applicant; the I-829 petition carries a single USCIS filing fee of $3,750 and an $85 biometric services fee per applicant. Costs for legal representation will vary based on whether the applicant hires only an immigration attorney or securities, business, and/or tax counsel as well. As a result, legal fees may range from $15,000 to $50,000. A more specific estimate of all costs involved in obtaining this immigrant visa requires consultation with an immigrant attorney.

What criminal convictions make a person inadmissible?

Serious crimes and those involving moral turpitude make a person inadmissible. A pattern of lesser charges may also be a problem. Someone concerned about past criminal convictions should consult an immigration attorney before pursuing the EB-5 Program or any other immigrant visa.

How can an EB-5 investor obtain a copy of the I-829 receipt notice?

An EB-5 investor may request a copy of his or her I-829 petition receipt notice from USCIS directly or have his or her attorney make the request.

How might a prior mental illness diagnosis affect an EB-5 investor's admissibility?

Whether or not a past diagnosis of mental illness will affect a foreign national's admissibility depends on the nature of the nature of the mental illness and the extent of recovery. A mental health screening by a panel physician may be required to determine admissibility. It may be prudent for a potential EB-5 investor with past mental illness to consult an immigration attorney concerning his or her likelihood of being barred from entry.

What source of funds requirements are there for regional center fees, legal fees, and USCIS filing fees?

While EB-5 regulations require source of funds documentation for the investment funds only, the best practice is to have lawful source of funds documentation for all money used in the EB-5 process, including money used for administrative fees, legal fees, and filing fees.

Can an employer make an EB-5 investment in an NCE on behalf of an employee?

No, an EB-5 investment must be made using the personal assets of the investor. If an employer is interested in helping an employee make an EB-5 investment, the funds would have to be transferred to the investor in some way. For example, the money could be paid out to the investor as salary or dividends; it could be loaned to the investor, for instance, through a shareholder loan; or it could be given as a gift to the investor.

Does it matter which spouse is the principal EB-5 applicant?

No, either spouse may serve as the principal applicant; this will have no real bearing on the EB-5 application. If the spouses are from different nations, for instance, either spouse's home nation can be used as the nation of chargeability. As for the source of funds, the personal assets of one spouse, the other, or both may be included in the investment—their assets are interchangeable. That said, when deciding which spouse will serve as the principal applicant, a couple should consult with an experienced EB-5 immigration attorney to ensure the I-526 petition and source of funds documentation are as clean and clear as possible to avoid any unnecessary delays and/or RFEs.

Job Creation Requirement

Can an EB-5 investor get a job in an EB-5 regional center?

Yes, but there are two (2) main issues to consider here: (i) the EB-5 investor cannot be employed illegally; he or she must wait until the receipt of the conditional green card in order to be authorized work in the United States (for the EB- regional center), and (ii) the job that the EB-5 investor creates/takes at the EB-5 regional center will NOT count toward the 10 jobs required for the EB-5 investor to receive removal of conditions on his or her future I-829 petition with USCIS.

Which EB-5 investors' I-829 petitions will be approved if the project fails to create the necessary number of jobs?

For a project sponsored by a regional center, the project documentation should include a job allocation schedule. Typically, jobs are allocated on a first-in, first-out basis. If a project does not create the required number of jobs by the I-829 stage, an investor and his or her family members may still be able to obtain unconditional permanent resident status if it can be demonstrated that the project will produce the necessary jobs within 12 months.

Where can the employees of an EB-5 project live and work?

While the EB-5 Program's regulations do not indicate where employees must be located, several factors may affect whether USCIS considers these positions eligible for the EB-5 Program. The jobs created by the new commercial enterprise must be doing business principally within the region—which is particularly important for projects in TEAs. The employees should be living near enough to commute and be working in the area. Some traveling job positions and off-site work may be permissible depending on the nature of the business.

What does the 40% growth requirement mean when making an EB-5 investment in an existing business?

According to EB-5 regulations, the 40% growth must occur in either the net worth or number of employees. This is a complex and confusing area of the EB-5 Program—with few successful petitions—and so it is best for anyone considering an investment in an existing business to consult experienced EB-5 immigration counsel.

How can investors count indirect jobs toward the EB-5 employment requirement?

In order to include indirect jobs when calculating employment creation, the EB-5 investment must be made in a project sponsored by a regional center. Without investing through a regional center, only direct jobs may be counted.

Can an investment that does not create jobs qualify for the EB-5 Program?

No, job creation is the primary purpose of the EB-5 Program and is essential to an EB-5 petition's approval. Without meeting the employment creation requirement, an investor will be unable to gain permanent resident status.

Does purchasing commercial property count toward the minimum EB-5 investment amount?

Whether commercial property can be counted as part of an EB-5 investment depends on several factors. For all EB-5 investments, the key issue is whether the business will create the necessary number of jobs. For direct investments, job creation is calculated directly, and so the purchase of property may be permissible as long as the business plan demonstrates the connection between the property and the jobs. For regional center investments, jobs are often calculated from expenditures—in such cases, the expenditures cannot include land or property acquisition since real estate transactions do not generate jobs.

What are the potential consequences if an EB-5 project is unprofitable or experiences losses?

The EB-5 Program is primarily concerned with job creation, and so if a business fails to make a profit—or even suffers losses—as long as the necessary number of jobs are created within the two-year period of an investor's conditional permanent residence, USCIS will likely approve the investor's I-829 petition.

When must the required jobs be created for EB-5 purposes?

While USCIS has recently considered changes to the job creation timeline, the current requirement is that the jobs be created within 30 months of I-526 petition approval.

Can the jobs created by the tenant of a property purchased using EB-5 funds count toward job creation?

For a project sponsored by a regional center, the jobs created by a tenant may, depending on certain factors, be counted as indirect job creation—but this is complicated and would require careful guidance from a qualified EB-5 immigration attorney. For direct EB-5 investments, however, the new commercial enterprise created through the investment must be the entity that creates the required jobs. Therefore, for direct investments, jobs created by tenants cannot be counted.

How might existing jobs from an investor's U.S. business be counted toward EB-5 job creation?

Existing jobs from an investor's previous investment in a business may be able to be counted toward EB-5 job creation, but anyone in this situation should consult with an experienced EB-5 immigration attorney due to the potential for problems. The primary concerns here include whether the jobs were created as the direct result of the investor's capital and whether that capital's lawful source of funds can be demonstrated.

Under what circumstances can part time jobs be counted toward EB-5 job creation?

Part time positions cannot be counted toward EB-5 job creation; the 10 jobs must be full time and permanent. Generally speaking, however, job sharing is permitted, and so two or more workers may fill a full time position.

If an EB-5 investor exits a direct investment project after I-829 approval, how might this affect the job creation calculation for the project's other EB-5 investors?

In direct investment projects with more than one EB-5 investor, each investor is responsible for the creation of 10 permanent, full-time job positions. In other words, each investor must be able to demonstrate the connection between his or her investment and the jobs that were created. If an investor exits the project and withdraws his or her principal investment after receiving I-829 approval, the effect on the business's job creation could be substantial. This highlights the importance of a carefully constructed exit strategy that protects all investors. An experienced EB-5 immigration attorney would likely be needed to advise the remaining investors on how to best proceed.

Could purchasing rental property and employing property managers qualify as an EB-5 investment?

Because real estate purchases do not involve job creation, the purchase of multiple houses by itself will not likely work for EB-5 purposes. If along with the purchase of the rental properties a business were created to manage the properties—and that business employed 10 or more full-time employees—it may be possible to qualify for the EB-5 Program. An immigration attorney would need to review the specific circumstances to determine if such an investment plan would constitute an approvable project.

For investments in troubled businesses, how does USCIS determine whether jobs have actually been preserved?

When determining whether a troubled business's jobs have been preserved, USCIS may evaluate the economic analysis of the business as well as examine the employment numbers to see if jobs were indeed preserved. USCIS may, at its discretion, consider any and all available information when making its determination.

How long must job positions exist to be considered "permanent" and count toward EB-5 employment creation?

Generally speaking, in order for a job position to be counted toward EB-5 employment creation, the job must exist at the time the I-829 petition is filed—or must be expected to exist within a "reasonable period" thereafter. While the EB-5 Program requires jobs to be "permanent," this doesn't mean they must exist indefinitely—the requirement is that the jobs are not temporary or seasonal in nature.

Does an EB-5 investor already need to have created 10 jobs at the time of the investment?

No, the purpose of the EB-5 Program is that an investment from a foreign national result in the creation of 10 full-time job positions. These jobs need to be newly formed based upon the investment of the EB-5 applicant. Jobs that exist prior to the investment cannot be counted as new jobs for EB-5 purposes.

How might an EB-5 investor count preserved jobs?

In order to count existing jobs that are preserved due to an EB-5 investment, the NCE must qualify as a troubled business. For EB-5 purposes, a troubled business is one that has existed for more than two years and has, in the past 12 to 24 months, experienced a net loss of at least 20% of its net worth. Apart from investments in troubled business, only newly created job positions may be counted toward the EB-5 employment requirement.

Change of Status

Can a foreign national in the United States with a pending asylum petition pursue the EB-5 Program?

Both an asylum claim and the EB-5 Program can be pursued at the same time; however, a foreign national with an asylum case pending should consult an experienced immigration attorney before proceeding to ensure he or she understands the potential consequences and risks.

Is there a limit to the number of visa types a foreign national can apply for?

Technically, no, but several factors must be considered. First, any visa application must be legitimate and non-frivolous. Second, if a foreign national is in the United States already, he or she must maintain legal status to be able to adjust to permanent resident status. Additionally, if the foreign national is currently in the United States on a nonimmigrant visa, a pending immigrant visa may affect his or her ability to renew the nonimmigrant visa.

What is an EB-5 investor's immigration status with a conditional green card?

A conditional green card holder has conditional permanent resident status, which affords the immigrant all the rights granted to permanent residents. A conditional green card holder may live and work anywhere in the United States, and he or she may enrol in education programs as a domestic student.

How can an EB-5 investor and any derivative beneficiaries abandon their conditional green cards?

To abandon their conditional green cards, an EB-5 investor and his or her family should appear at the U.S. embassy or consulate in their home nation, complete the interview, and file the proper paperwork (Form I-407).

Can an EB-5 investor with conditional permanent resident status apply for citizenship?

Yes, EB-5 investors with pending I-829 petitions may apply for U.S. citizenship if they meet all other naturalization requirements. The application for naturalization, however, will not be approved until the I-829 is approved. Applying for citizenship will force USCIS to adjudicate the I-829. It may be prudent to consult immigration counsel before proceeding since forcing USCIS to adjudicate the I-829 may, depending on the reasons for delay, result in denial.

Can an EB-5 investor transfer the application to his or her spouse?

No, once a foreign national files Form I-526 as the principal applicant, his or her spouse cannot become the principal applicant. The investor could withdraw the application and refile, but this will have financial repercussions (e.g., filing fees, legal fees, administrative fees, etc.) as well as an effect on immigration (e.g., a new priority date and, therefore, longer wait for permanent resident status).

What happens to an EB-5 applicant's priority date when the case is transferred to the IPO?

When the California Service Center (CSC) forwards a case to the Immigrant Investor Program Office (IPO), the priority date, which is the date the case was filed by USCIS, should not change.

Are EB-5 investors required to apply for advance parole when filing Form I-485?

While not required, unless an investor has a valid H or L visa, he or she should not travel abroad without advance parole. Without one of these two visas or a travel document, leaving the United States will be considered an abandonment of the investor's I-485 adjustment of status application.

Can an EB-5 investor in the United States on a visa waiver adjust status upon I-526 approval?

No, a foreign national who enters the United States on a visa waiver is not eligible to adjust status using Form I-485; the investor must consular process in his or her home nation.

Can an EB-5 investor extend P-3 status once an I-526 petition is filed?

As long as the P-3 visa holder is not classified as support personnel, USCIS generally allows P-3 extensions for applicants with pending immigrant petitions.

How might a pending I-526 petition affect an application to change from F-1 to F-2 status?

The F-1 and F-2 visas do not allow for immigrant intent, and so changing status to F-2 after an I-526 petition has been filed may prove challenging. Immigration counsel should be consulted regarding the specific facts and timeline of the case to determine whether changing status might be a viable option, and if not, to discuss what other options may be available.

What happens when an EB-5 investor withdraws a pending I-829 petition?

Withdrawing an I-829 petition would result in an abandonment of conditional permanent resident status for the principal applicant and all derivative beneficiaries, which would require them to leave the United States. This action with USCIS will likely have no bearing on the other aspects of the investment, such as its exit strategy, and so whether the investor will be able to get his or her principal investment back will depend on the investment's subscription agreement.

US Tax Treatment

At what point should an EB-5 investor expect to receive a K-1 tax form?

While this depends on the terms of the regional center, typically a K-1 will not be issued until after Form I-526 is approved since, in most cases, the invested funds will not be taken from escrow until USCIS approves the petition. In some cases, investors may receive a Schedule K-1 whenever the new commercial enterprise files its annual tax return.

When does tax residence start for an immigrant?

Tax residence is not the same as permanent residence, and determining when an immigrant's tax obligation in the United States begins can involve some level of complexity. Generally speaking, however, a person becomes a resident for tax purposes after both gaining permanent resident status and physically residing in the United States for six months.

When does an EB-5 investor become subject to U.S. taxes and other laws?

Whenever a foreign national is in the United States, he or she is subject to all local, state, and federal laws. An EB-5 investor's U.S. tax obligation generally begins when he or she obtains conditional permanent resident status and is physically residing in the United States—though investors residing in the United States under a nonimmigrant status may already be subject to U.S. taxes.

US Citizenship

For naturalization purposes, when does an EB-5 investor's period continuous residence begin?

The continuous residence requirement for naturalization begins when an EB-5 investor is granted conditional permanent resident status.

When is an EB-5 investor able to apply for U.S. citizenship?

An EB-5 investor may apply for U.S. citizenship after 4 years and 9 months in the United States. This period begins when the investor is granted his or her conditional permanent residence and is noted on the investor's green card. The investor must also meet certain other requirements, such as being physically present in the country at least 50% of the time and not abroad for any period of more than six months.

What are the continuous residence requirements for naturalization for EB-5 green card holders?

For an EB-5 investor, continuous residence for naturalization purposes begins when conditional permanent resident status is granted. The residence requirements are otherwise the same as for any other green card holder: more than 30 months of presence accrued over five years with no absences of more than six continuous months.

Why does the EB-5 visa lead to permanent residence while other visas do not?

The United States issues two general types of visas: nonimmigrant visas, which are issued to foreign nationals who wish to visit, study, or work in the United States on a temporary basis, and immigrant visas, which allow foreign nationals to enter the United States and obtain a green card (permanent resident status). The EB-5 visa is an immigrant visa that allows a foreign national to make an investment in a U.S. enterprise and, if all of the criteria are met, gain permanent resident status.

What is the process for becoming a U.S. citizen through the EB-5 Program?

The first step in becoming a U.S. citizen through the EB-5 Program is to gain lawful permanent resident status, which requires making an eligible investment and filing Form I-526. Upon I-526 approval, the foreign national is granted conditional permanent residence, which is identical to lawful permanent residence except that it is conditioned on the successful completion of the EB-5 Program. After two years of conditional permanent resident status, the investor files Form I-829 to remove conditions—which will be adjudicated based on whether the EB-5 investment was sustained and the employment creation requirement was met. If Form I-829 is approved, the EB-5 investor will be able to apply for naturalized citizenship four years and nine months after first receiving conditional permanent resident status—assuming all other requirements are met.

Family Member Treatment

Are family members of an EB-5 investor granted conditional permanent residence?

The EB-5 Program enables investors, their spouses, and unmarried children under age 21 to receive conditional permanent resident status through investment. The number of family members is not a consideration. For older children, as long as Form I-526 is filed before age 21, they will be able to apply for conditional permanent residence.

How does the EB-5 Program work for married couples?

The EB-5 Program allows the principal applicant and his or her spouse and unmarried children under age 21 to gain permanent resident status. Therefore, only one spouse needs to submit Form I-526 and make a qualifying investment. Depending on the situation, the spouse with the greater income may be better suited to submitting Form I-526 in order to more easily demonstrate lawful source of funds. If the spouses are of different nationalities, certain considerations may apply, such as visa backlogs, consular processing times, etc.

How might an EB-5 applicant visit the United States before receiving his or her conditional green card?

An EB-5 applicant and his or her dependent family members can temporarily enter the United States using B-1/B-2 visas while waiting to gain conditional permanent resident status. This shouldn't be a problem as long as they disclose their pending immigration petition and express their intent to return to their home country for consular processing.

If the principal I-526 applicant is living in the United States on a different visa and plans to adjust status through Form I-485, how can dependents living abroad file for the EB-5 visa?

After the principal applicant has adjusted his or her status, it should be possible to file for following-to-join benefits for any dependent family members. It may be quicker, however, for the principal applicant to return home and process at the consulate at the same time as his or her family. Since each case is different, it would be best to retain immigration counsel to determine the best course of action.

Can someone file Form I-485 as an EB-5 investor and Form I-485 as an EB-2 immigrant?

While a person can pursue both the EB-2 and EB-5 immigrant visa paths, when submitting Form I-485, he or she can file under only one employment-based category. When choosing which category might be best, timing is one consideration since, depending on the circumstances, one path may be quicker than the other. Another significant consideration is that permanent resident status through EB-5 is conditional for two years while the status granted through EB-2 is not.

Can a teenager apply for an EB-5 visa?

While there is no statutory age requirement for the EB-5 Program, in order to make the necessary investment, the investor must be able to legally execute a contract (e.g., a subscription agreement). Therefore, the investor could not be considered a minor under applicable state law. If unmarried, however, a teenager would qualify as a dependent of an EB-5 investor and could thereby gain permanent resident status through his or her parent's successful EB-5 investment.

After filing an I-829 petition, at what point are the dependents of an EB-5 investor given an extension of their status?

Shortly after the EB-5 investor files his or her I-829, USCIS will issue a receipt notice that allows the investor and any dependents to reenter the United States. The status extension lasts for one year and may need to be renewed if the extension expires before the investor's I-829 petition is adjudicated.

Can an unmarried adopted child under age 21 be included on an EB-5 application?

This depends on several factors. An adopted child can be a derivative beneficiary if he or she was adopted before the age of 16 and has been in the legal and physical custody of the parent(s) for at least two years. The parent(s) must also demonstrate that the adoption was full and final. Several other factors may affect eligibility, and exceptions may apply depending on the circumstances.

Will divorce affect the permanent resident status of an EB-5 investor's spouse?

If an EB-5 investor and his or her spouse have already obtained conditional permanent resident status through an approved I-526 petition, then a divorce will not affect the spouse's resident status or his or her ability to file Form I-829 to remove conditions.

When can a principal EB-5 applicant add a spouse to the application?

Generally, the spouse of an EB-5 investor applies for an EB-5 visa at the same time as the principal applicant—after Form I-526 is approved and the applicant files a DS-260 immigrant visa application (if living abroad) or an I-485 application to adjust status (if living in the United States).

At what point in the EB-5 process may a dependent child marry, and will the child's spouse become a derivative beneficiary?

If a dependent child marries before obtaining conditional permanent resident status, he or she will no longer be an eligible dependent. Once the child has a green card, he or she is free to marry, but the spouse will not be a derivative beneficiary of the principal EB-5 investor and would need to pursue an F2A or some other visa in order to immigrate.

Can a B-1 visa holder travel to the United States after receiving I-526 approval but before obtaining a green card?

With an approved I-526 petition, entry on a B-1 visa may be denied. If a B-1 visa holder with an approved I-526 petition needs to travel to the United States for business purposes before obtaining permanent resident status, he or she may be able to—but it will likely be necessary to have documentation stating the urgency of the visit and an itinerary that includes a departure date or some other indication of intent to return. Before attempting to travel, the B-1 visa holder should get the opinion of the U.S. embassy or consulate in his or her home country.

Can a derivative file Form I-485 after the I-829 petition is approved?

If a derivative was listed on the I-526 petition but simply failed to adjust status or consular process at the time of I-526 approval, it may be possible to apply for the adjustment of status through Form I-485 after approval of the I-829 petition. Alternatively, the derivative may have to file for following-to-join benefits, or the principal applicant might have to file Form I-130, petition for Alien Relative. The specific course of action will depend on the circumstances of the case, and so it is important to retain experienced immigration counsel.

What happens if a dependent child turns 21 before the I-526 petition is approved?

As long as an I-526 petition is filed before a dependent child is 21, and as long as he or she adjusts status or consular processes within one year of I-526 approval, the child will still be considered the principal applicant's dependent and will be eligible for an EB-5 visa as a derivative beneficiary.

What should an investor do if a family member's fee bill is missing?

If a fee bill is missing for one family member and not others, the investor or his or her attorney should contact the National Visa Center (NVC) immediately. Typically, the NVC issues fee bills within days of a request. In the meantime, it makes sense to continue processing the other family members' paperwork.

How long must an EB-5 business be maintained?

An EB-5 investment must be sustained throughout the conditional residence period. If the investment was sustained and created 10 job positions, the investor will be able to petition to have the conditions removed from his or her status. After the investor obtains unconditional permanent resident status, he or she is no longer required to maintain the investment/EB-5 business.

Can the principal EB-5 investor abandon his or her green card without affecting the family's green cards?

Once lawful permanent resident status is given to the investor and his or her family members, each person's status is independent of the others'. If, however, the principal EB-5 investor abandons his or her conditional green card before Form I-829 is approved, the investor and all derivative beneficiaries will be unable to remove conditions and obtain permanent green cards.

How soon after gaining conditional resident status can an EB-5 investor file an F2A spousal petition?

If an EB-5 investor gets married sometime after filing Form I-485, upon receiving conditional permanent resident status, he or she has the right to petition for his or her spouse. To sponsor his or her spouse, the investor must file Form I-130. If the investor's I-829 petition is denied, the spouse's F2A may also be terminated.

Can a same-sex married couple apply for EB-5 visas?

Yes, as long as the couple was married in a jurisdiction that recognizes same-sex marriages as legal, the principal applicant may claim his or her spouse as a derivative beneficiary.

Is an EB-5 applicant's stepchild considered a derivative beneficiary?

As long as a stepchild was under age 18 when his or her parents married, he or she may be included as a derivative beneficiary. The stepchild must also be under age 21 and unmarried at the time of filing Form I-526.

If a green card holder gives birth to a child while abroad, what is the child's immigrant status?

If a child is born to a U.S. green card holder while she is abroad, a record of lawful permanent residence will be created for the child as long as the following two conditions are met: (i) the child enters the United States with his or her mother on the mother's first reentry into the United States, and (ii) the child is under two years old upon entry. If these conditions are not met, a parent will have to file Form I-130, petition for Alien Relative, in order to obtain a green card for the child. On the other hand, if the child is born in the United States, he or she will be a citizen at birth.

At what point in the process do EB-5 applicants have access to resident tuition rates?

Once an EB-5 investor and his or her derivative beneficiaries have obtained conditional permanent resident status, they may live, work, and study anywhere in the United States. The right to study in the United States does not necessarily mean access to resident tuition rates—the residence requirements for in-state tuition vary by state.

What is the immigration status of an EB-5 investor and any derivative beneficiaries after the I-526 petition is approved?

An approved I-526 petition does not, by itself, confer any immigration status to the petitioner or his or her derivatives—after receiving I-526 petition approval, the petitioner must file either Form I-485 to adjust status (if already in the United States) or Form DS-260 to consular process (if living abroad). After successfully adjusting status or consular processing, the investor and any derivatives will be granted conditional permanent resident status.

Must each of an EB-5 investor's derivative beneficiaries fill out Form DS-260?

Yes, the EB-5 principal applicant and each derivative family member must complete the online Form DS-260, pay the fee, and submit all the necessary documents.

Why might an attorney advice against pursuing the EB-5 Program?

While thousands of foreign nationals have successfully gained permanent resident status through the EB-5 Program, this program is not for everyone. An attorney might advise against pursuing an EB-5 visa if other immigrant visa options are better suited to the client or if he or she foresees challenges to a successful petition, such as an inability to prove lawful source and path of funds. It is also possible, however, that an attorney advises against EB-5 simply out of ignorance—the EB-5 process requires specific knowledge of a fairly complicated area of law.

When should the derivatives of an EB-5 investor file Form I-485?

Unless there is a compelling reason not to, the principal applicant and all derivatives should file their I-485 applications at the same time. If a derivative chooses not to file at the same time as the principal applicant, he or she may file Form I-485 up to six months after the principal applicant is granted permanent resident status. After six months, the derivative must file for following-to-join benefits via Form I-824, Application for Action on an Approved Application.

How will I-526 approval affect a derivative's ability to obtain or renew an F-1 visa?

Depending on the timing, it is possible that an I-526 approval will have no effect on a derivative's application for an F-1 visa. Until a derivative files his or her own Form DS-260, he or she has not expressed immigrant intent. It may, however, be necessary for the derivative to disclose the potential of future immigration based on the family member's EB-5 petition. If a derivative has already applied for an EB-5 visa, he or she may be denied the F-1 visa. Due to the complex nature and timing of such cases, it would be best for the investor and/or derivative beneficiary to consult their immigration attorney before proceeding with the F-1 application.

How is a derivative child's age calculated, particularly in light of visa retrogression?

In order for a child of a principal EB-5 investor to be eligible for an EB-5 visa as a derivative, he or she must be unmarried and less than 21 years old. For immigration purposes, the child's age is determined by taking his or her age at the time his or her visa number becomes available and subtracting the length of time the I-526 petition was pending (from filing date to approval date). Time spent waiting due to visa retrogression—which presently affects only Mainland-born Chinese nationals—is not subtracted. For example, if a child is 22 years and 3 months old when a visa number becomes available and Form I-526 was pending for 16 months, then for immigration purposes, the child's age is 20 years 11 months. Such a child could be claimed as a derivative beneficiary.

Can a derivative beneficiary living in the United States as a nonimmigrant adjust status even if the principal applicant consular processes?

Until the principal applicant has completed consular processing and received his or her conditional green card, the derivative would be unable to file to adjust status. It would be best for the principal applicant and all derivatives to consular process together.

When can an EB-5 investor file Form I-130 on behalf of relatives?

Form I-130 may be filed by any lawful permanent resident or U.S. citizen. Therefore, once an EB-5 investor has obtained conditional permanent resident status, he or she may file Form I-130.

Can the EB-5 Program help a derivative who has overstayed a visa?

Because derivative beneficiaries must obtain their own EB-5 visas, even though their visa applications are all based upon the same approved I-526 petition, their admissibility is determined individually. Unless a waiver is obtained, a derivative who has overstayed his or her visa will be temporarily or, in some cases, permanently barred from entering the United States.

Will divorce during conditional residence affect an I-829 petition?

Generally speaking, divorce will have no effect on a conditional permanent resident's ability to file Form I-829. The principal applicant may include the former spouse on his or her I-829 or, if necessary, the spouse can file his or her own I-829 petition.

Who is allowed to gift funds to an EB-5 investor?

Currently, the EB-5 Program does not restrict the gifting of funds to any particular relationship between the benefactor and the investor. As long as the gifted funds were obtained and transferred lawfully, they can be used by the EB-5 investor.

Can an EB-5 investor add a spouse to his or her application after obtaining a conditional green card?

A spouse cannot be added as a derivative beneficiary after the principal applicant has received conditional permanent resident status. At that point, the investor will need to petition for the spouse using Form I-130—but the spouse will not obtain a visa until his or her priority date becomes current.

Can an EB-5 investor's partner in a civil union apply for an EB-5 visa as a derivative?

USCIS will not recognize a partner joined through civil union. If a same-sex couple is not married due to the marriage laws in their home nation, the solution is to get married in a nation that recognizes same-sex marriage. USCIS recognizes same-sex spouses as long as the couple was married where same-sex marriage is legal.

When can the derivative family members of the EB-5 investor apply for their green cards?

Typically, all derivatives apply for the EB-5 visa and green card at the same time as the principal applicant. This application process takes place after the I-526 petition is approved.

How might an expected grandchild be included as an EB-5 derivative beneficiary?

Only the spouse of the principal applicant and his or her unmarried children under age 21 can be included as derivatives under EB-5 law. If an investor's unmarried daughter is expecting a child, the immigration options for the child are limited. Once the daughter obtains permanent resident status, she can petition for the child.

Does an EB-5 investor have to include his or her spouse on the application if the spouse does not intend to pursue the EB-5 visa?

An EB-5 investor is not required to list his or her spouse as a derivative beneficiary, but it is better to list all eligible family members in the I-526 petition because it is much more difficult to add them later in the EB-5 process. Regardless of whether the spouse is included as a derivative beneficiary, the applicant should truthfully answer any questions about marital status and submit any requested documents (e.g., the marriage certificate).

How will a derivative abandoning his or her conditional permanent residence affect the principal EB-5 applicant and other derivatives?

A derivative may file Form I-407, Abandonment of Lawful Permanent Resident Status, to be removed from the pending I-829 petition. Doing so will have no effect on the principal EB-5 applicant or other derivatives.

When is the child of an EB-5 investor too old to be included as a derivative beneficiary?

The child of anEB-5 investor may be included as a derivative beneficiary as long as he or she is unmarried and under age 21 when USCIS receives the I-526 petition. Note, however, that this issue becomes more complicated for the children of Mainland-born Chinese investors due to visa retrogression. For EB-5 purposes, a child's age is frozen while the I-526 petition is pending, but this is not the case while waiting for an available visa.

If an EB-5 investor marries or has a child after filing his or her I-526 petition, will the new family member be eligible for a green card?

As long as the new family relationship exists before the principal applicant applies for the EB-5 visa/green card—whether by adjusting status through Form I-485 or by consular processing through Form DS-260—the new family member should be able to apply as a derivative beneficiary. The main consideration here is timing, and so any EB-5 investor planning to marry or anticipating the birth of a child should consult an immigration attorney.

Can someone in the United States as a spouse on a nonimmigrant dependent visa, such as F-2, J-2, or H-4, apply for EB-5?

Yes, anyone who meets the requirements for the EB-5 visa may apply. If someone on a dependent visa applies for the EB-5 visa, his or her spouse—the primary nonimmigrant visa holder—may be listed as a derivative beneficiary on the EB-5 application.

How might a stepchild be included as a derivative beneficiary of an EB-5 investor?

It is possible to include a stepchild as a derivative beneficiary as long as (i) the child is unmarried and under 21 years old at the time of filing, (ii) the child was under 18 years old when the marriage took place, and (iii) sufficient documentation is provided, including but not limited to the marriage certificate, divorce decree or death certificate of the biological parent, and the child's birth certificate and any other necessary proof of legal custody.

How might an EB-5 investor sponsor elderly parents as dependents?

The EB-5 Program allows the principal applicant to include as derivative beneficiaries his or her spouse and any unmarried children under age 21. The principal applicant's parents, or any other relatives, may not be sponsored through EB-5. After an EB-5 investor becomes a resident, however, he or she may petition for relatives using Form I-130.

Can an EB-5 investor and his or her family move to the United States before the I-526 petition is adjudicated?

Because no immigration status is granted while the I-526 petition is pending, an investor and his or her family may only enter the United States using a valid nonimmigrant visa. Note, however, that unless the nonimmigrant visa being sought carries dual intent, it is less likely to be approved once the I-526 is filed. Immigration counsel would be able to help determine what nonimmigrant visas an EB-5 investor and his or her family are eligible for.

If a derivative child turns 21 before Form I-829 is approved, will the child be eligible for the permanent green card?

The age requirement for derivative children is that they be under age 21 at the time the I-526 petition is filed. A derivative child may still age out if a visa is not immediately available after I-526 approval (which currently only affects Mainland-born Chinese nationals). Once a derivative child receives a conditional green card, however, age is no longer a factor—the conditions on his or her green card will be removed when the I-829 petition is approved.

Can a married couple file two separate I-526 petitions and include one another as derivatives?

Yes, both spouses may file separate EB-5 petitions as principal applicants and list each other as derivatives; however, only one petition may serve as the basis for the EB-5 visa application. So, while possible, such a plan can only improve the chances of I-526 petition approval—it will not increase the likelihood of I-829 petition approval. Two EB-5 applications is no substitute for competent immigration counsel and careful due diligence.

How might an EB-5 applicant and/or derivatives postpone entering the United States after I-526 approval in order to complete business, academic, or other obligations?

Depending on the length of delay required, consular processing may be postponed; note, however, that delaying the visa application process can result in a child aging out. Once an EB-5 visa is issued, the visa holder has six months to enter the United States. In order to avoid any undesirable consequences, any foreign national considering intentionally delaying consular processing or entrance into the United States should consult an experienced immigration attorney.

How might derivatives spend more than six months abroad after obtaining an EB-5 visa?

Once EB-5 visas are issued to an investor and his or her family, it would be best for all visa holders to enter the United States within the six months that the EB-5 visa is valid. If more time is necessary, or for extended absences, an EB-5 visa holder should obtain a reentry permit, which would allow the immigrant to remain abroad for up to two years; if more time is required, another reentry permit will need to be issued. The primary concern for permanent residents spending extended periods abroad is proving an intent to reside in the United States—any permanent resident considering an extended absence should consult an immigration attorney to ensure sufficient ties to the United States exist and that he or she will not jeopardize his or her status.

Can a derivative beneficiary on a nonimmigrant visa travel abroad with a pending I-526 petition?

Until an I-526 petition is approved, an EB-5 investor's derivative beneficiaries are free to leave and reenter the United States on any valid nonimmigrant visas they may have as long as the purpose for their reentry is consistent with their nonimmigrant visas. For example, a derivative with a valid F-1 student visa may enter the United States to pursue his or her academic program.

Is there a limit to the number of family members who can apply for EB-5 visas as derivative beneficiaries?

There is no specific limit to the number of family members who can apply for EB-5 visas as derivatives; however, the only family members eligible as derivative beneficiaries are the principal applicant's spouse and any unmarried children under age 21 at the time the I-526 petition is filed.

How might a parent who shares custody of a child include the child as a derivative beneficiary on an EB-5 application?

If an EB-5 investor wishes to obtain a visa for a child from a previous marriage in which he or she and the other parent share custody, the investor will likely have to first acquire consent from the other parent.

Visa Availability

How is EB-5 visa availability determined?

Other than for Mainland China, all countries have current visa availability. A total of 10,000 EB-5 visas are available each year, and up to 7.1% of these are available to investors from any given nation. This limit can be exceeded if there are unused visas, but no nation except China has approached/exceeded the 7.1% limit.

What is the current minimum EB-5 investment and when will it change?

Currently, the investment threshold for projects located in TEAs is $500,000, while the threshold for projects outside of TEAs is $1,000,000. These minimums may be changed by Congress, but it is unclear when and by how much. In February 2019, Congress extended the program for seven more months without alteration; the program is up for reauthorization on September 30, 2019, and may at that point be changed.

Is Hong Kong considered part of Mainland China for EB-5 purposes?

No, applicants born in Hong Kong are considered separately from Mainland-born Chinese and are not subject to the current EB-5 visa availability delays for Mainland-born Chinese nationals.

What is the success rate for EB-5 investors obtaining visas?

USCIS website offers updated statistics regarding the approval and denial rates of I-526 and I-829 petitions. The approval rate for I-526 petitions generally ranges from about 75% to above 80%. It can be assumed that an investor who receives I-526 approval will apply for conditional permanent resident status. The approval rate for I-829 petitions is generally above 90%.

Are foreign nationals from certain countries restricted from applying for EB-5 visas?

No, the EB-5 Program is open to applicants from all nations. Practically speaking, however, there are certain limitations. For example, applicants from Mainland China are subject to visa retrogression due to high participation and limited numbers of visas. Also, the economic and immigration policies of some nations create specific obstacles for potential EB-5 investors.

China Retrogression

Why do Mainland China EB-5 applicants face a longer wait time to receive their conditional green cards?

This is a simple question of supply and demand. The current demand for EB-5 visas from China has exceeded the fixed number of visas available for Chinese applicants. The mechanics of this deal with the immigrant visa quota system. Today there are only 10,000 EB-5 visas available worldwide per (USCIS) fiscal year. The Department of State has allocated 7% of the total available visas to Chinese investors, plus any un-claimed visas from all other countries. Demand in China is significantly greater than in any other country, but it is facing rising competition from countries such as India, Venezuela, South Korea, and Brazil. As evidence, Chinese investors claimed 83% of the 10,000 visas available in 2015 but only 48% in 2018. Despite this drastic decrease, the visa supply for Chinese applicants must still be kept in check so that there are visas available for EB-5 applicants from the rest of the world. This is done by instituting a "cut-off date" each month (i.e., only applicants with priority dates before the cut-off date can receive an immigrant visa/green card for that month). Currently, no other countries are facing a "cut-off date" or other type of processing delay and this is unlikely to change in the near future due to lower EB-5 visa demand outside of China.

What can Mainland-born Chinese EB-5 investors do to get green cards more quickly?

EB-5 investors from Mainland China can do nothing to more quickly obtain their green cards. The wait time, which is currently about five to six years, is due to the limited number of visas available through the EB-5 Program in a given year and the high participation among Chinese investors. While Congress and/or USCIS could implement changes that might reduce the wait, it is unlikely they will do so.

Does EB-5 visa retrogression for Mainland-born Chinese applicants affect other Chinese applicants?

No, EB-5 visa retrogression currently affects Mainland-born Chinese nationals exclusively. Other Chinese nationals, such as those from Taiwan or Hong Kong, are not subject to EB-5 visa retrogression.

Visa Comparison/Overlap

Is the L-1 or EB-5 visa better for me?

Which visa is best depends on several factors. One of the main differences between the two visas is that the L-1 is a nonimmigrant visa while the EB-5 is an immigrant visa. If the goal is to become a permanent U.S. resident, the EB-5 may be the better option. Timing is another consideration since EB-5 petitions have a backlog of more than a year. A number of additional factors are involved, and retaining an experienced immigration attorney is an excellent first step.

Can an EB-5 investor apply for an E-2 visa while waiting for I-526 approval?

Nothing bars an EB-5 investor with a pending I-526 petition from applying for an E-2 visa, and applying for an E-2 visa won't jeopardize the I-526 petition. It may, however, be hard to prove the nonimmigrant intent necessary for the E-2 visa with a pending I-526 petition, which demonstrates intent to immigrate.

What are the consequences of an H-1B visa holder filing an I-526 petition?

Because H-1B visas allow for dual intent, submitting Form I-526 will not affect a foreign national's H-1B status. While awaiting adjudication, an H-1B holder should maintain his or her status, and once the I-526 is approved, the foreign national can apply for an adjustment to status through Form I-485.

Can a foreign national pursue the EB-5 Program and register for the Diversity visa Lottery at the same time?

Yes, a person can pursue both immigration avenues at the same time; however, once an EB-5 investment is made, it may or may not be retrievable depending on the specific details of the project's offering documents. The EB-5 Program has a high rate of success, while the chances of gaining a green card through the DV Lottery are slim—but there is no harm in pursuing both, and doing so only increases the likelihood of gaining permanent resident status.

Can an EB-5 investor with a pending I-526 petition enter the United States on an I visa?

Because the I visa is a nonimmigrant visa that does not allow for dual intent, entering or reentering the United States on the I visa may be problematic with a pending I-526 petition since that petition clearly demonstrates immigrant intent. If a foreign national filed his or her I-526 petition after entering the United States on an I visa, it may be necessary to return home and complete consular processing upon receiving Form I-526 approval.

Can an EB-5 applicant apply for an F-1 visa?

The F-1 student visa is a nonimmigrant visa, and so a pending I-526 petition will likely result in an F-1 visa application being denied since pursuing the EB-5 Program demonstrates immigrant intent. If a foreign student is already in the United States on an expired F-1 visa, even if his or her status is current, leaving the country with a pending EB-5 application might make reentry on a new F-1 visa difficult or impossible.

Which country should an EB-5 investor with dual citizenship apply from?

In most cases, the differences between applying for an EB-5 visa from one country or another are negligible. Certain countries, however, have restrictions on transferring funds, more complicated source of funds requirements, longer consular processing times, etc. Experienced immigration counsel will be able to help an EB-5 investor with dual citizenship to determine which country it would be better to apply from.

Can a married couple from two different nations use either nation as their nation of chargeability?

Yes, if the principal applicant and his or her spouse are from different nations, the applicant can apply for the EB-5 visa from his or her home nation or cross charge to the home nation of his or her spouse. For many EB-5 investors, the nation of chargeability will have little effect except for Mainland-born Chinese nationals, in which case cross charging may carry significant advantages due to the visa backlog facing Chinese investors.

What is a foreign national's status while appealing H-1B termination, and how could such circumstances affect an EB-5 petition?

When H-1B status expires or is terminated, the foreign worker is out of status. Being out of status can have significant effects on applying for the EB-5 visa: (i) too much time spent in the United States while out of status will result in a foreign national being barred from reentry for 3 or more years; (ii) a foreign national without a legal nonimmigrant status cannot file to change status to permanent resident; and (iii) any income earned in the United States while out of status will be ineligible for EB-5 investment since it was gained through unauthorized employment. It would be best for anyone in this type of situation to seek the counsel of an immigration attorney as soon as possible.

Can other immigrant visa petitions be paused during EB-5 conditional residence and resumed if theI-829 petition is denied?

While an immigrant may pursue multiple immigrant visa paths, once conditional residence is granted, other visa petitions are no longer valid since an immigrant visa was approved and status was changed.

How might someone in the United States on a C-1/D visa fulfil the requirements of the EB-5 Program?

The C-1/D visa does not allow the visa holder to work in the United States or manage a business—so a direct EB-5 investment would not likely be possible. It would, however, be possible to pursue an EB-5 visa through an investment in a project sponsored by a regional center. Further, it is unlikely that a C-1/D visa holder will be able to adjust status to conditional permanent resident and will most likely have to return to his or her country of origin to consular process.

How might a denied F-1 visa application affect a pending I-526 petition?

An EB-5 investor with a pending I-526 petition may file for an F-1 visa, but it is unlikely the visa will be granted due to the obvious immigrant intent demonstrated through the I-526. A denied F-1 visa application will not affect an I-526 petition unless the petitioner is already in the United States and the denial could result in loss of status, in which case the EB-5 investor will need to do whatever is necessary—possibly returning to his or her home nation—to avoid any time in the United States without legal status.

Can a person file both EB-2 and EB-5 petitions, and if so, which should be filed first?
EB-2 and EB-5 petitions may be filed simultaneously—the order of submission does not matter. Which petition is adjudicated first will depend on one's country of chargeability. It would be prudent to discuss these options with an immigrant attorney experienced in both EB-2 and EB-5 matters.

For H-1B visa holders, what is the benefit of filing an extension while awaiting Form I-485 approval?
Form I-485 is an application to adjust status, and so the applicant must have a current status in order for it to be adjusted. An H-1B visa holder should maintain current status until his or her status is adjusted to conditional permanent resident. In addition to the need for current status, maintaining the H-1B visa also serves as a fallback in case Form I-485 is denied.

What are the differences between EB-2, EB-3, and EB-5 visas?
The primary difference between the EB-5 visa and the EB-2 and EB-3 visas is that the EB-5 visa is based upon the investment of the applicant creating jobs, whereas the EB-2 and EB-3 visas are based upon the applicant being sponsored to work by a U.S. employer. A number of other differences exist between these three options, including the qualifications of the applicant and visa availability based on country of chargeability. When determining which options may be viable, quickest, and/or least risky, it is best to consult with an experienced immigration attorney.

Can someone other than the EB-5 investor pay the legal and filing fees for the EB-5 application?
There is no regulatory requirement that the EB-5 investor must pay his or her own legal fees or even the filing fees for the petition. The only requirement is that the investor is able to document the legal source and path of funds for the investment capital.

How might an L-1 visa application affect a pending I-526 petition?
Because the L-1 visa carries dual intent, it is possible to apply for the L-1 with a pending I-526 petition. Applying for the L-1 visa will not adversely affect the I-526 petition, nor will the I-526 petition prevent a foreign national from obtaining or renewing an L-1 visa.

How might a pending EB-5 petition affect an H-1B extension application?
Because the H-1B visa allows for dual intent, a pending I-526 petition should not adversely affect an investor's ability to file for H-1B extension. When filing for the extension, the investor must simply disclose the pending EB-5 case.

How might a past tourist visa denial affect an EB-5 petition?

Unless the B visa was denied for reasons of inadmissibility—such as criminal activity, fraud, misrepresentation, an overstay, etc.—it is unlikely the past denial will affect an EB-5 petition. Anyone interested in the EB-5 Program should retain an experienced immigration attorney, who would also be able to answer any questions about admissibility and past visa issues.

What are the differences in financial requirements between E-2 and EB-5 visas?

The EB-5 visa requires an investment of at least $1,000,000; however, for projects located in TEAs, the minimum investment is $500,000. An E-2 visa, on the other hand, has no specific minimum investment threshold—and many E-2 investments are well below the minimum possible EB-5 investment of $500,000. Because these two visas differ greatly in their other requirements, anyone weighing which visa to pursue should retain experienced immigration counsel.

How might an I-526 petition affect a current F-1 student's application for CPT or OPT?

Since Curricular Practical Training (CPT) and Optional Practical Training (OPT) are temporary forms of employment authorization based on the F-1 status, an I-526 petition will not have any bearing on either unless the petitioner must renew his or her F-1 visa. If F-1 status is expected to expire before the petitioner is granted conditional permanent residence, it may be difficult to maintain nonimmigrant status and remain in the United States. An F-1 student should consult a qualified immigration attorney before pursuing the EB-5 Program.

Can Form I-140 be filed for an EB-5 investor with a pending I-526 petition?

Yes, foreign nationals may pursue multiple immigrant visas simultaneously; however, if both petitions are approved, only one can be used as the basis for the I-485 adjustment of status application.

Can an L-1 visa holder remain in the United States while applying for EB-5?

Yes, an L-1 visa carries dual intent, which means an immigrant visa petition will not adversely affect visa renewal. An L-1 visa holder, however, can only be in the United States using that status for a maximum of seven years—if the visa cannot be extended, then the EB-5 investor will have to either gain another legal status or return home until an EB-5 visa is obtained.

When is an EB-5 investor able to attend a U.S. college or university?

Unless a foreign national enters the United States on an F-1 visa before applying for EB-5 through the I-526 petition, the investor will likely have to wait until he or she gains conditional permanent resident status to attend a college or university in the United States. Generally speaking, an EB-5 investor will not be able to obtain or renew an F-1 visa because the F-1 requires nonimmigrant intent, and EB-5 is an immigrant visa program.

Can someone in the United States on a temporary worker visa sell personal assets and use the proceeds for an EB-5 investment?

Regardless of the type of temporary worker visa, the sale of personal assets should not be a form of unauthorized employment, and so as long as the assets were lawfully obtained, the money earned selling the assets should be a viable source of funds for an EB-5 investment.

Can an EB-5 investor with an approved I-526 petition travel on an H-1B visa?

Because the H-1B visa allows for immigrant intent, an H-1B visa holder with an approved I-526 petition should be able to travel outside the United States as long as his or her H-1B visa is still valid and the visa's underlying conditions (e.g., the visa holder still works for the sponsoring employer) are still met. The EB-5 investor should apply for adjustment of status (Form I-485) and advance parole (Form I-131) as soon as possible.

Should an EB-5 investor with an approved I-526 petition maintain a current nonimmigrant visa?

If an EB-5 investor has current nonimmigrant status, he or she should maintain that status since the process of adjusting to conditional permanent resident status is easier than consular processing. If nonimmigrant status is abandoned, it will be necessary for the foreign national to return to his or her country of origin in order to avoid accruing unlawful presence and to file for the EB-5 visa at his or her embassy or consulate.

What are the restrictions and limitations of conditional permanent resident status?

Conditional permanent resident status affords foreign nationals with all the rights, privileges, and responsibilities of permanent resident status—the only difference is that conditional permanent resident status expires after two years and must be renewed yearly until the I-829 petition is adjudicated. If the I-829 petition is approved, the investor and any derivative beneficiaries will be granted permanent resident status without conditions, which does not expire—though the permanent resident card (green card) requires renewal every 10 years.

How might an EB-5 investor apply for a B-1/B-2 visa with a pending I-526 petition?

B-1/B-2 visitor visas carry nonimmigrant intent, and so for an EB-5 investor with a pending I-526 petition, it may be difficult to obtain a B visa. That said, an EB-5 investor is allowed to apply for a B-1/B-2 visa but will likely have to demonstrate sufficient need for the visa and should also be prepared to provide evidence of his or her intent to return home upon the visa's expiration. The investor should also truthfully disclose the pending I-526 petition.

How might a foreign national who is out of status apply for EB-5?

While a foreign national who has overstayed his or her visa can apply for EB-5, he or she will likely be unable to file for adjustment of status and may be temporarily or permanently inadmissible pending on the amount of unlawful presence accrued. Also, any money earned while out of status cannot be used in an EB-5 investment.

Should someone in the United States seeking asylum apply for EB-5?

Whether or not a foreign national seeking asylum in the United States should apply for an EB-5 visa will depend on a number of circumstances. An asylee may concurrently pursue an EB-5 investment, but if the investor does not have current nonimmigrant status when the I-526 petition is approved, he or she will have to consular process in his or her home country. Experienced immigration counsel should be able to help an asylee determine the best course of action based on the specific facts of his or her asylum case and other relevant information.

How might a B-1/B-2 visa holder operate a business with a pending I-526 petition?

A B-1/B-2 visa does not provide work authorization, and therefore a B-1/B-2 visa holder cannot legally work or actively engage in the operation of a U.S. business. A B-1/B-2 visa holder may, however, appoint an agent or hire a business manager to operate a business on his or her behalf.

Can a J-1 or J-2 visa holder apply for EB-5?

J-1 and J-2 visa holders are allowed to apply for EB-5 visas; however, if a J-1 or J-2 visa holder's status is subject to the two-year home residence requirement, then before he or she can adjust status, the investor will either have to meet the home residence requirement or obtain a waiver.

How might someone simultaneously apply for H-1B status as self-employed and for an EB-5 visa based on an investment in the same company?

Filing an H-1B visa application in itself would not pose any problems with filing an I-526 petition; however, filing as a self-employed H-1B worker and as an EB-5 investor may pose some challenges. It may be possible to structure the company in such a way that both applications can be approved, but the specific details would need to be discussed with an immigration attorney.

Can someone in the United States on an H-1B visa apply for an EB-5 visa?

Yes, an H-1B visa holder may apply for an EB-5 visa—in fact, anyone in the United States on a nonimmigrant visa may apply. One of the primary concerns for nonimmigrant visa holders, however, is maintaining status while the I-526 petition is pending. Because the H-1B visa carries dual intent, maintaining H-1B status with a pending I-526 petition is not problematic;

renewing a nonimmigrant visa that does not allow for immigrant intent, on the other hand, may pose significant challenges.

Should a derivative beneficiary in the United States on an F-1 visa file Form I-485 or consular process with the principal applicant?

If a derivative beneficiary of an EB-5 investor is already in the United States on a nonimmigrant visa but the principal applicant is not, the best option is, most likely, to have the derivative return home and consular process with the principal applicant. Alternatively, the derivative in the United States can wait for the principal applicant to receive permanent resident status, at which point the derivative will be able to file Form I-485 to adjust status.

What are the primary differences between the L-1, E-2, and EB-5 visas?

The main difference between the L-1 and E-2 visas and the EB-5 visa is that the former are nonimmigrant visas while the latter is an immigrant visa leading to permanent resident status. The L-1 visa allows a foreign national to work for his or her company in its U.S. office; this visa allows for a maximum stay of seven years. The E-2 visa, on the other hand, allows a foreign investor from a treaty nation to make a "substantial investment" in a U.S. company and then manage that company; this visa must be renewed every two years but can be renewed indefinitely. The EB-5 visa is different from the L-1 and E-2 visas in that it confers permanent resident status contingent upon an investment that results in the creation of 10 or more jobs.

How might a past L-1 visa rejection affect an EB-5 application?

A past L-1 visa rejection will not have any effect on an I-526 petition since Form I-526 deals with the investor's compliance in terms of investment amount, job creation, and source of funds. Unless the L-1 visa was rejected due to inadmissibility, the past rejection should have no bearing on the approvability of an EB-5 visa application.

How might an F-1 visa holder with a pending I-526 petition exit and reenter the United States?

It is possible for F-1 visa holders with pending I-526 petitions to leave the United States and reenter—but EB-5 investors who intend to adjust status through Form I-485 would be prudent not to leave the United States. If the investor indicated on the I-526 petition that he or she intends to consular process upon I-526 approval, reentering the United States is less likely to be problematic. Note, however, that because a pending I-526 petition indicates immigrant intent, a Customs and Border Protection officer can, at his or her discretion, deny entry.

How might applying for EB-5 affect a pending family petition?

Pursuing an EB-5 visa will have no bearing on any other pending immigrant petitions, including a family petition. If one of the petitions fails, the other(s) will not be affected.

Can a foreign national in the United States on a visitor visa apply for EB-5?

Yes, a foreign national visiting the United States on a nonimmigrant visa may apply for the EB-5 Program and may engage in all the activities necessary to do so—such as retaining legal counsel, conducting due diligence, etc. Depending on the nature of the nonimmigrant visa, however, the foreign national may have to return home before the EB-5 petition is approved.

Visa Application/Approval Timing

How soon after receiving a loan can the funds be used for an EB-5 investment?

An EB-5 investor may use loaned funds for his or her investment as long as the money can be traced to a lawful source and is secured by the investor's personal assets assessed at fair market value. Once the loaned funds are in the possession of the investor, they can be used as capital for an EB-5 investment.

What is the typical timeline for EB-5 investors from I-526 petition to receiving a permanent green card?

The current adjudication time for I-526 petitions is about 14–16 months. Once Form I-526 is approved, the investor must either have his or her status changed (if already in the United States) or go through the visa application process through his or her nation's consulate or embassy. The application to adjust status (for those in the United States) is typically approved within 12–18 months. The visa application process with the National Visa Center (NVC), on the other hand, generally takes between 6–12 months. Once conditional resident status is granted, the foreign investor can apply for permanent resident status two years later through Form I-829.

What do the terms "processing" and "adjudication" mean in reference to the I-526 petition?

The term "processing" refers to USCIS reviewing the I-526 petition and all supporting documentation to determine if the EB-5 investor made a qualifying investment in an EB-5 compliant project that will create at least 10 jobs per EB-5 investor. The USCIS officer, or adjudicator, will render a decision based upon the submitted documentation. This decision is referred to as "adjudication." Adjudication results in acceptance, denial, or an RFE. Due to a backlog of pending I-526 petitions, the delay between filing and adjudication is now typically 12 months or more.

What happens once an EB-5 investor files Form I-829?

If the I-829 petition is filed on time, the investor should receive a receipt within 10 to fourteen days. With the receipt notice, the investor's conditional status is extended for one year. If the I-829 petition is not adjudicated within that year, the investor will need to have his or her passport stamped again to remain in status. Once adjudicated, the investor will, if approved, have the conditions removed from his or her status or, if denied, face immigration proceedings and possibly deportation.

Can a foreign national submit an I-526 petition while abroad?
The I-526 petition can be submitted from anywhere in the world; the EB-5 investor does not need to be in the United States or even in his or her home country. Most EB-5 investors make their investments through regional centers and with the assistance of immigration attorneys, and so the only real requirement is that they have the ability to communicate with the necessary people.

Does an EB-5 project have to receive USCIS pre-approval?
EB-5 projects that receive pre-approval from USCIS are called exemplars, and while they offer certain advantages, pre-approval is not required. As long as the regional center has been approved by USCIS, EB-5 investors can invest in the regional center's project and submit their I-526 petitions.

How long does it take USCIS to pre-approve exemplar projects?
Currently, regional center exemplar projects are adjudicated and may receive pre-approval within about 12 months.

How is the filing date of an I-526 petition determined?
The filing date of an I-526 petition is the date that USCIS receives the petition package, including fees, and files the petition in order to create a new case. USCIS issues a receipt notice in which the filing date and payment amount are recorded. The filing date is also known as the receipt date or priority date.

Why might anI-526 petition be adjudicated later than other petitions from the same project filed at the same time?
While the stated policy of USCIS is first in, first out, sometimes there is a delay between the adjudication of petitions filed close together from investors in the same project. The delay may be caused, for instance, by greater scrutiny of an investor's source of funds or by RFEs, but a delay can also be inexplicable.

On the USCIS processing time website, what does the "Processing Cases as of Date" column indicate?
The information listed on the USCIS website under the "Processing Cases as of Date" column indicates the approximate processing times for I-526 petitions, I-829 petitions, and I-924 applications. The "Processing Cases as of Date" column may contain a length of time given in months, which represents the average time it takes for the respective form to be adjudicated, or it may contain a date, which would mean USCIS is currently reviewing cases that were filed on or before that date.

How long does it take for USCIS to adjudicate an investor's I-526 petition after the project receives exemplar status?

It is impossible to know how long USCIS will take to adjudicate any given petition; this remains true even if a project obtains exemplar status. If an investor's I-526 petition has been pending longer than the current average processing time, the investor's attorney should ask for a status update and, if applicable, indicate that the project has received exemplar status. An investor living in the United States on a nonimmigrant visa should not make plans based on a hoped-for adjudication date since there are no guarantees of when a petition will be adjudicated.

When is an EB-5 investor's priority date determined?

The priority date is the date that the I-526 petition was received and filed by USCIS. This date should be included in the receipt notice (Form I-797). Sometimes, however, the priority date is not noted in the receipt notice, but this does not mean the priority date hasn't been set.

What is the order in which I-526 petitions are processed by USCIS?

USCIS has indicated that it processes I-526 petitions on a first-in, first-out basis. Practically speaking, however, some petitions simply take longer to process than others due to level of complexity, the need for clarification, etc.

How will an EB-5 investor know his or her I-526 petition was filed?

When an EB-5 investor files Form I-526, USCIS will issue a receipt notice (Form I-797). If an attorney files the petition on behalf of an investor, he or she may receive the receipt notice and should provide the investor with a copy.

What is the normal processing time for I-526 petitions?

Average processing times change based on a number of factors, but the current average is available at the USCIS website. Processing times beyond the average, however, may still be considered "normal" since some petitions simply take more time to adjudicate than others. If an investor's petition is taking longer than average, it would be safe to inquire as to the status of the petition.

How long does it take for an EB-5 petition to be prepared, filed, and adjudicated?

The length of time it takes to prepare and file an I-526 petition varies based on a host of variables, including the investor's source of funds and the project's level of readiness. Once filed, adjudication times vary greatly, but the average time between submission and adjudication is generally more than one year.

Which date is used to determine if an investor can file Form I-485, the "date for filing" or the "final action date"?

Each month, USCIS publishes which date may be used—and so whether an investor may submit an I-485 adjustment of status application will depend on the details of the investor's case and which date USCIS is using at the time.

What is the maximum length of time an investor will have to wait for I-526 petition adjudication?

There is no maximum processing time for I-526 petitions. If an investor's petition has been pending for longer than the current average processing time, his or her attorney should make an inquiry with USCIS.

How much money must an investor have in escrow in order to be considered "in the process of investing"?

Generally, USCIS requires the entire investment amount to be either invested in the new commercial enterprise or placed in escrow when the I-526 petition is filed. The basic expectation is that the entire investment amount is irrevocably committed to the enterprise. That said, promissory notes may also be accepted depending on the value and payment term.

What can be done if an EB-5 investor's nonimmigrant visa is expected to expire before I-526 adjudication?

If an EB-5 investor anticipates his or her nonimmigrant visa will expire before I-526 adjudication, the options are limited. There is no way to expedite a decision on an I-526 petition, and so the investor may either seek an extension of his or her current visa, apply for a different nonimmigrant status, or return to his or her home country and consular process.

How long does it take USCIS to adjudicate direct investments?

Adjudication times vary on a case-by-case basis, and so it is impossible to predict how long a given petition will take to process. USCIS provides current processing time estimates, but these are based on all petitions and do not distinguish between direct investments and regional center investments.

What happens to an investment if USCIS denies the EB-5 investor's I-526 petition?

For direct investments, there may be little recourse in the case of a denied I-526 petition since much if not all of the investment funds will likely have been spent by the time the I-526 is adjudicated. For investments in projects sponsored by regional centers, however, a refund mechanism may be in place for denied I-526 petitions. Generally speaking, such refunds do not include any administrative fees paid by the investor to the regional center.

I-829 Approval Requirements/Timing

How might investors' I-829 petitions be affected by an incomplete project?

An incomplete project may pose a significant threat to the approval of investors' I-829 petitions, particularly if the project has not proceeded according to the business plan filed with investors' I-526 petitions. But an incomplete project may not pose a substantial risk in some cases—particularly when the project has significant job cushion built in. Generally speaking, as long as an EB-5 investor can prove that he or she invested the necessary amount of

319

capital into an eligible project, that the investment was sustained throughout the conditional permanent residence period, and that the investment produced the necessary number of jobs, his or her I-829 petition should be approved, even if the project is not complete.

How do delays in I-485 processing affect I-829 petitions?

Conditional permanent resident status does not begin until the I-485 application is approved, and the I-829 petition to remove conditions cannot be filed until 21 months after I-485 approval. Thus a delay in I-485 processing will result in a corresponding delay in an investor being able to file Form I-829.

What level of scrutiny does USCIS apply when adjudicating I-829 petitions?

When USCIS examines an investor's I-829 petition, the primary concern is program compliance. Generally speaking, the investor must prove that an NCE was created, that the minimum required investment was made and sustained throughout the conditional residence period, and that the investment resulted in the creation of at least 10 full-time, permanent jobs. The level of scrutiny is high, and so these facts must be clearly demonstrated. Adherence to the original business plan is also important, but some minor changes may be permissible depending on the nature of those changes.

If the principal applicant abandons his or her I-829 petition, what happens to the immigrant status of derivative beneficiaries?

Abandoning an I-829 petition will result in an inability to renew the conditional green card. Without the pending EB-5 case, the principal applicant and any derivatives will have no basis for renewing their conditional green card or for removing conditions, and therefore will have to either obtain a different status or leave the United States.

How much does it cost to file an I-829 petition?

The filing fee for Form I-829 is currently $3,750, and the biometric services fee is $85 per applicant. Any associated legal costs will vary based on the attorney(s) hired by the EB-5 applicant.

Personal Investor Requirements

Is age a factor in EB-5 eligibility?

The age of an EB-5 applicant is only a factor if the investor cannot legally execute a binding contract. Generally speaking, this means the investor must be 18 years old or older—but there is no upward age limit.

Can someone with a salary of less than $200,000 apply for the EB-5 Program?

Generally speaking, a person must be an accredited investor to invest in a project sponsored by a regional center. In order to be classified as an accredited investor, a person must either have a net worth of more than

$1,000,000 without including the value of his or her primary home or must have earned $200,000 in each of the past two years. For direct investments, however, depending on the specific nature of the investment, being an accredited investor is not required. In such cases, the investor must simply have $500,000 to invest that can be traced to a lawful source.

How much of an investor's wealth must be included in source of funds documentation?

Typically, USCIS requires only the investment amount of $500,000 or $1,000,000—and potentially the administrative fee for regional center investments—to be included in source and path of funds documentation.

What are the age requirements of the EB-5 Program?

The laws and regulations of the EB-5 Program do not stipulate any age requirement or limit. Age is only a factor as it relates to signing contracts; if an applicant is younger than 18, he or she cannot sign a legally enforceable contract. It may be possible for someone under age 18 to have his or her legal guardian co-sign the paperwork.

How is the admissibility of an EB-5 applicant with a health problem determined?

Whether or not a foreign national with health concerns can immigrate will be determined through the physical examination required as part of the immigrant visa process. If an immigrant has been treated and is no longer contagious, he or she should be permitted to enter the United States.

What financial requirements does the EB-5 Program have for investors?

The current minimum investment is $1,000,000—or $500,000 for projects in TEAs. While the investment capital is the only requirement of the EB-5 Program, practically speaking, investors will generally accrue legal fees, filing fees, and in some cases administration fees. Typically, regional center investors must also be considered accredited investors, which means they must meet certain net worth or annual income requirements.

How might a non-accredited EB-5 investor invest in a project sponsored by a regional center?

Because a regional center is engaged in a securities offering when raising funds for an EB-5 project, the investment activity is subject to federal and state securities laws and regulations. Most regional center projects operate under a securities exemption and thereby can only accept investments from accredited investors. This requirement is not optional. Anyone interested in investing through a regional center must be accredited—the only likely alternative for a non-accredited investor is to make a direct investment.

What documents will an EB-5 investor need in order to invest through a regional center?

When investing through a regional center, all project documentation will be provided, and so an EB-5 investor will need only the personal documentation required by the I-526 petition. This documentation primarily deals with proving the lawful source and path of the investor's funds—though the specific documents needed will depend on the source(s). The foreign national will also need to be able to prove he or she is an accredited investor.

Can someone with no employment history apply for an EB-5 visa using gifted funds?

A foreign national may apply for an EB-5 visa using gifted funds, in part or in whole, as long as the gift is accompanied by lawful source of funds documentation and a deed of gift proving the funds do, in fact, belong to the investor. Employment history and/or management experience are not required by the EB-5 Program—though for direct EB-5 investments, business experience may play an important role in meeting the program's employment creation requirement. Also, because regional center investments generally require investors to be accredited, any EB-5 investor with no employment history whose investment is based solely on a gift may need to consult securities counsel to determine whether a regional center investment is possible.

What medical issues will make an EB-5 applicant inadmissible?

Generally speaking, visa applicants are rendered inadmissible for medical reasons if they have communicable diseases or certain mental illnesses. In some cases, a visa applicant may be inadmissible due to a physical/mental condition that, in combination with other relevant factors, makes the applicant likely to become a public charge. An EB-5 investor and his or her derivatives, however, are at low risk of becoming public charges due to their high net worth.

Investor USCIS Filings

Is Form I-130 used within the EB-5 process?

No, Form I-130 is used by those currently living in the United States as citizens or permanent residents to request immigrant status for family members living outside the United States. Since the EB-5 Program grants permanent resident status to the principal applicant and his or her spouse and unmarried children under age 21, Form I-130 is not needed. Form I-130 can, however, be used by an EB-5 investor after receiving permanent resident status to petition on behalf of any other qualified family members.

What is Form DS-260?

Form DS-260, Immigrant Visa Electronic Application, is a form submitted after the approval of the I-526 petition by EB-5 investors who do not have a current nonimmigrant status in the United States. The form is submitted to the National Visa Center from the investor's consulate or embassy and is the first step in consular processing, which is how the investor and his or her dependent family members obtain their EB-5 visas.

What forms are involved with filing an EB-5 application?

The primary forms are as follows: Form I-526, Immigrant petition for Alien Entrepreneur, is the first and arguably most important form that will be submitted in the process. Once the I-526 petition is approved, the next form will depend on whether or not the investor is currently living in the United States on a nonimmigrant visa. If living abroad, the investor must submit Form DS-260, Immigrant Visa Electronic Application. If living in the United States, Form I-485, Application to Adjust Status, must be filed to change from nonimmigrant to immigrant status. Concurrently, Form I-765, Application for Employment Authorization, and Form I-131, Application for Travel Document, may be submitted. With an approved DS-260 or I-485 application, the investor gains conditional permanent resident status, which after 21 months requires the submission of Form I-829, petition by Entrepreneur to Remove Conditions from Permanent Resident Status. Once Form I-829 is approved, the investor has unconditional permanent resident status and has successfully completed the EB-5 process.

Does USCIS issue a single RFE for all concerns in a petition or one RFE for each concern?

Typically, USCIS will review an entire petition and, if deemed necessary, issue a single RFE that addresses all of their concerns. USCIS is not, however, limited in its ability to issue RFEs, and so they can issue any number of RFEs pertaining to any or all concerns they have regarding a particular petition.

Residence Requirements and Benefits

How can an EB-5 investor gain a homestead tax exemption?

Homestead tax exemptions vary by state, and so each state might have different requirements. Generally speaking, an EB-5 investor will have to prove that he or she has been granted permanent residence, which can be done after the I-526 petition has been accepted and the petitioner has successfully adjusted his or her status. It may be necessary to retain the counsel of a real estate attorney and/or CPA specializing in taxes and immigration.

What should an investor do after filing his or her I-526 petition?

Regarding the EB-5 process, the only thing to do after filing Form I-526 is to wait. If still living outside the United States, a foreign national might consider preparing for consular processing by compiling the necessary documentation and seeking the help of immigration counsel. This wait may also be an ideal time to engage in estate and tax planning.

How soon must an EB-5 investor enter the United States after gaining his or her green card?

The immigrant visa specifies how long it is valid—typically 180 days from the date of the consular interview. It is best to enter the United States, at least for a short time, within this period. After this, it is possible for the immigrant to return to his or her home nation and apply for a reentry permit. Permanent residence, however, can be jeopardized by too much time spent abroad.

What is the difference between U.S. conditional permanent resident status and permanent resident status without conditions?

The conditional permanent resident status granted to an EB-5 investor upon approval of Form I-526 gives the immigrant all the rights and privileges of permanent resident status, including the right to work, live, and study anywhere in the United States. The main distinguishing characteristic of the conditional status is that it is effective for only two years, and at the end of this two-year period, Form I-829 must be submitted to remove the conditions from the status.

Where can an EB-5 investor with a conditional green card work?

For employment purposes, the conditional green card is no different than a green card without conditions. Therefore, EB-5 investors with conditional permanent resident status may live and work anywhere in the United States.

Can a J-1 or J-2 visa holder become an EB-5 investor to avoid the two-year home-country physical presence requirement?

No, the EB-5 Program does not negate the two-year home-country physical presence requirement. If a J-1 or J-2 visa holder is required to fulfill the two-year home-residence requirement, he or she must either return home at the end of his or her exchange visitor program or obtain a waiver. Without fulfilling the two-year home-country physical presence requirement (or obtaining a waiver), the J-1 or J-2 visa holder may not adjust status to conditional permanent resident through the EB-5 Program.

How much time can an EB-5 investor spend abroad while a conditional permanent resident?

The amount of time that can be spent abroad involves several factors, such as the reason for being out of country and the conditional permanent resident's ties to the United States. Generally speaking, one should not spend more than 180 continuous days outside the United States, but if a longer absence is required, the conditional permanent resident should apply for a reentry permit prior to leaving. Reentry will be denied if it is determined that the conditional permanent resident has abandoned his or her U.S. residence.

At what point is an EB-5 investor able to permanently reside in the United States?

An investor may apply for conditional permanent resident status upon the approval of his or her I-526 petition, but this status is temporarily granted on the assumption that the investor will meet all the requirements of the EB-5

Program. The conditions are removed from the investor's status upon the approval of Form I-829, at which point the immigrant may permanently reside in the United States barring any action that might result in removal.

How might an illegal stay in another country affect an EB-5 petition?

While an unlawful presence in a foreign country has no direct effect on whether an applicant is eligible for the EB-5 visa, the issue may come up during the visa application interview. Also, if a prospective EB-5 investor is currently living illegally in another nation, he or she will likely need to return to his or her home nation to consular process. It would be best for anyone in such circumstances to consult a U.S. immigration attorney before proceeding with an EB-5 investment.

How much of the year must an EB-5 green card holder live in the United States?

The key issue is whether the green card holder can demonstrate that he or she intends to permanently reside in the United States. Extended absences can result in the assumption that the lawful permanent resident has abandoned his or her status. Generally speaking, if a green card holder stays out of country for six continuous months or more, he or she will need to prove intent to remain a permanent resident of the United States and may need to obtain a reentry permit.

What happens to a foreign national's U.S. property when abandoning a green card?

Relinquishing a green card will have no effect on the ownership of a foreign national's property in the United States. While he or she will be required to leave the United States or obtain a valid nonimmigrant status, any real estate or other property owned by the foreign national remains his or her property. There may, however, be a number of tax issues to consider, and it would be prudent for anyone thinking about relinquishing his or her green card to retain a tax attorney.

How soon after DS-260 approval must an EB-5 investor move to the United States?

The EB-5 visa is valid for six months, so once the visa is issued, the investor should enter the United States within this period. An extension may be granted if the investor can demonstrate he or she did not or will be unable to enter the United States due to circumstances beyond his or her control.

Can an EB-5 investor stay in the United States while the I-526 petition is pending?

The I-526 petition does not grant the petitioner any immigration status, and therefore the only way an EB-5 investor will be able to legally enter and remain in the United States is through a separate nonimmigrant visa. Also, if a nonimmigrant visa does not carry dual intent, the investor would likely have to obtain that visa before Form I-526 is filed and may be unable to renew it once the EB-5 case is pending.

How might an EB-5 investor move to the United States prior to receiving an EB-5 visa?

Filing the I-526 petition—or even receiving I-526 approval—does not grant an investor any immigration status. The most likely way for an EB-5 investor to move to the United States prior to receiving the EB-5 visa is to obtain a visa that carries dual intent, such as an H-1B, L-1, or E-2 visa. Nonimmigrant visas, such as B-1/B-2 and F-1 visas, are not likely to be approved or renewed once an I-526 petition has been filed.

At what point in the EB-5 process are EB-5 investors required to be physically present in the United States?

At no time during the EB-5 process is an EB-5 investor required to be in the United States. All communication between the investor and his or her attorney can take place via phone, email, etc., and the attorney will be able to handle the process on behalf of the investor. Physical presence is required only after the investor receives permanent resident status.

How much time can a conditional permanent resident remain out of the United States?

The general rule is that a green card holder should not spend more than six months out of the United States in a year without first obtaining a reentry permit. That said, the primary consideration is whether the green card holder can prove his or her intent to reside in the United States. Prolonged absences can be perceived as the abandonment of permanent resident status. Green card holders traveling abroad should maintain strong ties to the United States, which can be demonstrated through home ownership, employment, the presence of family, school attendance, bank accounts, tax documents, etc.

What are the potential consequences if a conditional permanent resident is away from the United States for more than six months?

If a permanent resident is away from the United States for longer than six months, USCIS may make a rebuttable presumption that the investor no longer intends to permanently reside in the United States. The investor can overcome this presumption by offering evidence of sufficient ties to the United States— these ties may include a family presence, permanent residence, vehicle ownership, bank accounts, tax documents, etc. For absences longer than one year, the permanent resident should obtain a reentry permit.

After becoming a permanent resident, how frequently can an EB-5 investor travel abroad?

The primary concern for permanent residents travelling abroad is whether they can clearly demonstrate to USCIS their intent to permanently reside in the United States—this is accomplished by establishing obvious ties to the United States, such as family, housing, employment, bank accounts, etc. Travel frequency is less of an issue than length of time spent abroad—any absences of six months or more will raise a rebuttable presumption that permanent resident status has been abandoned. Absences of more than a year require a reentry permit.

EB-5 Project Selection/Diligence

How can an investor know if an EB-5 regional center project is a viable investment with low immigration risk?

While USCIS grants businesses the regional center designation, the agency does not post a list of approved projects. Proper due diligence should be conducted to determine if a project is viable from a business perspective and low risk from an immigration perspective. It may be best to hire an experienced due diligence specialist and an immigration attorney with EB-5 experience.

Can an H-1B visa holder pursue the EB-5 Program?

Yes, a foreign national in the United States on an H-1B visa may make an EB-5 investment. The best option here is likely a regional center investment since an H-1B worker would not be permitted to manage a direct investment. A direct investment is possible, however, since the H-1B visa does not restrict a foreign national from owning a company in the United States, and once the I-526 is approved and status is adjusted, the investor would be allowed to manage the company.

How safe is the EB-5 Program?

The financial and immigration risk of the EB-5 Program depends on the specific project in which a foreign national invests. While every EB-5 project must comply with all EB-5 laws and relevant securities regulations, some projects carry greater risk than others. The best projects have virtually no immigration risk and limited financial risk. It is vital that a prospective EB-5 investor retain an experienced EB-5 immigration attorney and conduct sufficient due diligence on any potential investment.

How likely is it that an EB-5 investor's principal investment will be returned?

An EB-5 investment must be considered at risk until after the investor's Form I-829 has been approved. At that point, whether the investor will be returned his or her principal investment depends on the exit strategy and track record of the regional center. Financial due diligence should be conducted to determine the viability of the exit strategy and the likelihood that funds will be returned to EB-5 investors.

What passive investments qualify for the EB-5 Program?

By nature of the program, passive investments—such as stock ownership—aren't allowed. That isn't to say that all EB-5 projects are high maintenance for investors. On the contrary, the requirement is either day-today management of the business or a role in policy formation and decision making. As a result, most projects sponsored by regional centers are structured as limited partnerships, and so each investor has the role of limited partner, which generally requires minimal involvement in the daily management of the business.

How should an investor evaluate an EB-5 project?

An EB-5 investor considering a project should retain an immigrant attorney to perform due diligence on the project from an immigration perspective. The investor should also retain an investment advisor to perform due diligence on the project from a business and investment perspective. The track records of the regional center and the developer are also important, as is the structure of the capital stack (i.e., the percentages of developer equity, loaned funds, EB-5 investor capital, etc.).

Must an EB-5 project be pre-approved before investors can file Form I-526?

While project pre-approval can be beneficial to investors as they file their I-526 petitions, the pre-approval process is not a prerequisite to investors I-526 submissions. As long as the project documents are ready for filing, investors may submit their I-526 petitions.

What is an I-924 application and how does it affect EB-5 projects and investors?

Form I-924, Application for Regional Center under the Immigrant Investor Pilot Program, is the form used by an organization to apply for regional center designation. Projects sponsored by regional centers benefit from being able to count indirect and induced job creation along with direct job creation, which in turn can make it easier for EB-5 investors to meet the program's job creation requirements. Form I-924 can also be used to create an exemplar project, a designation that indicates USCIS approval of a project's documentation—which can reduce the risk associated with investing in the project.

How can an investor determine if a project site is inside a TEA?

The EB-5 regulations define a TEA as an area of low population (outside a metropolitan statistical area and any city of 20,000 people or more) or an area of high unemployment (50% higher than the national average). Each state has a different process by which investors can determine whether an area is or is not classified as a TEA. In some states, if an area is not already classified as a TEA, it may be possible to gain special TEA designation. It would be prudent for an EB-5 investor to retain an experienced immigration attorney to help determine whether a project qualifies for the lower TEA investment amount.

Can an EB-5 investor invest in a project that already has I-526 approvals?

Yes, the presence of approved I-526 petitions does not mean a project is no longer open to EB-5 investment. As long as the subscription period remains open, new investors may join the project.

What are the benefits of investing in a project that already has some approved I-526 petitions?

A project with approved I-526 petitions has had its documentation reviewed and accepted by USCIS. For investors considering such a project, this means that the project documentation will not likely result in a denied petition. Prior I-526 approvals do not, however, indicate that a project is a safe or good investment—nor does it mean that the project will succeed and that investors' I-829 petitions will be approved. Every project is unique, and an investor should consider hiring third party due diligence professionals to carefully scrutinize a project before the investor enters into an agreement.

How can a potential EB-5 investor find available projects?

Projects can be found by using online databases, by calling regional centers, or by employing a licensed investment advisor. The best first step for a potential EB-5 investor, however, is to retain an experienced immigration attorney. Good immigration counsel will be able to guide the potential investor through the process and help connect the investor to other qualified professionals.

How secure are EB-5 investments?

The amount of risk involved in an EB-5 investment depends wholly on the project and, if applicable, the regional center. While all EB-5 investments must be considered "at risk" in order to comply with the EB-5 Program, careful due diligence should be conducted to determine how much financial and immigration risk a given project carries. Good projects carry virtually zero immigration risk and very little financial risk; others may be quite risky. Consulting qualified, third party professionals—such as due diligence experts and immigration attorneys with EB-5 experience—can help investors navigate the EB-5 market to find low-risk projects.

How should an investor go about performing due diligence on an EB-5 regional center project?

Because of how complicated the EB-5 Program is, and because of what is at stake for investors, an EB-5 investor should hire a qualified third-party professional to conduct due diligence on his or her behalf. Typically, the due diligence process can be started by the investor's immigration attorney, who will likely involve the services of a due diligence expert.

What criteria must an existing company meet in order to qualify as an NCE?

An existing business can qualify as an NCE as long as it is restructured in such a way that a new enterprise is formed or expanded in such a way that either the net worth or the number of employees is increased by 40%. A business may also qualify if it is considered "troubled"—meaning it has experienced a net loss of 20% over the past 12 to 24 months.

Can a foreign national make an EB-5 investment into a family business?

Yes, an EB-5 investor may make an investment in any qualified business, regardless of his or her relationship to the business's owner. As long as the investor and business comply with all EB-5 regulations and laws, such an investment should not be a problem.

How quickly can an investor obtain an EB-5 visa and enter the United States?

The time it takes for an investor to obtain an EB-5 visa depends on several factors. First, the investor must find a suitable project, conduct sufficient due diligence, make an investment, and prepare the I-526 petition—all of which may take several months to complete. The processing time for I-526 petitions is more than a year; upon I-526 approval, the investor will have to apply for the visa, which is usually issued within six months. An EB-5 investor should expect it to be two years or longer before he or she obtains the EB-5 visa.

Can the purchase of an apartment work as an EB-5 investment?

The purchase of real estate for EB-5 purposes is problematic for a number of reasons. Because real estate is a fixed asset with definite value, it does not represent an at-risk investment. Also, purchasing real estate does not, in itself, produce jobs.

Can investing in a residential real estate development project work for EB-5?

While the purchase of real estate does not qualify as an EB-5 investment, investing in a real estate development project may qualify as long as the necessary amount of capital is invested in an NCE and results in the creation of at least 10 full-time, permanent jobs. Residential real estate developments don't typically meet the job creation requirement through operating jobs, and so construction expenditures are often used to calculate employment creation.

Can financing be the source of an EB-5 investment?

EB-5 investment funds can be financed through a loan as long as the loan is secured by the personal assets of the investor and not, for example, the assets of the NCE.

Can an EB-5 investor split an investment between two businesses?

An EB-5 investment must be made into a single NCE. The NCE, however, may be a holding company with multiple subsidiaries. If structured properly, all of the jobs created by the subsidiaries would be credited to the investor.

Does the I-526 processing time differ between EB-5 regional center investments and direct investments?

The processing time estimates provided by USCIS do not distinguish between projects sponsored by regional centers and those that receive direct investments. That said, the more complex a project, the more work it is for USCIS to adjudicate. If the business plan and source of funds documentation are simple and clear, a direct investment may be adjudicated more quickly than the average processing time; however, the same can be said of an I-526 petition for a regional center investment. Unlike most regional center investments, however, direct investments do not involve economic analysis as part of calculating job creation, and so processing time may be saved in that regard. Generally speaking, though, simpler and clearer petitions will be adjudicated more quickly than those that are more complex and/or result RFEs—and this is true regardless of whether the petition is based on a direct or a regional center investment.

How can EB-5 investors ensure the success of their investments?

The EB-5 Program requires the invested capital to remain at risk throughout the duration of the conditional permanent residence period. No project is guaranteed success, and so there is always an element of risk involved—and a regional center can offer no assurances that an EB-5 investor's capital will be returned at the end of the process. Immigration and financial risk can be limited through careful due diligence, but no EB-5 project is totally risk free.

How might a potential EB-5 investor find active projects?

USCIS does not maintain a list of projects, but it does provide a list of current regional centers on its website, which may be one place for potential investors to start looking for projects. Searching for regional centers and open projects using online search engines is another option. Additionally, while an immigration attorney should not refer a client to a particular regional center or project, he or she may be able to help a potential EB-5 investor find a project— or otherwise direct the investor to someone who can help.

How can an EB-5 investor be sure a project is a good investment?

The primary safeguard for EB-5 investors is careful due diligence. All investments carry risk, and so it is vital that a potential investor investigate that risk to determine if the investment is a suitable choice. A potential EB-5 investor may want to hire a financial advisor and/or due diligence professional to help determine if a particular project meets the investor's investment criteria.

Investor Involvement in the Business

How much involvement can investors have with EB-5 projects sponsored by regional centers?

Typically, EB-5 projects sponsored by regional centers are structured as partnerships, and the EB-5 investors become limited partners who are not involved in the day-to-day management of the business. The level of involvement, however, depends on the regional center. An EB-5 investor who desires a more active role in his or her investment should consider a direct investment.

Can an EB-5 investor visit the regional center project that he or she has invested in?

Whether or not an EB-5 investor may visit the site of the regional center project will depend on the agreement between the investor and the regional center. Some regional center projects install webcams that allow their investors to monitor the construction 24/7.

How do EB-5 regional center investors fulfill the program's "active participation" requirement?

The EB-5 Program's requirement that investors be actively involved in the new commercial enterprise can be satisfied by day-to-day management and operation of the business, as is the case with most direct EB-5 investments, or through policy formation. Most regional center projects are structured as limited partnerships in which the EB-5 investors are limited partners; the role of limited partner satisfies the requirement for active participation.

Does an EB-5 investor have to be the sole owner of the NCE?

No, the EB-5 Program does not require an investor to be the sole owner—or even the majority owner—of an NCE. No minimum percentage of ownership is required.

How can an investor use his or her invested EB-5 capital to operate the NCE while living abroad?

In order to run an NCE from abroad, it may be necessary for the EB-5 investor to hire a manager—this could also fulfil part of the employment creation requirement of the EB-5 Program. Due to the complex nature of direct EB-5 investments, a potential investor should hire competent immigration counsel with EB-5 experience before making any decisions about the company's structure and management.

Is an EB-5 applicant who invests in an existing business required to have a certain share of ownership?

While ownership is involved in any equity investment, the EB-5 Program does not dictate any minimum ownership percentage requirement—whether the investor is starting a new business or investing in an existing one. One consideration for direct EB-5 investors is that their ownership share should be consistent with an active management or policy formation role.

What is the typical management role of an EB-5 investor who invests in a project sponsored by a regional center?

While each regional center has the prerogative to determine the role of its EB-5 investors, most form limited partnerships or limited liability companies in which the EB-5 investors take on limited management responsibilities. Regional center investors typically have a role in voting on certain policy measures, which satisfies the USCIS requirement of "active participation" without day-to-day operational involvement.

Direct EB-5 Qualification

How close to an EB-5 investment must an investor live?

Technically, the EB-5 Program allows investors to live anywhere in the United States. The program does, however, require that investors be actively involved in managing the enterprise, either through day-to-day operations or through policy formation. For regional center investments in which the EB-5 investor is a limited partner, living near the project generally has no bearing on an investor's ability to take part in policy formation. For direct investments in which the investor must manage the daily operations of the enterprise, it may be impractical to live far from the project.

For direct EB-5 investors, when must the full investment be made?

While EB-5 law specifically states that investors may be in the process of investing the necessary amount of capital, in practice, USCIS expects to see the entire amount already at risk at the time the I-526 petition is filed. Depending on the business plan, incremental payments may be permitted—but it would be advisable to consult an experienced EB-5 immigration attorney about this before proceeding.

When must a direct EB-5 investor have a completed business plan?

The business plan must be submitted with Form I-526, but it is best to have the plan ready well before then. Because it takes time to create a compliant business plan—which must be comprehensive, feasible, based on verifiable information, and credible—it is important to begin drafting the plan early in the process. Once filed along with Form I-526, the business plan cannot undergo any material changes.

How does consular processing time affect the length of time allowed for EB-5 job creation?

Generally speaking, job creation for EB-5 purposes needs to take place within two years of an investor receiving conditional permanent resident status. Thus consular processing times have no real effect on the length of time permitted for creating the necessary number of jobs. Another way of looking at this is that the necessary number of jobs should be created by the time the I-829 petition is filed, which is approximately 21 months after conditional permanent resident status is granted.

Can a foreign worker be hired by an EB-5 investor?

While it is possible for an EB-5 business to sponsor a foreign worker, doing so is complex and unadvisable. If, however, a foreign worker is successfully sponsored, he or she may or may not fulfill the requirements of a qualified U.S. worker, in which case the position filled by the foreign worker would not be counted for job creation purposes. Anyone considering such a plan should consult an experienced EB-5 immigration attorney before proceeding.

Can a foreign business owned by a potential EB-5 investor somehow qualify for a direct EB-5 investment?

No, a foreign business cannot qualify as an NCE under the EB-5 Program; the NCE must be a U.S. business. That said, funds earned through a foreign business could be used as an investment. Alternatively, if the business is owned by the investor, its assets may be able to be used as collateral for a loan that could fund an EB-5 investment.

How might an EB-5 direct investor create two businesses in separate locations using EB-5 funds?

Although more complicated, an investment may be used to create two separate businesses and still qualify for the EB-5 Program. The most likely way to successfully structure such an investment would be to create a holding company or corporation, which would serve as the NCE, and to create the separate businesses as wholly-owned subsidiaries of the NCE. Due to the complex nature and need for strict compliance with EB-5 laws and regulations, anyone considering such an investment should consult with experienced EB-5 immigration counsel.

How can an EB-5 investor legally operate a direct investment with a pending I-526 petition?

Because filing Form I-526 does not grant immigration status, a direct EB-5 investor may have difficulty operating the new commercial enterprise unless he or she has or can obtain employment authorization. Alternatively, the investor may hire or partner with someone in the United States to manage the business, at least temporarily. Due to the complexities of the EB-5 Program, particularly for direct investors, anyone considering such an investment should retain experienced EB-5 immigration counsel in order to work out the details before investing.

Can multiple investments in unrelated businesses qualify an investor for an EB-5 visa?

Multiple investments in unrelated businesses are not likely to meet the requirements of the EB-5 Program. It is possible, however, to create multiple businesses through an EB-5 investment—the separate businesses would need to be wholly-owned subsidiaries of a single entity, which would be the NCE and actual recipient of the EB-5 funds.

What are the business plan requirements for direct EB-5 investors?

As with all EB-5 petitions, an I-526 petition for a direct EB-5 investor must be accompanied by a business plan that meets the standards set forth in *Matter of Ho*. Generally speaking, this means the business plan must be comprehensive, feasible, and credible. The plan must detail what jobs will be created, when, and how.

How might a direct EB-5 investor obtain TEA designation for a project?

States are responsible for determining whether or not an area qualifies as a TEA, and every state has a different process for designating TEAs. A direct investor will need to contact the appropriate state agency and follow its instructions to apply for TEA designation.

How might a direct EB-5 investor get his or her principal investment back after obtaining a green card?

While a number of viable exit strategies may be available to an investor depending on the nature of the project, the most common way for an investor to be returned his or her capital after I-829 approval is for the investor to sell his or her equity interest in the business.

How likely is an investor's EB-5 petition to be denied?

The specific details of every EB-5 case are different, but generally speaking, if an EB-5 investor fully complies with all EB-5 laws and regulations and has his or her I-526 petition prepared by competent counsel, the likelihood the petition will be denied is relatively low. The success of an I-526 petition ultimately depends on whether the investor can prove he or she made the necessary investment using lawfully obtained funds, and that the investment is or will be responsible for creating 10 new full-time jobs.

How might an EB-5 investor change a direct investment during the conditional residence period?

USCIS will likely consider any change to the business to constitute a material change, which will result in a denial of Form I-829. If a business needs to be changed for whatever reason, the EB-5 process will likely have to be restarted—a new I-526 petition will need to be filed based upon the new material facts of the altered business.

How might all of an investor's funds fulfill the "at risk" requirement if only a portion of the investment is needed to start the NCE?

If a direct EB-5 investor is able to start a business for less than the required investment amount, the remaining funds must be irrevocably committed to the business. The simplest way to accomplish this is to have the remainder of the investment placed in the NCE's operating account. For example, if a business is started in a TEA for $200,000, the remaining $300,000 would need to be placed in the business's account as operating capital. Because of the importance of demonstrating the connection between the investment and job creation, any direct investor in a situation like this should consult an immigration attorney to ensure he or she is complying fully with these foundational requirements of the EB-5 Program.

Can a foreign national transfer a business to the United States and invest in that business to qualify for an EB-5 visa?

In order for a foreign national to qualify for an EB-5 visa, he or she must invest in an NCE in the United States that creates at least 10 new full-time, permanent jobs for U.S. workers. Simply transferring a business to the United States and infusing capital is not sufficient. Because of the complexities involved in both transferring a business and pursuing an EB-5 visa, qualified business and immigration counsel should be retained before making any decisions.

Does the EB-5 Program expect applicants to make their investments before visa approval?

Yes, the EB-5 Program requires that investors' funds be at risk and irrevocably committed to a new commercial enterprise in order to qualify for an EB-5 visa. Some projects sponsored by regional centers place the funds in escrow pending the adjudication of the investors' I-526 petition. For a direct investment, placing funds in escrow may or may not be an option. An investor should consult appropriate business and immigration counsel to determine how best to protect his or her EB-5 investment while limiting immigration risk.

Can an EB-5 investment made in a single business with multiple branches count the total number of jobs created by all branches?

Yes, provided the corporate structure is that of a holding company with subsidiaries or a single business with multiple locations, all job creation should be attributable to a single EB-5 investment. If planning to invest at the lower threshold of $500,000, then all subsidiary companies or separate business locations must be within TEAs.

How might someone in the United States on an H-4 visa make a direct EB-5 investment and operate the NCE while awaiting I-526 adjudication?

Because H-4 status does not offer any employment authorization, an H-4 visa holder may not legally work or operate a business in the United States. Operating the business may require hiring a business manager or appointing some agent to act on behalf of the investor. An H-4 visa holder in a scenario like this should consider seeking some form of work authorization.

When should an EB-5 investor transfer investment funds into the NCE?

For projects sponsored by regional centers, the investment timeline is likely part of the subscription agreement. For direct investments, funds should be invested in the enterprise or in escrow before the I-526 petition is filed.

Can an EB-5 business be established in phases?

It may be possible to formulate a business plan in which an NCE is created in multiple phases, but experienced EB-5 immigration counsel and business counsel should be consulted before doing so. The biggest obstacle to such a plan will likely be the time constraints of the EB-5 Program: the EB-5 petitioner must have invested or be in the process of investing all required funds into the NCE at the time of I-526 filing—and generally speaking, the employment creation requirement must be satisfied by the time the I-829 petition is filed.

What kind of business is eligible for EB-5 investment?

Any for-profit enterprise engaged in lawful business activities can qualify for an EB-5 investment. The business must be classified as an NCE, which generally means it must have been established after November 29, 1990. In order to work for EB-5, the business must also be able to generate 10 or more full-time, permanent job positions.

Where must an EB-5 business be located?

An EB-5 business may be located anywhere in the United States. If an EB-5 investor wishes to make an investment at the lower threshold of $500,000, the business must be located within a TEA.

When must the 10 job positions be created by a direct EB-5 investment, and how long must they exist?

Generally, USCIS requires that all 10 jobs must be created within thirty months of I-526 petition approval. These jobs must then be maintained until the conditions are removed from the investor's permanent resident status.

Source of Funds

Can funds for an EB-5 investment be gifted from someone outside the United States to someone in the United States?

A foreign national living in the United States can be gifted funds from someone outside the United States as long as the nation in which the benefactor lives allows such transfers. The key is that a lawful source of funds can be traced from its origin to the EB-5 investor. This means the investor must demonstrate both that the money was gained lawfully and that it was transferred into the EB-5 investor's account lawfully.

What information needs to be provided with gifted EB-5 investment funds?

When the source of an EB-5 investment is a gift, the gifted funds must be accompanied by a deed of gift and documentation demonstrating the lawful source of funds—in other words, the documentation must show how the money was obtained. Such documentation might include employment history, wage statements, etc. If part of the gift originates from a loan secured by personal assets, such as a house, the source of funds documentation will also need to demonstrate where the funds used to purchase these assets came from.

Can an EB-5 investment be comprised of funds from multiple sources?

Yes, but the more sources an EB-5 investment has, the more complex its source of funds documentation becomes. Each source of capital must be traced from the EB-5 investor back to its origin, and the source of funds documentation must demonstrate that all funds were earned and transferred legally. Any gifts must be accompanied by a deed of gift, and any loans must be enforceable and secured by the lawfully obtained personal assets of the investor.

337

What can an EB-5 investor do if unable to provide direct source of funds evidence?

If an investor wants to use funds for an EB-5 investment, the source of those funds will be required by USCIS. Without direct, primary evidence, an investor may be able to demonstrate lawful source of funds through secondary evidence and a totality of the circumstances. A sworn affidavit explaining where the funds originated may be suitable in certain circumstances. Because lawful source of funds is a key requirement of the EB-5 Program, it is important to retain an experienced EB-5 immigration attorney to help compile the necessary documentation.

What source of funds requirements apply to EB-5 administration fees?

While only the EB-5 investment itself requires source of funds documentation, if the investment and the administration fees are paid together, the best practice would be to demonstrate lawful source of funds for the entire amount.

What is the easiest source of funds to prove?

A salary earned from lawful employment accompanied by payroll records and/or tax information would be one of the simplest sources to document, but no single source of funds is universally easier to prove than another. Each investor's financial background is different, and so the easiest sources to prove are those that involve the simplest and clearest paper trail.

How much source of funds documentation must someone have for an inheritance?

Demonstrating lawful source of funds for an inheritance typically requires the applicant to document that he or she has a right to the assets in question and that, by a preponderance of the evidence, the deceased obtained those assets legally. If no direct documentation exists, notarized affidavits from reliable sources may be used.

Can an EB-5 investment include funds won gambling or through the lottery?

Yes, as long as the gambling was legal and the necessary taxes were paid on the winnings, such funds can be used in an EB-5 investment. The source of funds documentation for gambling winnings might include a copy of the bank check, bank statements, Form 1099-G, and any other document that demonstrates where the funds came from.

Does the EB-5 definition of capital include non-cash assets?

Yes, for EB-5 purposes, capital includes equipment, inventory, and other forms of tangible property. These assets must be properly appraised, and the source of funds for such assets must be carefully traced to demonstrate that they were obtained lawfully. Another key consideration, however, is whether or not it can be clearly demonstrated how these assets will fit into the business plan and job creation of the new commercial enterprise.

Who must prove lawful source of funds in the case of a loan or gift?

USCIS requires lawful source of funds documentation from any lender or benefactor. In the case of a loan, the recipient must also be able to demonstrate that the collateral used to secure the loan was obtained lawfully.

When must an EB-5 investor transfer funds into the escrow account?

If an EB-5 project has an escrow account set up for EB-5 funds, investors will likely be required to have all investment funds and any administrative fees transferred before their I-526 petitions are filed. USCIS also expects investors' funds to be irrevocably committed to a project when adjudicating Form I-526.

Should money gifted to an EB-5 investor be transferred directly from the benefactor into escrow?

The key issue when dealing with gifted funds is demonstrating that the funds in question are, in fact, the investor's funds. It is generally better to have a gift be deposited into the investor's account and then transferred to the project's escrow account, but this is not required. In either case, the investor must be able to clearly show lawful source and transfer of funds.

Can venture capital be the source of an EB-5 investment?

Because an EB-5 investment must be derived from the investor's personal assets, funding an EB-5 investment in part or in whole with venture capital is unlikely to be accepted by USCIS. It may be possible to use venture capital to fund an EB-5 investment, but doing so would prove complicated and challenging. It would be best to consult an experienced EB-5 immigration attorney before proceeding with an EB-5 investment derived from venture capital.

Can money gained trading binary options be used for an EB-5 investment?

Yes, money obtained by trading binary options may be used as long as the initial capital was lawfully obtained. As always, the source and path of funds documentation is vital. Because binary options are a less well known investment vehicle, it may be prudent to include some description of binary options trading in the I-526 petition.

What potential problems can arise if someone in the United States gifts funds to an EB-5 investor living abroad?

Source and path of funds is one of the main considerations when gifting funds for EB-5. The gift should be accompanied by a deed of gift, and the gift giver must be able to demonstrate that the money was legally obtained. If the gift is being given from someone in the United States to an EB-5 investor living abroad, any applicable tax, remittance, or other financial regulations must be carefully observed. Anyone thinking about gifting funds for EB-5 purposes should consult experienced immigration and international tax counsel.

Can money earned through the sale of bitcoins be used to fund an EB-5 investment?

USCIS should accept an investment derived from the sale of bitcoins as long as the bitcoins were lawfully obtained and legally exchanged for U.S. currency. As with all other fund sources, the key is documenting the legal source and path of funds.

How might U.S. real estate owned by a foreign national be used in an EB-5 investment?

Other than serving as the location of a new business that creates the number of jobs required by the EB-5 Program, real estate itself does not qualify as a form of capital for EB-5 investment purposes. The real estate could, however, be used to secure a loan, which could then be used in an EB-5 investment.

What specific documentation is needed to prove source of funds?

The exact source of funds documentation will depend on the source. If, for example, the money is derived from salary, the documentation will likely need to include five to seven years' worth of tax returns. On the other hand, for funds derived from the sale of some asset, the documentation will need to include the deed of ownership and purchase agreement. Because source of funds documentation is essential to successful obtaining an EB-5 visa, a U.S. immigration attorney should be hired to handle this step in the process.

What source of funds documentation does USCIS require of non-EB-5 investors?

USCIS requires lawful source and path of funds documentation only from EB-5 investors. Any other investors involved in a project that receivesEB-5 funding are in no way required to meet the requirements of the EB-5 Program.

Can a foreign national borrow money from a U.S. bank to fund an EB-5 investment?

It is possible to use loaned funds for an EB-5 investment as long as the loan is secured by the investor's personal assets other than his or her primary residence; the EB-5 project cannot be used as collateral. The location of the lender is not necessarily restricted—the main concern is that the funds can be traced to a lawful source—and so investors may secure loans from U.S. institutions.

What are the restrictions for the place of origin of EB-5 funds?

Generally speaking, as long as the capital is obtained and can be transferred legally, the nation in which the money is earned is not relevant. Even money earned in the United States by a foreign national on a nonimmigrant visa is eligible if the worker had employment authorization.

Can a retirement fund be used as a source for an EB-5 investment?

Yes, an investor may use retirement funds as a source for the EB-5 investment. Documenting this source will require proof that the capital invested into the fund was obtained lawfully. Of course, depending on when the retirement fund is accessed, there may be fees and taxes associated with the withdrawal.

Can lottery winnings be a source of funds for EB-5 investment?

Yes, as long as the lottery winnings can be documented as a lawful source of funds, they can be used in an EB-5 investment.

Can gifted funds derived from the sale of real estate be used in an EB-5 investment?

As long as the funds given to an investor can be traced to a lawful source, they can be used as part of an EB-5 investment. The gift would have to be accompanied by a deed of gift and proof that the real estate was originally purchased using lawfully obtained funds and that the sale was also conducted legally.

What source of funds requirements exist for U.S. citizens investing in a project alongside EB-5 investors?

Generally speaking, U.S. citizens who invest in a business alongside EB-5 investors are not required to prove lawful source of funds to USCIS. They are, however, required to abide by all applicable state and federal securities laws.

Can venture capital raised in the United States be used by an EB-5 investor to obtain a green card?

Generally speaking, no, venture capital cannot be used to fund an EB-5 investment because the EB-5 Program requires the foreign national to make an investment of his or her personal assets. Venture capital invested in a company would not qualify.

Can a foreign national's company be the source of EB-5 investment funding?

An EB-5 investment must be made out of the personal assets of the investor. If the investor already owns a company, that company's revenue cannot be directly used to fund his or her EB-5 investment. The investor may, however, use any personal income derived from that business (in the form of salary or distributions) as the source of funds for an EB-5 investment.

Can a loan used to fund an EB-5 investment be repaid early?

Yes, the early repayment of a loan used to fund an EB-5 investment will have no effect on the investor's EB-5 case.

How might a Chinese EB-5 investor most efficiently transfer funds to the United States?

The most important consideration in transferring funds is that the transfer is handled legally and in such a way that compliance can be easily demonstrated to USCIS. For Chinese investors, who face restrictions on funds transfers, one option is to have family and friends help by transferring funds on behalf of the investor. To best understand the legal options available and to ensure every transaction is handled and documented properly, a Chinese EB-5 investor should retain immigration counsel before taking action.

Can money gifted to a foreign national from someone living in the United States be used in an EB-5 investment?

Money gifted to a foreign national from someone in the United States can be used as EB-5 investment funds as long as the gift is accompanied by a deed of gift, is transferred legally, and can be traced to a lawful source.

Can income earned by a foreign national while in the United States be used in an EB-5 investment?

As long as income earned in the United States was gained lawfully, it may be used as a source of EB-5 funds. Documentation that clearly demonstrates proper work authorization and payment of taxes is essential.

Can an EB-5 investor's current business invest in an NCE on his or her behalf?

No, the funds used in an EB-5 investment must be the personal funds of the investor. A business's funds cannot be used as the source of an EB-5 investment, even if that business is owned by the investor. Funds from the business may, however, be paid out as salary or a distribution to the investor, or the business may loan the funds to the investor in the form of a member or shareholder loan.

Can computer screenshots and emails serve as proof of an online transaction for source of funds documentation?

While there is no reason a screenshot or email would not be accepted as part of an EB-5 investor's proof of funds documentation, the issue is whether the screenshot or email contains sufficient information. For instance, if an EB-5 investor sells an asset through an online transaction, proof of the sale by itself is not enough documentation—the investor will also need proof that the asset itself was lawfully obtained, that the investor actually owned the asset, and that the funds were legally transferred from the buyer to the investor's account.

Visa Interviews/Consular Processing

When will USCIS interview an EB-5 investor and his or her family?

The only interview that occurs during the EB-5 visa process is after the I-526 petition is approved and the investor files for conditional permanent resident status with the National Visa Center. The interview will be scheduled by the U.S. consulate in the investor's home nation. The investor and each family member applying for a conditional green card (except children under 14 years old) will be interviewed.

What questions can an EB-5 visa applicant expect during the consulate interview?

Interview questions generally relate to personal information (e.g., name, date of birth, relationship to the principal applicant, etc.), employment history, civil and police records, and basic information about the EB-5 investment. The principal applicant should review the cover letter, memorandum, and source of funds document that were submitted to USCIS. In order to be better prepared for the interview, it may be prudent to retain immigration counsel.

What can an investor expect at an I-829 interview?

USCIS announced the implementation of I-829 interviews in April 2016. These interviews involve questions on investors' work and immigration histories, the origins of their funds, and their EB-5 projects. An investor should prepare for this interview by reviewing the status of his or her investment, particularly the use of the invested funds and the project's current employment creation.

Who decides whether or not an EB-5 applicant is in good health?

USCIS requires all foreign nationals applying for permanent resident status to undergo physical examination. The medical exams are conducted by physicians designated by either USCIS or the State Department. An applicant may not use his or her own doctor.

When is a medical examination required in the EB-5 process and who is required to be examined?

Medical examinations are performed after the EB-5 investor's I-526 petition is approved and are required for the investor's status to be changed to permanent resident. The investor and any derivative beneficiaries must get the physical examination done.

Who determines whether or not a change of status (green card) interview was successful?

EB-5 investors who are already in the United States may be required to attend a change of status interview in order to obtain their conditional permanent resident status and green card. The outcome of the interview is generally determined by the interviewing officer, whose decision is reviewed by his or her supervisor.

Where are I-485 applications for EB-5 cases processed?

While I-485 applications are processed at various USCIS locations, those filed based upon I-526 petitions are all processed at the California Service Center.

Is it better to adjust status or consular process?

Generally speaking, if someone is in the United States on a valid nonimmigrant visa, it is better to file Form I-485 and adjust status rather than return home and consular process. The processing times for both methods vary, and in most cases, it is difficult to determine which is faster. The advantage of adjusting status in the United States is that the applicant can also file for work authorization and a travel permit, which will be issued within about 90 days.

Selecting EB-5 Professionals

What professionals should a foreign national consult before pursuing an EB-5 visa?

Anyone interesting in the EB-5 Program should retain a U.S. immigration attorney with EB-5 experience. Based on the foreign national's specific circumstances, the immigration attorney will be able to recommend other trusted professionals, such as an investment adviser, third-party due diligence expert, or international tax attorney.

For a company that wants to receive EB-5 investments, either directly or through a regional center, what are the most important considerations in selecting an EB-5 attorney?

The most important considerations are experience and record. A company that is trying to determine whether to pursue direct investments, become sponsored by a regional center or apply for regional center status needs a lawyer with experience and a track record of success in each of these areas. Involvement in one or two EB-5 cases is insufficient.

How can foreign nationals living abroad work with U.S. EB-5 attorneys?

EB-5 attorneys represent clients from all over the world. The physical presence of an EB-5 investor is not required—all the necessary communication can be done via telephone, email, skype, etc.

What professionals do regional centers provide EB-5 investors?

Generally, regional centers do not provide investors with the professionals needed to conduct proper due diligence and to prepare the documentation needed for an EB-5 investment. Investors should hire an immigration attorney to represent his or her interests, and may also consider hiring a tax advisor and financial analyst. A good immigration attorney will be able to recommend which professionals an EB-5 investor should hire.

Where should an EB-5 investor's immigration attorney be located?

The geographic location of an immigration attorney is unimportant—all work can be completed and filed from anywhere. The attorney is in no way required to be located near the EB-5 project or regional center and, thanks to modern communication technology, does not even need to live near his or her client. Having a competent immigration attorney is much more important than where the attorney is located.

Who should prepare an EB-5 investor's source of funds documentation?

An EB-5 investor should retain a U.S. immigration attorney with EB-5 experience to prepare his or her entire I-526 petition and all supporting documentation—which includes the source of funds documentation. A qualified attorney will be able to help the investor compile the necessary evidence for establishing lawful source and path of funds.

When should a foreign national considering an EB-5 investment hire an immigration attorney?

The earlier a potential EB-5 investor hires a U.S. immigration attorney, the better. A qualified attorney with EB-5 experience will be able to help the foreign national determine if the EB-5 Program is the best immigration option available—and if so, the attorney will then be able to help guide the investor through the rest of the process, from diligencing a regional center to preparing the I-526 petition, answering any questions the investor has along the way.

Who should a potential EB-5 investor consult before applying?

The first professional a potential EB-5 investor should consult is an immigration attorney with EB-5 experience. After discussing the investor's goals and plans, the immigration attorney will be able to recommend other professionals as needed, which may include securities counsel, a business plan writer, an accountant, and possibly others.

Do immigration attorneys typically offer EB-5 clients investment advice?

Immigration attorneys advise clients regarding immigration issues, offering related due diligence and ensuring compliance. Generally speaking, immigration attorneys do not give investment advice to clients—though they may help a client find a qualified investment adviser. If an immigration attorney offers investment advice, it would be prudent for the investor to inquire about any financial interest the attorney may have in the regional center or project in question.

Troubleshooting Problems

Can an I-526 petition be changed once approved?

The information provided by investors in their I-526 petitions should be carefully reviewed prior to submission since the I-829 petition will be approved based on the same material facts. As a result, any foreign national considering an EB-5 investment should consult immigration counsel and, possibly, international tax counsel.

How does failing to appear at a biometrics appointment affect an EB-5 investor's I-829 petition?

Failure to appear at the biometrics appointment will result in the denial of Form I-829. If a scheduling conflict exists, it is best to reschedule as soon as possible. If the principal applicant misses the biometrics appointment, his or her family's I-829 petitions may also be denied.

What happens to EB-5 investors if the JCE goes bankrupt?

If the necessary number of jobs were created by the JCE and the EB-5 investors filed their I-829 petitions before the JCE went into bankruptcy, the EB-5 investors' I-829 petitions may be approved. If, however, the JCE went bankrupt before creating the necessary number of jobs, the investors will not be able to petition for unconditional residence. Any foreign national in this situation should seek the counsel of an experienced EB-5 attorney.

What are the potential consequences of attorney disbarment to a pending I-526 petition?

An EB-5 investor's attorney being disbarred will not necessarily have an impact on a pending I-526 petition. If, however, the attorney was negligent in preparing or filing the I-526 petition, this could result in an RFE or denial. Also, the reason for disbarment might cause USCIS to more carefully scrutinize the petition. The best course of action would be to retain new counsel and have that attorney file a notice of appearance as the new attorney of record. The new attorney should also review the submitted I-526 petition to ensure it was complete and accurate.

What happens if Form I-829 is denied?

If Form I-829 is denied, the case will be referred to immigration court, where the investor will have another chance to gain I-829 approval. If the judge does not approve Form I-829, the decision can be further appealed. If, however, the petition is not approvable, the investor will either need to find another EB-5 investment or some other means to maintain lawful status in the United States—or face deportation. An experienced EB-5 immigration attorney will be able to guide an investor through this process.

In what ways might a pending I-829 petition affect an H-1B visa application?

The H-1B is a dual intent visa, and so an application for the H-1B visa will not be affected by a pending immigrant visa petition. An immigrant investor with a pending I-829 petition, however, has conditional permanent resident status and is not eligible for the H-1B visa until the I-829 petition is either abandoned or denied.

How can an EB-5 investor be certain an EB-5 immigration attorney is not affiliated with a regional center?

The best way to discover whether or not an immigration attorney is affiliated with a regional center is simply to ask. An investor should ask if the attorney is affiliated with, compensated by, or working for a regional center. If a regional center offers a list of recommended attorneys, this does not necessarily indicate affiliation. Regional centers tend to prefer working with attorneys they know have the necessary experience to navigate the complexities of the EB-5 Program.

How might a previous overstay affect an application for an EB-5 visa?
A previous overstay may result in the EB-5 visa being rejected. Whether or not the application is rejected will depend on several factors, including the length of the overstay, how long ago the overstay took place, and the reason for the overstay. It is important to consult with an experienced EB-5 immigration attorney concerning how an overstay might affect an EB-5 application prior to filing Form I-526.

How might filing a Writ of Mandamus affect a pending EB-5 petition?
Filing a Mandamus may force USCIS to adjudicate a pending EB-5 petition, but doing so does not guarantee approval—and depending on the reason for the delay, may actually result in a denial. For instance, if the reason for the delay of an I-526 adjudication is an un-adjudicated project exemplar application, the I-526 petition will likely be denied. Filing a Writ of Mandamus may be an option in some cases—but this action should be discussed with an experienced EB-5 immigration attorney.

How might a past SEC lawsuit affect an investor's EB-5 visa eligibility?
Civil court cases do not generally have a bearing on one's eligibility for permanent resident status. Depending on the nature of the SEC lawsuit, however, USCIS may be concerned about whether the suit affects lawful source of funds and may issue an RFE. Because of how the previous lawsuit could affect an EB-5 case, it would be best to retain an experienced EB-5 immigration attorney before proceeding.

What can be done if an EB-5 petition is denied?
Depending on the reason the petition was denied, which should be indicated in the denial letter, an EB-5 investor may be able to appeal the denial decision. If an appeal isn't possible, it may be possible to file a new petition. In such cases, investors should consult with experienced immigration counsel before going forward.

How long does it generally take USCIS to forward an EB-5 case to the National Visa Center (NVC)?
The time between USCIS approving an I-526 petition and the NVC receiving the case varies widely. Generally, cases are forwarded within five to six weeks. Occasionally, cases aren't received by the NVC for two to three months. In rare cases, the delay is longer.

What should an EB-5 investor do if the National Visa Center (NVC) hasn't received his or her petition from USCIS?

If the NVC has not received an investor's approved I-526 petition from USCIS after about five or six weeks, the investor should contact the Immigrant Investor Program Office (IPO) and wait for a response. At this point, the investor may also want to consult with the attorney who filed his or her I-526 petition or retain new counsel to handle the delay.

If an EB-5 project fails, can an investor keep his or her priority date?

If an EB-5 project fails before an investor receives I-829 approval, he or she will not be able to remove conditions based on the same I-526 petition, and so the only option within the EB-5 Program would be to file a new I-526 petition based on an investment in a new project. The priority date established by the earlier I-526 petition is not transferable. Depending on the circumstances, it may make sense for the investor to contact USCIS to see if there is a way to keep the earlier priority date—but there is no guarantee USCIS will have a solution.

What is a Writ of Mandamus and when might it be an option in an EB-5 case?

In the context of EB-5, a Writ of Mandamus is a federal lawsuit that forces USCIS to take action on a case that has been unreasonably delayed. Filing a Writ of Mandamus forces adjudication, which does not necessarily mean approval, and so this action should not be taken lightly. Mandamus is, however, an option, particularly in cases that have been pending beyond the normal adjudication time without any clear reason from USCIS. Anyone considering a Writ of Mandamus should consult an immigration attorney with experience filing such actions.

What is the Immigrant Investor Program Office (IPO) and how is it different from the California Service Center (CSC)?

The IPO is the USCIS office in Washington, D.C., created specifically to process EB-5 petitions. While the CSC still receives EB-5 petitions, as of 2015, all such petitions are transferred to the IPO for adjudication.

What does it mean when an I-526 petition is pending with the Immigrant Investor Program Office (IPO)?

A "pending" I-526 petition is one that has been filed but has not yet been adjudicated by USCIS. As of 2015, the adjudication of all I-526 petitions takes place at the IPO, which USCIS created specifically to handle EB-5 petitions.

What are the consequences to an EB-5 investor if the regional center closes?

The consequences of a regional center closing—whether due to bankruptcy, termination of USCIS designation, or some other cause—will depend somewhat on the timing of the closure relative to the investor's EB-5 case. If the I-526 petition is not yet adjudicated, it is likely to be denied. If the I-

526 is approved, it could be very difficult to obtain I-829 petition approval. If, however, it can be demonstrated that the necessary number of jobs have been created at the time the I-829 is filed, the investor may be able to obtain I-829 approval.

What should an EB-5 investor do if the I-526 petition has been pending beyond normal processing times?

Beyond making inquiries as to the status of the petition, an investor may consider filing a Writ of Mandamus—which would force USCIS to adjudicate. Filing a Mandamus action may carry some risks, however, and so any investor considering this course should seek the counsel of an immigration attorney with relevant experience.

Will an EB-5 investor be refunded the investment if the I-526 petition is approved but the EB-5 visa is denied?

Whether or not an EB-5 investor is returned his or her investment—either upon I-526 petition denial or EB-5 visa denial—will depend entirely on the subscription agreement between the investor and the regional center. Many regional centers offer a return of the investment if an investor's I-526 petition is denied; however, regional centers are unlikely to return capital if the investor's EB-5 visa is denied due to inadmissibility. Potential EB-5 investors should carefully review the subscription agreement before signing and investing in a project.

What are the most common reasons an EB-5 petition might be delayed or denied?

I-526 petition delays can simply be due to the backlog of pending applications, but other common reasons for delay can involve authenticating the investor's lawful source of funds, verifying that the necessary investment was made and is truly at risk, and the need for additional documentation. Generally speaking, petitions are denied due to noncompliance with the EB-5 Program.

What immigration options exist for EB-5 investors if their I-829 petition is denied or is not approvable?

As long as the EB-5 investor did nothing to make himself/herself inadmissible, failure of an EB-5 case does not restrict the investor from applying for any nonimmigrant or immigrant status, including EB-5. If an EB-5 investment fails for some reason, the investor may pursue any immigrant visa path for which he or she is eligible—and may even choose to pursue multiple immigrant visa options simultaneously.

How might prior drug charges affect a potential EB-5 investor's admissibility?

How prior drug charges will affect a person's admissibility depends on the nature of the charges. A potential EB-5 investor with prior drug charges should consult an immigration attorney, preferably one with criminal law experience, who will be able to provide specific counsel upon reviewing the arrest report and disposition of the case.

What is a notice of intent to deny (NOID)?

A notice of intent to deny (NOID) is a warning that unless some issue with the EB-5 case is rectified, USCIS will deny the EB-5 investor's petition. Such a notice should be handled by competent immigration counsel in a timely manner.

What options does an EB-5 investor have if the project fails at some point in the EB-5 process?

If a project fails prior to I-526 petition approval, the investor will be unable to meet the requirements of the EB-5 Program—particularly sustaining the investment during conditional residence and creating 10 or more job positions. The only viable option in such cases is to re-file based on an investment in a different project. If a project fails sometime after I-526 approval but before I-829 petition approval, it may still be possible to successfully remove conditions depending on the timing and if sufficient job creation can be demonstrated. After I-829 approval, the success or failure of a project will have no bearing on an EB-5 investor.

How might an EB-5 investor discover why an I-526 petition is delayed?

If an EB-5 investor believes his or her I-526 petition is taking longer to process than normal, the first step would be to check the USCIS website to determine what the current I-526 adjudication time is. If the petition is, in fact, past the current listed adjudication time, an investor should ask the attorney who filed his or her I-526 petition about any communication between the attorney and USCIS—and request that the attorney make an inquiry regarding the delay. If the investor invested through a regional center, he or she may also consider asking the regional center whether the project is having difficulty receiving I-526 approvals.

What happens to EB-5 investors if a regional center's designation is terminated?

If a regional center loses its designation with USCIS, the consequences for investors will likely be severe. Pending I-526 petitions will not be approvable. Investors with approved I-526 petitions will likely have to file new I-526 petitions based on new EB-5 projects. For investors with pending I-829 petitions, however, it may be possible to receive approval if the necessary jobs were already created through project expenditures. Any EB-5 investor with a pending I-829 petition who invested through a regional center that lost designation should consult an experienced EB-5 immigration attorney to determine what options may be available.

Regional Centers

General Questions

Do regional centers operate from a physical location, and if so, what governs where a regional center is located?

Every EB-5 regional center must have a physical address within the United States. This location may or may not be within the regional center's geographic area of operation, which is where the EB-5 projects it sponsors must be located.

Can multiple regional centers exist in the same geographic area?

Yes, any number of regional centers may exist in a given area, and the areas in which they are approved to operate may overlap with the geographic scope of other regional centers.

How many projects can be offered by an EB-5 regional center at a time?

EB-5 regional centers may sponsor any number of projects at a given time. The number of projects being offered and how the investor quotas for those offerings are filled is up to the discretion of the regional center.

Does USCIS approval of a regional center mean a project is a safe investment?

An organization seeking regional center status must submit Form I-924 to USCIS along with various disclosures and project documents. USCIS is primarily concerned with the compliance of the regional center to applicable laws and regulations. The agency does not conduct thorough due diligence on the regional center principals or project principals, nor does it assess whether a given project is a good investment. When selecting a USCIS-designated regional center, individual investors should conduct their own due diligence to ensure minimal immigration and financial risk.

Can a regional center use EB-5 funds that aren't yet allocated to job creation to trade stocks?

No, EB-5 funds are required to be irrevocably committed to the new commercial enterprise and at risk until USCIS adjudicates the investors' I-829 petitions.

What is a government-affiliated EB-5 regional center?

While all regional centers in the EB-5 Program are approved by USCIS, some regional centers are established by public or government agencies (e.g., city governments, development commissions, universities, etc.) or by public-private partnerships. Public and government organizations are permitted to apply for regional center designation, but the projects they sponsor are not necessarily safer investments, nor are they treated differently by USCIS. EB-5 investors should conduct the same due diligence on government-affiliated regional centers as they would on any other regional center.

What is a regional center and what role does it play in the EB-5 process?

An EB-5 regional center is defined as an economic unit that promotes the economic growth of a specific geographic region. Anyone is eligible to apply for regional center designation with USCIS, but it is a lengthy and expensive process. Regional centers sponsor projects, and investors in these projects are able to count direct, indirect, and induced job creation—whereas direct EB-5 investment projects can only count jobs created directly by the new commercial enterprise.

What is the purpose of an EB-5 regional center?

The main function of an EB-5 regional center is to facilitate economic growth in a region. This goal is accomplished in a couple of primary ways: (i) regional centers tend to sponsor projects that pool several EB-5 investors, which means greater economic impact, and (ii) regional centers have a greater ability to attract investment since indirect and induced jobs can be counted toward EB-5 job creation.

Do projects have to affiliate with a regional center in order to receive EB-5 funding?

No, a project is not required to be sponsored by a regional center—though regional center sponsorship is often advantageous. Projects not sponsored by regional centers, referred to as direct investments, must directly create at least 10 jobs per EB-5 investor.

How do regional centers earn revenue?

Regional centers can earn revenue in various ways, including through administration fees paid by EB-5 investors and through accrued interest from the projects they invest in. This latter form of revenue is often accomplished through the use of a loan model in which the NCE receives the funds from EB-5 investors and loans those funds to the JCE. A regional center should retain the necessary business, securities, and immigration counsel to ensure compliance with all applicable laws and regulations.

What steps should a regional center take to enlist qualified brokers?

Selecting qualified brokers involves careful due diligence. A regional center should select credible, licensed/registered brokers with track records of success. When considering a broker's history, a regional center should look for any disciplinary actions or administrative hearings by regulatory agencies. A regional center should also consider the number and type of investors a broker will be able to source. An experienced EB-5 attorney will likely prove invaluable to a regional center looking for credible brokers.

How might a regional center use foreign migration agents to source investors?

For U.S. citizens and residents serving in this capacity, SEC requirements dictate that the finder must be licensed and registered if he or she is to be paid a finder's fee. As long as a migration agent is not a U.S. citizen or legal permanent resident, however, he or she may be paid to source investors for a regional center even if the agent is not licensed and registered. A regional center should consult with both EB-5 immigration counsel and securities counsel before sourcing investors to ensure compliance with all applicable laws and regulations. An immigration attorney may also prove an invaluable source of information in finding credible migration agents.

What are the costs associated with applying for EB-5 regional center status?

While the specific costs of setting up a regional center vary greatly depending on the circumstances, the following expenses can be expected: (i) Form I-924, Application for Regional Center Designation, has a filing fee of $6,230; (ii) preparing the I-924 application through immigration and securities counsel may cost anywhere from $30,000 to $50,000; and (iii) hiring other professionals, such as a business plan writer and an economist, may cost as much as $50,000 if done by separate professionals. The total cost can be expected to range from $100,000 to $150,000—possibly more in rare circumstances if done outside of EB5 Affiliate Network.

How might someone sell a regional center?

Because a regional center is a business entity, such as a limited partnership or limited liability company, it can be sold like any other business according to all relevant local, state, and federal laws. A regional center might be marketed by contacting immigration attorneys, brokers, and other regional centers. Before a buyer can take ownership of the regional center, however, an I-924 application requesting the transfer of ownership must be approved by USCIS.

How do migration agents fit into the EB-5 process?

Generally speaking, migration agents serve as finders who refer potential EB-5 investors to regional centers. This is one of the ways regional centers source investors, particularly from China. Both regional centers and potential EB-5 investors should be cautious when engaging the services of migration agents—it is best to first consult an experienced immigration attorney. In the United States, the services typically offered by migration agents are regulated by the Securities and Exchange Commission (SEC); however, foreign migration agents must comply only with the laws of their respective countries.

Do regional centers profit from the projects they sponsor?

Regional centers are for-profit business entities, but this does not necessarily mean they are all profitable. The ways in which regional centers earn profit—and how much profit they earn, if any—vary from project to project.

Create a Regional Center

Can a person establish an EB-5 regional center without hiring an attorney?

While it is possible for a person to apply to USCIS for regional center designation without an attorney, it is unadvisable to do so. Establishing an EB-5 regional center is complicated and typically involves the expertise of numerous attorneys and professionals.

What kinds of organizations can apply for regional center designation?

A regional center can be any economic unit, private or public, as long as it promotes economic growth, job creation, and improved productivity in its region. As a result, almost any organization can apply for regional center status. Examples include for-profit businesses, states, cities, chambers of commerce, and universities.

How can a potential EB-5 investor find a project sponsored by a regional center?

While USCIS lists all regional centers on its website, it may be better for a foreign national interested in the EB-5 Program to contact an immigration attorney with relevant experience since a good attorney will be able to help a potential investor find a project as well as guide the investor through the entire process. Potential investors may also be able to find projects online or through due diligence agencies, brokers, orEB-5 consulting firms.

What fees can a regional center use to cover operational costs?

To cover their operating expenses, regional centers typically charge investors administrative fees; in some cases, they also earn a portion of each investor's return on investment. Regional centers may structure their fees however they wish as long as they remain compliant with SEC and EB-5 laws and regulations.

How much does it typically cost to become a regional center?

The cost of setting up a regional center varies greatly based on an assortment of factors, including the specific professionals engaged and the amount of work to be done. One of the key factors is whether the project filed with the I-924 petition is hypothetical, actual, or exemplar. And so anyone seeking to establish a regional center should expect to spend at least $35,000 and perhaps, in rare cases, as much as $80,000.

How large an area can a regional center cover?

The geographic size of a regional center is not specifically limited by any EB-5 regulation; however, practically speaking, the larger a regional center's geographic scope, the more challenging its size will be to justify to USCIS. Generally, if a regional center is larger than a single county, the combined counties must be contiguous and economically interdependent. A regional center's industry scope must also be specified, which may, depending on the region, effectively limit the size of the regional center's geography.

What are the requirements for a hypothetical project in an I-924 application?

A hypothetical project proposal requires a business plan and an economic impact analysis that includes a job creation study. For hypothetical projects, the business plan should be fairly comprehensive, but it need not be compliant with *Matter of Ho*. An EB-5 immigration attorney should be retained to ensure all of the elements of the hypothetical project proposal and I-924 application meet USCIS requirements.

Can a foreign national establish a regional center?

Yes, anyone may form a business entity and apply for regional center designation. There are no regulations that restrict regional center ownership to U.S. citizens. As long as the applicant complies with all relevant laws and regulations, the I-924 application should be approved. Note, however, that it may be difficult for one or more foreign nationals to operate a regional center without either a U.S. partner or employment authorization.

Can an EB-5 investor form a regional center?

While no law or regulation presently restricts an EB-5 investor from starting his or her own regional center, such a venture would add a substantial upfront cost—both in time and finances—to the EB-5 process. A potential EB-5 investor considering whether to apply for regional center designation should consult immigration counsel with relevant EB-5 experience in order to fully understand the risks, costs, and time involved.

Types of Projects

Can a regional center offer incentives to EB-5 investors?

While no law or regulation prohibits regional centers from offering incentives to EB-5 investors, USCIS may consider the value of any incentive to reduce the value of the invested, at-risk capital. As long as it can be demonstrated that it does not affect any investor's principal investment, a regional center may offer some form of incentive—though it would be prudent to consult with an experienced EB-5 immigration attorney about such a plan before proceeding.

What guarantees are regional centers allowed to offer EB-5 investors?

The EB-5 Program expressly prohibits the guaranteed return or repayment of investors' funds, in part or in whole. Any promises that can be construed as a guaranteed repayment—whether the return of the principal investment or an incentive like guaranteed housing—will lead to the denial of investors' I-526 petitions.

What steps should a developer take to submit a project proposal to a regional center?

While there is no set process and every regional center is different, generally speaking, a developer should first retain an EB-5 immigration attorney to create a compliant and marketable project. The developer will then need to approach a regional center about the project—the regional center will review the project proposal to determine whether or not it is interested.

Regional Center Responsibilities

What fiduciary duties do EB-5 regional centers have?

While the fiduciary duties of regional centers are not presently well defined, best practice is for regional centers to perform sufficient due diligence on projects they sponsor, maintain good investor records, and act in the best interests of both investors and projects. The specific fiduciary duties of a regional center should be specified in the agreement made between the regional center and each investor.

What factors might disqualify a person from becoming an EB-5 regional center principal?

While no specific statute or regulation bars anyone from managing a regional center on the basis of previous criminal convictions, previous bankruptcies, a history of civil judgments, etc., such factors may pose a challenge to the success of the regional center. A regional center would have to disclose any such background information in the private placement memorandum of any project it sponsors.

Can EB-5 regional centers accept administrative fees?

Generally speaking, regional centers are able to accept administrative fees to cover their management costs, but certain uses of the fees may or may not be permitted. The offering documentation should specify what the administrative fees are being used for—any questions or concerns regarding regional center administrative fees should be directed toward qualified securities counsel.

How are indirect and induced jobs documented?

Typically, indirect and induced jobs are calculated using project expenses. Project expenditures should be documented using accounting records, which might involve the services of a professional accountant and/or third-party fund administrator.

Is an EB-5 regional center required to own an NCE, or can they be unrelated entities?

A regional center may own an NCE, but this is not required. When an NCE seeks sponsorship from a regional center, however, an agreement should be entered into for both parties' benefit.

Timing of EB-5 Capital

When are an EB-5 investor's funds used by the regional center project?

The exact timeline depends on the specific project's documents, such as its subscription agreement or escrow agreement. The use of investor funds may not carry any conditions at all, but often funds are released when an investor's I-526 petition is filed. The best projects release the funds only upon approval of the petition and return funds to the investor if his or her I-526 is denied.

At what point do EB-5 investors pay regional center administrative fees?

While the fee amount and payment requirements are determined by each individual regional center, most require the entire fee (typically around $50,000) paid upfront and in full.

Where does transferring funds into escrow fit into the EB-5 process?

The first step in any EB-5 investment is for the investor to hire an EB-5 immigration attorney. With the attorney's help, the investor can then find a suitable project and perform due diligence on both the project and the affiliated regional center. Once an investor settles on a project, he or she will be expected to sign the necessary paperwork and invest the required capital. Once the capital is committed to the project, the I-526 petition can be submitted to USCIS.

Can an entity seeking regional center designation accept investments before I-924 approval?

An investment may be accepted prior to I-924 approval, but the investor's I-526 petition should not be submitted until after the I-924 is approved and the regional center is officially formed. The invested funds should also be placed in an escrow account until the I-924 is approved.

At what point in a project's development can EB-5 funds be invested and used?

When the funds are invested—and when they are used by the project—will depend on the agreement between the regional center and investors. While funds may be placed in escrow until I-526 petition approval, depending on the agreement, funds may instead be used upon filing or even before the I-526 petition is filed.

USCIS Compliance

How might missing securities and due diligence information affect an I-526 petition?

If necessary information is missing from the I-526 petition, USCIS is likely to issue an RFE rather than outright deny the petition. Securities documentation is required for regional center projects, and so any missing securities documents will probably result in an RFE. Due diligence information, on the other hand, is for the investor's benefit and is not required in the I-526 petition.

Do foreign nationals have to work with USCIS to find regional center projects?

No, foreign nationals do not work directly with USCIS to find and select projects sponsored by regional centers. Instead, a foreign national interested in the EB-5 Program should consult with an immigration attorney who will be able to guide the investor regarding how to choose a regional center project.

Repayment of EB-5 Capital

When do regional centers return EB-5 funds to investors?

An EB-5 investment must be considered at risk for the duration of the investor's two-year conditional resident status. The return of the invested capital is governed by the project's offering documents and exit strategy, but the standard term is five years. A regional center should not return the principal of any EB-5 investment until all I-829 petitions have been adjudicated.

What is the typical exit strategy of an EB-5 investment?

No guarantee can be made concerning the return of an EB-5 investment, but the project's offering documents should specify the exit strategy. Depending on the project, the exit strategy may involve the sale of the investor's interest in the project at fair market value, but an equity-based investment might instead involve only annual distributions of investment returns proportional to the investor's ownership interest in the entity.

What repayment requirements are there for loans used to fund EB-5 investments?

The EB-5 Program does not govern the specific nature of loaned money used to make EB-5 investments except that it must be legal and secured by lawfully obtained personal assets at fair market value. The repayment term of any such loan would be based solely on the agreement made between the lender and the EB-5 investor.